THE VIDEO EDITOR'S GUIDE TO SOUNDTRACK PRO

Dedications

Thanks to my beautiful wife Jenny for putting up with long hours and late nights. I couldn't have done it without you! I'd also like to dedicate this to Adam, Jacob, and Hannah – the finest kids one could wish for.

—Sam McGuire

I'd like to dedicate the book to my wife Angela and son Caleb.

—David Liban

THE VIDEO EDITOR'S GUIDE TO SOUNDTRACK PRO

Workflows, Tools, and Techniques

SAM MCGUIRE AND DAVID LIBAN

Routledge
Taylor & Francis Group

LONDON AND NEW YORK

First published 2010 by Focal Press

This edition published 2015 by Focal Press

Published 2017 by Routledge
2 Park Square, Milton Park, Abingdon, Oxon OX14 4RN
711 Third Avenue, New York, NY 10017, USA

First issued in hardback 2017

Routledge is an imprint of the Taylor & Francis Group, an informa business

Copyright © 2010, Taylor & Francis.

Notices
Practitioners and researchers must always rely on their own experience and knowledge in evaluating and using any information, methods, compounds, or experiments described herein. In using such information or methods they should be mindful of their own safety and the safety of others, including parties for whom they have a professional responsibility.

Product or corporate names may be trademarks or registered trademarks, and are used only for identification and explanation without intent to infringe.

British Library Cataloguing in Publication Data
A catalogue record for this book is available from the British Library

Library of Congress Control Number: 2009939163

ISBN 13: 978-1-138-41942-1 (hbk)
ISBN 13: 978-0-240-81173-4 (pbk)

CONTENTS

Supplementary Resources Disclaimer

Additional resources were previously made available for this title on DVD. However, as DVD has become a less accessible format, all resources have been moved to a more convenient online download option.

You can find these resources available here: www.routledge.com/ 9781138419421

Please note: Where this title mentions the associated disc, please use the downloadable resources instead.

INTRODUCTION

Audio post-production can be an intimidating process for a video editor. Hopefully the audio on your project will receive the appropriate attention from a skilled audio engineer, but that doesn't mean you won't be working with audio all along the way. This book is written for the video editor using the tools in Final Cut Studio. It makes no assumptions about your knowledge of the world of audio, but does assume that you know how to use Final Cut Pro. What we have done is collect a number of experts in the field and bring them together to provide you with real world examples and a resource that will help you understand the audio process and what you can do when using Soundtrack Pro 3.

As we progress through the text, you will notice that a good amount of emphasis is placed on explaining the process; this is not simply a glorified software manual. The goal is to inform your work as a video editor, enable you to do some basic audio editing, and allow the more adventurous among you to complete the entire audio mix. Not every project is going to have a big budget for audio, and more than once I have been asked to help a video editor learn enough to spend the hours required to complete the audio portion of the project. Well, this is the result of those requests. Instead of pushing you to a separate audio application, the text enables you to use Soundtrack Pro 3 for all of your audio tasks. Not only is it a powerful tool, but it will also be instantly familiar to you because it works a lot like Final Cut Pro.

In the text many topics are covered, but we have spent a lot of time narrowing them down to things you need to know. Some of the topics don't translate well to the written text, so we've also created a DVD with an example project that you can copy to your computer and video clips that you can view on your computer or any DVD player. The clips walk you through some of the functions that make more sense when learned visually. We've covered all of the bases and hope that you'll work with the example project as you read through the text. The project is an excerpt from a film by David Liban about an artist named Erik Rieger. Erik Rieger works in many mediums but is best known for working with his grinder as seen on the video. He is also a fine artist, a furniture and wood craftsman, and a musician. He has performed as an opening act for Santana and has done hundreds of shows as you will see on the video.

In addition to things related to the text, the DVD also includes sections on composing music with Apple Loops, mixing in surround, and demonstration of effects not listed in the text.

Each time there is a section of the text that relates to a sample on the DVD, you will see the DVD logo on the side of the page.

Another thing we've done is to include sidebars and extra boxes that provide alternate interpretations and insights from David Liban's personal experience. An Internet search on David Liban will show you just how much experience he has.

As an additional resource, I have made arrangements with VTC.com to open up several additional tutorials on effects from Soundtrack Pro 2 and 3. This is another project I worked on in the past, but the information remains relevant. Go to http://www.vtc.com/products/Apple-SoundTrack-Pro-2-Effects-Tutorials.htm to access these clips.

As you read this book, keep in mind that, although working on audio post-production is not an exercise in voodoo wizardry, it is a specialized skill that takes specific equipment and lots of practice. If you want to be able to work on both the audio and the video, then keep at it and learn what Soundtrack is capable of; it has a lot of tools that can make a huge difference to your project.

Most importantly, have fun with it.

Sam McGuire

THE VIDEO EDITOR

What does it mean to be a video editor? It means finding order amongst the chaos. There are infinite possibilities to every edit you make and, while there are accepted practices, there is no right and wrong, just subjective interpretation. This is why editing is an art form most analogous to writing music mixed with writing fiction. The viewer knows if they like it or not, but it is up to the editor to guide them to a particular thought or emotion. Do you want them to be jolted into a perception or eased into a realization? Do you want them to feel uncomfortable or do you want them to feel content? The editor has this power to manipulate. Film as we know it is editing. The reason we love films and are engaged in the storytelling is because of the editing. A film that is not edited well and crafted with care is a film we may disregard or simply dislike.

Figure 1-1 The video editor (photograph by David Liban).

But to have this sort of control and awareness of your audience means you must have control and awareness of the media at hand. The editor is usually given the material they are editing, so they must work within this world. I believe those people who have edited projects with mediocre or poor footage will be better directors and better editors because they have seen the problems and hope not to have to revisit them.

Know Your Material

Not only do you need an awareness of your audience, but you must really know your footage. I don't mean that you recall it when you see it, I mean you *know* your footage. The nuances of a moment; a meaningful glance; a train in the background. Having this sort of awareness is the difference between the good and bad editor. And, if you are like me, you don't have a photographic memory, so you must find a way to organize your media so that you can instantly access it. Spending time scanning the same footage over and over is also the mark of an inexperienced editor. Some of this practice is hard to avoid, but if you sift through your media and segment it into small bits, and categorize those bits into ideas that you place in folders with appropriate labels, you are on your way to a thorough edit. Even the most creative of filmmakers cannot imagine what they might have missed by not going through this task. It's this organization that provides for magical juxtapositions in the editing room. The script might have called for a particular edit from one shot to another, but because you know that one shot has the essence of a particular sound or image you can make connections far beyond what can be found in the script. This is why the edit is often called the 'third rewrite,' meaning the final delivery of the shooting script, then the result of what is actually shot, and finally the result when the editor has pieced together the story with those bits. This is what it means to be an editor.

Unfortunately, very little of the actual time an editor is working is pure creative work – there are loads of tedious and busy tasks to be carried out. The aforementioned organization, the client/director relationship, the cleaning of the image, and the sweetening of the sound are all aspects of the job. This is not a bad thing – it is just how it is, and I believe that it is all integral to obtaining the most effective final product. You need to know your footage and organize it; you need to know what the director/producer wants; you need to have the awareness of what constitutes a good image and a bad image, and what can be used or not; and of course you need good quality sound. The audience will forgive a poor quality picture before they forgive poor quality sound, so you as an editor must be able to identify these problems. Then you need to address them either by collaborating with an audio specialist or learning the tools and doing the work yourself. We as filmmakers are really quite fortunate to have these wonderful tools at our fingertips. Just 15 years ago it was unthinkable to have a full editing system in your home.

So in short, you, the editor, are an artist, a manipulator, a technician, and a magician. It's all done with slight of hand, or a keyboard shortcut.

Workflow

The editor's usual workflow may vary slightly according to whether they are acquiring footage on tape or a media card. You will need to refer to your camera's manual in order to properly digitize and store its media on your computer's hard drive. But, assuming that you have done that, the workflow is as follows. Capture; organize; reorganize; subclip; identify theme; identify easy scenes to work on and work on those first. I would always suggest avoiding starting at the beginning of your story, because that is always the first thing to change. Start with the easy things first because often we need to get into the flow of editing. If you start at the beginning, it seems like a monster that you simply cannot handle. Just think in little increments, and you'll gain momentum and make natural transitions from scene to scene, given that you know your footage well. Do not get into trying to finish your film the first time around – that is not possible. Also, if you find yourself stuck on an edit for more than five minutes, move on. Come back to it with fresh eyes and you'll see obvious answers reveal themselves. Just lay down shots at a reasonable pace knowing that you are going to clean the sequence up later. There may be times when you'll have to focus on a cut to see if it will work, but most of the time make it quick and dirty. Do this with the notion of creating your 'first assembly.' This is not a cut you really want to show anyone, it's just the framework or outline of the project. From here you can start to fine-tune and begin to make it slick.

The next milestone of your edit would be the rough cut. This means the edit's more-or-less in place, but with little or no attention given yet to audio mix or color correction. It's the cut you'll show people for feedback. This is where you get ideas from others on what is working and what is not. Take notes and try to distinguish between what of the feedback is useful and what is not. I often find that the critiques that are the most painful are the ones that probably are the most valid. Try not to dismiss comments because they hurt. Put them aside and come back to them – perhaps there is something there.

Picture Lock

Next you begin the process of making your fine cut, with the idea of trying to reach 'picture lock.' This is when you are done with all your creative decision-making. It's all about going through moment by moment to see if the edit is cutting together well and achieving the goals everyone has set. Fine-tune each edit and, when you are either out of time or at a place where it's as good as it's going to get, call it picture lock. This is normally when you hand over the media to your audio person and let them begin work on it. If you change the picture after you have done this, it could mean costly changes that will hurt your pocket and annoy your collaborators. So be sure you're done when you say picture lock.

If you are using this book you may be doing the audio sweetening yourself, and that is a good thing. However, I would still try to reach picture lock and stay there. Although Final Cut Studio has great integration between Final Cut Pro and Soundtrack, changes can cause trouble. That said, the folks at Apple have tried to minimize the pain caused by changes to the picture after picture lock, but ...

Aside from the audio, the point when you reach picture lock is also when you should start your color correction process. I've seen many students spend hours on color correction before they've reached the rough cut phase. This might end up being a complete waste of time if that portion ends up being cut out, so try to refrain from spending that time until you've reached picture lock. There may be times when you mess around with color correction to get inspired or to try ideas, or to see if a shot is usable, but mostly I'd recommend holding off until it's time and your film is done.

When you've got your final audio mix and sweetening completed and your picture is color corrected, you will output to all the appropriate mediums. I am still a fan of mastering to the best quality tape format available to you. Should you lose your hard drive or your DVD back ups fail, you've always got your tape. Mastering out your product is an important step that you really must consider. How are you going to save your project and where will the film be screened and on what format? Ask yourself these questions to make sure you have a back up.

When editing, be organized on your timeline as much as possible. Keep your dialog on the same tracks (1,2), your nat-sound on (3,4), music on (5,6), and SFX on (7,8). This way you can make changes to individual stems if need be. I also see many students who have dozens of tracks of audio spread out all over the place. It's sloppy and careless and can come back to hurt you if you make a change and don't see that it affects audio on your timeline that is out of sight, often scrolled below the visible portion of your screen. Use as few tracks as you can get away with and as many as you must. Again, it's a simple task to achieve if you begin your edit this way, but if you have to move your audio clips around later it is easy to make mistakes that will cost time to fix.

Steve Stamps – Editor Profile

'I'm not what you would call a Final Cut Pro power user. I use it for making basic SD (standard definition) video cuts in my spare time. Last year I was hired by an organization to create a video that consisted mostly of talking head interviews. I have a two-camera setup and use a lavalier mic as the primary audio source. Normally, I use a special cable to put the mono audio signal on both channels. On one of the interviews I forgot the correct cable, so when it became time to edit, several of the clips had the audio in only the left channel. After stumbling around in Final Cut Pro for a while trying to get the audio on both channels with no success, I tried to solve the problem in Soundtrack. Within minutes, I was able to get the audio from one track to both and get the audio resource back into the video. I'm sure I could have accomplished the same thing in Final Cut, but it was just easier in Soundtrack Pro.'

Sound Editing with Final Cut Pro and Sound Editors

Video editors often work like me when it comes to manipulating audio. That is, unless I need something unusual, I might not ever use an application like Soundtrack Pro to do my audio editing.

You can actually accomplish a great deal within Final Cut with regards to audio. I think it goes without saying that your situation is always better if you have recorded good quality sound in the first place. That means a variety of things. For example, if you listened to your location on a location scout and heard many airplanes overhead, a train that goes by frequently, or an air conditioner in the space that cannot be turned off, you might want to choose another location. You really need to evaluate the sound before you commit to a location. Sometimes the problem audio can be handled by unplugging the device making the noise and other times you might be able to control the sound in question by using sound blankets. The point is that you need to have good ears when recording on location. If you do that, your sweetening process will be so much easier. (Oh, and turn off all phones!) Any audio post engineer will tell you there are no magic buttons to fix problem sounds, no matter how useful a piece of software may be.

So, you have a good, clean audio track. You capture your footage and make sure that you are using the track that has your good microphone, and not the camera mic. You do your video editing and right from the get-go it's in your best interest to monitor the levels as you go along. Listen to the sound carefully and make notes of things that you will want to address later and clean up or remove. These could be a hum, a background noise that might be reduced, or simply bringing greater clarity to a portion of the sound that you want to improve. I do want to stress here that you will want to make notes. Even the best editor will forget to revisit a problem area when they start working on other portions of the film. Write it down!

There are many decent audio filters right in Final Cut, so, as a video editor, I can usually do some preliminary audio sweetening without ever opening Soundtrack Pro. For example, I use the Apple AUGraphicEQ all the time. It has 31 bands of frequency adjustments to mess with. And, as a video editor, I admit that I 'mess' with those adjustments most of the time. For example, I know a smidgeon about the physics of sound and, if I hear a rumble on my audio, I know I can go into this filter and reduce the low frequencies to get rid of that rumble or hum. On the other end of

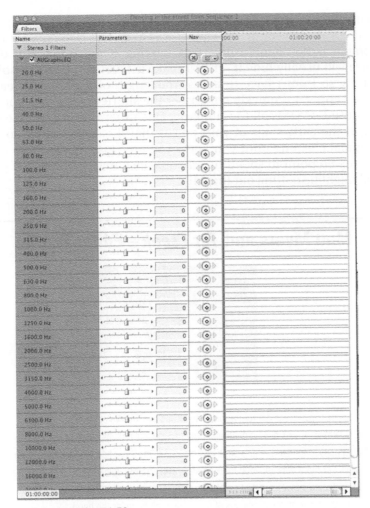

Figure 1-2 Apple AUGraphicEQ.

the spectrum, if there is a hiss or lots of 's' sounds, I can reduce the high frequencies without hurting the voice quality too much. Somewhere in my travels, I learned that the human voice lives around the 2500 Hz frequency, so I try to not alter sounds near that. Sometimes I will try to bring a little richness to the voice by playing with the 250 or 300 Hz sliders, and I have helped the audio in this way on occasion. This is also a good tool for making the all too well-known 'telephone voice.' Just bring down the low frequencies and bring up the high frequencies to make it tinny.

Another thing I do is to listen carefully to the edit points. If I can hear the edit, I know it is likely a bad edit. I do what I can to make the transition from one cut to the next as seamless as possible. As a video editor, the easiest way to do this is to create a 1 to 3 frame audio dissolve. If you are hearing a 'digital tick' this dissolve will usually hide it. Then I make a 'favorite' of this dissolve setting so I don't have to adjust the length of the dissolve each time I apply it. I quickly remember the shortcut for this favorite, because I use this all the time too. One other thing about cleaning at the early stage of your edit is that it is a good idea to do minimal cleaning until you know you are close to your fine cut. There's no point in spending any time cleaning your audio if you still might be cutting out that clip.

Matt Myers and *Tar Creek* – Editor Profile

'James Graves was the formation of my sound design. We shot James almost entirely while he was driving his truck. We put a lav mic on him, Director of Photography in the passenger's seat, and me in the back. We had the camera mic on as well, but there was still loud truck noise in every frame. James said some important stuff, including a few lines that summed up the issue at hand in *Tar Creek*. All of his lines interlaced with the rumblings of the straight eight under the hood.

'I am not a trained or educated filmmaker. My entry into filmmaking came about out of necessity, so I had to learn as I went along. I was thrust into the editing suite with the same gusto as the film itself, and when I tried to cut some things together with James Graves, I couldn't stand the audio transition from one guy sitting in a quiet room to a roaring Chevy engine with James at the wheel. Luckily for me the way out of this mess was to use James in places where we cut from – and back to – the driving footage. I couldn't pull this off in every instance but, for the most part, this allayed what I felt was a jarring experience from a studio sound to a big, honking, Oklahoma truck.

'*Tar Creek* is an environmental documentary, if it's anything, and being a writer I am constantly negotiating the relationship between form and content. They both need to live together peaceably and, given that, it made sense to bring the 'environment' into the interviews. Even when it was clear that the only noise in the interview setting should have been the hum of the camera and the A/C, I would bring in water, wind, birds, bugs, storms, sinkholes – whatever came from outside, I brought it in. As I'm writing this, I'm still not sure – or even aware – if that tack was breaking any fundamental filmmaking or audio rudiments. I didn't know much, or even many people who did, so I just had to go with what made sense to me. This made sense for an environmental documentary. A better filmmaker probably would have shot people outside so that the ambient sounds were never a question, but at the time of shooting I knew even less than I do now, which is saying quite a lot.

'Something interesting that I didn't even recognize until I sat down with an audio editor was that, while I fiercely avoided dissolves and cross-fades with the picture, I blended audio tracks the whole way through. To this day I don't have a justification for that. Being new to the process it just really bothered me jumping from one sound to another – as a straight cut – even when the correlative cut of the picture felt right. Something in the fluidity of the sound really kept the pace going for me in ways that were more congruent to the overall design than straight cuts or quick fades. Keeping the pace going was important because, one, we had a great deal of information to get through, and two, Oklahomans talk slow. So, if we were able to quicken the heart and mind a little bit by blending ambient and underlying sounds, then that tactic served the higher purpose of keeping the film going, which seemed a worthy sacrifice.

'When I first opened Final Cut, it defaulted to two picture tracks and four audio tracks, which was sort of an omen I failed to recognize. Getting the sound locked took twice as long as the picture, if not more. Documentaries are seemingly less visual than narrative films in that if you take away the picture most of the time there is still a story left, but it's usually not so the other way around. Perhaps the importance of the audio to me was only due to the fact that it was an environmental documentary, and that a different documentary with different circumstances would not require such heavy lifting and concentration on the audio. Perhaps. However, I don't think so. Even though I've only made one film, it strikes me that audio will always be a challenge and also a weapon to be wielded in any film. The trick is to find out *what* the audio needs to do for the film – beyond being audible and understandable – and then to figure out *how* to deliver that around all the other obstacles that the footage, the story, and *you* put in the way.'

Another set of audio tools in Final Cut Pro that I use all the time are the buttons for −1 Gain dB, −3 Gain dB, +1 Gain dB, and +3 Gain dB, which you can add to your timeline window for immediate access. In the button list, which you can get to via **Tools** > **Buttons** > **Audio**, you can select these settings and then drag them to your accessible buttons on your timeline window. Again, I use this *all* the time. Let's say you have a clip that just

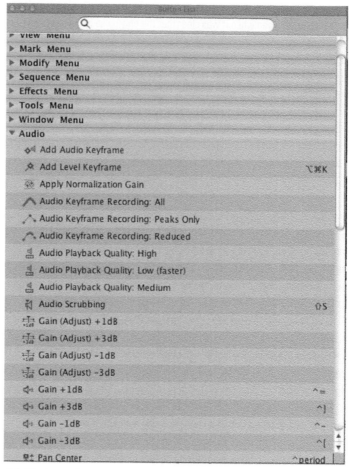

Figure 1-3 The button list.

Figure 1-4 Audio buttons on the timeline.

needs a little boost or reduction in volume. Select the clip in question and simply click these buttons and you've quickly made it louder or softer. While I edit, I watch my VU (Volume Unit) meter and try to keep my audio levels near $-12\,\mathrm{dB}$. Making this adjustment as I move along allows me to better listen to the quality of the sound in case I need to sweeten the clip later and, if not, I might have gotten the level to an acceptable place on the first go-round.

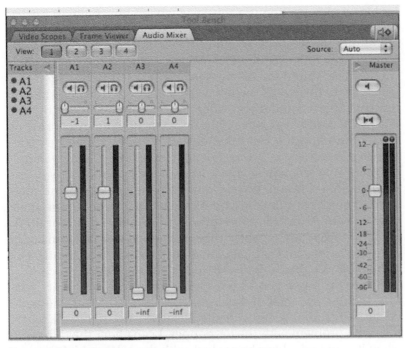

Figure 1-5 The audio mixer.

When you want to focus your editing on the audio, go to **Windows** > **Arrange** > **Audio Mixing** and the Final Cut interface will bring up the tools to do some basic mixing. You can also access the audio mixer by going to **Tools** > **Audio Mixer**. This gives you the ability see big sliders for each track you are using. You can even automate the level adjustments for pan and volume

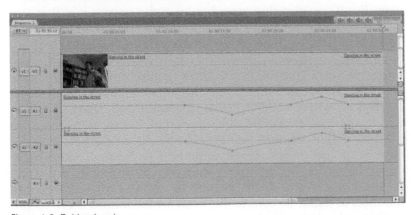

Figure 1-6 Rubber bands.

in this window. I often use this view when I am trying to finalize my mix in the fine cut stage of my edit.

Another audio tool I commonly use in Final Cut is the keyframe Rubber Band tool. At the bottom of the Final Cut timeline window is a button for Toggle Clip Overlays (Option + W). When you activate this you'll see a red line appear on the clips in your timeline, both in audio and video. You can then activate the Pen tool (p) and add keyframes right on your timeline by clicking on the red line with the Pen tool. Each of these keyframes (or dots) you create will act as a way to add and reduce levels by simply dragging that dot up or down like a rubber band, so you can have audio levels fade up and down where you want. You might need to make your timeline tracks bigger to give you more space to work with. I am really careful with my edits in terms of thinking about what audio needs to be primary and what needs to be more in the background, and this aspect changes constantly. This 'rubber banding' technique is essential for my editing process.

There are other good audio effects that are useful in Final Cut, such as the shelf and pass filters. A not-so-good one is the de-esser. I cannot seem to make this one work that well. I have the same problem with the de-popper. I can't hear the difference when it's applied. I have better luck with the AUGraphicEQ.

The Audio Post Personnel

So, as you can see, I spend a lot of time working on the audio as I am editing, but all video professionals know that what the basic video editor can do on their own is limited when compared with what a post-audio editor can do to improve their sound. The thing to remember is that, as you are editing, you become accustomed to the sound and it becomes familiar and seems okay. But if you give that sound to an audio person and they use Soundtrack or some other audio program to improve the sound, you'll hear that it can be improved even more. Because Final Cut Studio ships with Soundtrack, you have the tools at your disposal to do the work yourself, but it does require a bit of training on your ears as well as training with the software. Just like with color correction, where every shot can be improved no matter how well it was shot, every clip of audio can be improved as well. The trouble is that you may not be able to tell unless you play the clips with the improvement and then without, back-to-back. Often there is no budget to pay the audio person to do this work, so you may have to do it yourself, or do the best you can with the tools at hand. Be aware: this is an art form unto itself, so you really need to have good ears to do a good job.

I have made programs that have aired nationally on PBS for which I did all my own mixing and sweetening right in Final Cut. I may have opened Soundtrack to clean one or two clips using the Noise Reduction tool, but I had to do it myself since I did not have the budget to bring in an audio person. In the end, no one complained about how it sounded so I must have done something right.

There have been other films for which I did hire an audio post person to clean the audio and complete the mix. Again, unless I played the final mix back-to-back with my mix out of Final Cut Pro, even I couldn't hear the difference, but I know that there is one, especially when I see the waveforms of the particular clips change as the audio is processed. There have been numerous instances when the audio seemed fine, but then the audio engineer would apply a variety of filters to the clip and I'd see the waveform strength increase instantly. I could have boosted the level in Final Cut to get that volume, but in doing so I would have also increased the room noise. The process as completed by the audio engineer brought up the voice and minimized the background sound. Once you see and hear this, you know that your cut can be improved. And once you know that, you can't go back.

Now, when it comes to mixing sound, the outcome is very subjective. When my audio people have given me what they thought was a good mix, 90% of the time I have agreed with their decisions. At other times I felt the most important audio was too loud or soft, and I wanted to make adjustments. Because it costs so much to work with these professionals, what I like to do is to ask them to give me a set of audio tracks (stems) for dialog, another set for music and another for natural sounds and effects. This allows me to import the sweetened audio into a new Final Cut timeline, and then rubber band the audio to get the mix I prefer. It's more work for me, but it means I don't have to either bother the audio engineer and/or pay them more.

To help with this process, it is important to keep your tracks organized. Use the same two tracks for dialog, the same two for music, and the same tracks for sound effects and natural sounds. This way, when it becomes time to mix, you can easily adjust the sounds you want instead of hunting for the right track. If you are using more than ten tracks of audio for a video edit, the chances are that your timeline will be sloppy and may cause havoc when you are finishing. Be organized throughout!

An embarrassing anecdote I can share concerns my attempts to produce a 5.1 surround sound mix using just Final Cut and having only two speakers on the edit system. I had completed a 30-minute program that I was very excited about. I had been very organized with my audio tracks in the timeline window and was able to export the dialog, music, and effects tracks as separate AIFF files, with the mix levels as they were in Final Cut. I then brought those files into Compressor where I encoded a surround mix for the DVD I was authoring in DVD Studio Pro. Next, I burned the DVD and put it into my home system, in which I have a 5.1 surround sound amplifier, and watched the show taking notes. Based on those notes, I made adjustments in Final Cut, re-exported the various tracks, imported them back into Compressor, and then replaced the old tracks in DVD Studio Pro. I burned the new DVD and listened again on my home entertainment system. Long story short ... it took me ten tries, and probably still is not as good as it could be if I had just hired an audio professional. I won't *ever* be doing that again.

WHAT IS AUDIO POST?

Figure 2-1   Audio mix facility at 42 Productions. Reproduced with permission of 42 Productions – Boulder, CO.

One of the primary goals of this book is to help you as a video editor to understand the audio post-production process so that when you find yourself in a position where you are working on audio (either by choice or because the budget requires it) you will feel comfortable with the different audio tasks. Instead of jumping right into the features and tools available in Soundtrack Pro, it makes sense to present portions of the entire process to help you connect with the audio engineer's perspective. This is important because it will help you to understand the language and workflow of the audio post phase. It will also help you to understand the best-practice considerations to follow in case the audio ends up in the hands of an audio engineer later in the project. Keeping things organized according to how an audio engineer might do it will help such a transition proceed smoothly.

15

David Bondelevitch

I have invited David Bondelevitch to write a few pages about the audio post process. David is a veteran in the film industry and recently joined the faculty at the University of Colorado, Denver. You will find a full biography at the end of his section, along with a selected project history. I think you'll find his descriptions of dialog editing, music editing, and sound effects editing very informative. Most importantly, though, you will get a very accurate idea of how an audio engineer thinks and acts throughout the post-production phase. Keep in mind that these sections were written in an attempt to describe the traditional post-production process in which there is an editorial team working on picture and then, once the picture is locked, the entire project passes on to the audio team.

One other thing that you will notice immediately is that there are notes in the margins of the page. These briefly describe how the Final Cut Pro/Soundtrack Pro integration aids in the efficiency and strength of the audio post-production workflow. There are aspects that, when going from AVID to Pro Tools or from Final Cut Pro to Pro Tools, either don't exist as options or are more complicated.

Dialog Editing

It is not necessarily the concern of the picture editor to worry directly about the dialog editing. However, in order to accommodate the simplest workflow possible, it is best to talk to the sound editors about how they would like their dialog delivered, and attempt to deliver the best tracks possible.

Of course, in order to export the material properly, it must be imported properly. It is extremely important that the picture editors import the material correctly into their non-linear editing system so that the sound materials are of the highest quality to begin with, which will mean that there will be no need to re-digitize the materials later in the process.

The correct decisions rely on a number of outside factors:
• How the material was recorded in the field;
• How the sound editors will be working;
• How the final project will be delivered.

In general, the decisions you will be making will be to do with the following:
• File format;
• Sample rate;

- Bit rate;
- Channel format;
- Track layout.

The standard for file format has become .BWF (Broadcast Wave Format) but, again, you should confirm this with your sound editorial crew. Note that .BWF is essentially the same as .WAV (except that it includes added metadata which may be very useful to the sound crew, such as Scene, Shot and Take numbers). So if you cannot use .BWF as your option, .WAV is usually a close second.

The next most likely format would be .AIF, or AIFF (Audio Interchange File Format), which is the standard on audio CDs. It is also possible that editors working on older versions of Pro Tools may request SDII (Sound Designer II) files. You should avoid working with any data-compressed formats. These include but are not limited to MP3, MP4, AAC, or some types of WAVE files. These will create audible artifacts which may create problems that are not easily rectified if a distributor later complains about problems on the sound tracks.

For sample rate, you should choose the highest sample rate available (pending approval of your sound department). In general, the standard in film/television is 48 kHz. However, on some older non-linear picture editing systems, the only option may be 44.1 kHz. For bit rate, you should again choose the highest resolution possible. On most projects, this is 24-bit, but on older non-linear picture editing systems you may be limited to 16-bit. Channel format should be split-mono wherever possible because Pro Tools and most other editors will deal with two split-mono files (left and right, rather than a single stereo file) in a much better fashion. (Note a possible area of confusion here: stereo and split-mono both have two tracks, left and right; the difference is just a matter of how the software stores and reads the files.)

Production sound should be imported with as many files as is feasible. It is now common to split production tracks over eight or more tracks in the field. If possible, the picture editor should import and edit all of the tracks, even if they are only monitoring one track, such as a 'dailies mix' (which combines all other tracks), or a boom track, where the rest of the tracks are individual wireless mics. This will allow the most choice later on when editing sound. If this is not feasible, it is possible to edit only the mix or boom track and import the other tracks as needed later on, but this is usually much more labor-intensive than importing them directly early in the process. Note that music should *always* be imported and edited with both tracks, even if the file format is two mono files (left and right)!

File Formats

 When sending a sequence from Final Cut to Soundtrack, you don't need to worry about the file formats because Soundtrack is able to use every file that is useable in Final Cut. This applies to file type, sample rate, and bit depth. This is because Soundtrack uses the exact files that exist on the Final Cut sequence.

Track layout is perhaps the most complicated question of all, and is the most subjective choice. Picture editors will tend to cut three categories of material:

1. Synch production dialog;
2. Additional sound that is intended to be kept but did not come from synch production dialog, including voiceover, wild sounds, additional sound effects, or music that has been placed by the picture editor;
3. Temp materials that are intended to be replaced later on by the sound crew, which may include any of the elements listed in point two.

It is extremely important that the picture editors make clear to the sound editors in which category each sound falls, and the easiest way to do this is by separating the tracks as listed above, so that a temp effect is never on the same track as something that is intended to stay, and an added line is not placed on the same track as production sound.

Most sound crews will want dialog, music, and sound effects kept separate from each other as much as possible. Also, most crews will want all of the temp materials as well, not only as a reference for replacement, but also because occasionally the temp material becomes permanent, so it pays to keep it throughout the process, even at the final dub.

Within these three groups, it is also important to keep tracks as consistent as possible, especially on materials that are intended to be kept and not replaced. If you have voiceover, sound effects, and music, it is best to keep these on separate tracks, as they are likely to be covered by three different crews!

I fully understand that the more sound tracks there are, the more difficult it is to edit picture. For this reason, many editors will deliberately limit themselves to four tracks. This may be functional for editing picture but, when exporting material, it is necessary to split the tracks to a higher degree. This job of track-splitting is frequently handled by an assistant editor. In some cases this is a poor choice, as an assistant may have less experience and does not understand the basic concepts necessary for preparing the tracks properly for a sound editor.

Once the tracks are prepared, they are typically exported as an OMF (open media framework) file, with media embedded. One important choice that must be made is the number of 'handles' to be added to the media.

For dialog editing, the most important part of the job is to mask the audio edit point so that there is no clear sound change on the picture change. This is usually done most effectively by creating the longest sound cross-fade possible across the picture edit.

Organization

Organization is important even when working with Final Cut and Soundtrack. In fact, I recommend an extra layer of caution because all too often a video editor will plan on working in Soundtrack and assume that the material will never leave it, thereby introducing the chance to employ a certain amount of 'laziness' in organizing audio tracks. It almost always happens that the project ends up being sent to an audio engineer who has an impossible time figuring out the mess.

In order to do this, the export must have lengthy handles. If each take is its own sound file, the setting should be to export the entire file for each edit. This not only allows for long handles, but also allows the dialog editor to search the remainder of the take for other material, such as 'fill' or alternate lines to replace a bad section of audio.

If the sound files are not imported as separate takes, importing the entire file for each edit may be impossible, as many very large files would be imported. In that case, it may be necessary to choose the length of handles, for example ten seconds. Again, in this case, you should speak to the sound crew about their desires.

If you will be editing the sound yourself in your non-linear editing system (or Soundtrack Pro), you will want to split your tracks even more carefully. The tracks edited in category one above (synch production dialog) will need to be split on 8–12 tracks of their own.

When splitting production sound, it is very important to split the tracks by 'angle' and *not* by 'character.' The basic idea in track-splitting is to make it as simple as possible for the mixer. If the mixer is inserting processing (such as EQ [equalization], compression, or reverb) on a track, it is easiest to drop it onto a track and leave it there. Most of the processing on production dialog is done to remove extraneous background noise, which can shift drastically when the camera moves on each angle choice. So, if you are allowed eight tracks for splitting dialog, the track alignment would often be to split the dialog by shot amongst those tracks. Since shots are frequently identified by letter (49A and 49B are two different angles in the same scene), it is not uncommon to use letters to identify the tracks.

In addition, it is common to split sound effects from production (PFX) on to their own tracks, often using two tracks for overlaps, so that the mixer can choose to replace these with the sound editors' work at the mix if desired.

It is also typical to split out lines that are expected to be replaced in ADR (automated dialog replacement). It is important to leave these in the edit for several reasons, the most obvious being that the actor must hear the original lines in order to loop them well, but also because it is very common that the production ends up being more desirable than the ADR, even if it has some technical problems. In order to prepare the tracks properly, lines spotted for ADR must be moved to a separate track in case they are dropped, and must be filled with production background noise so that there is not an apparent 'hole' in the track. Yet they must still be edited in such a way that the lines are usable in the event the ADR is dropped.

Handles

One of the best aspects of sending Final Cut sequences to Soundtrack is that you never have to worry about handles because Soundtrack references the same media that Final Cut referenced, and always in its entirety. The only exception is if the Final Cut sequence is 'media managed' before sending to Soundtrack; be careful in this case to create long handles.

There are rare occasions when tracks should be split by character, for instance in animation, where all the dialog is essentially ADR and there is no background noise, or where an entire character is expected to be re-voiced or has recurring specific needs (will be pitch-changed to sound like a robot, or is always radio-miked because he has a very soft voice), but, in most cases, it is more important to match shot due to background noise. Note that on many picture editing systems the audio monitoring setup is not accurate enough to hear the mismatches between shots, so you should not assume 'everything is okay if I put it all on one or two tracks.'

Music Editing

After the editing of the production sound, the sound element that a picture editor is most likely to deal with is music. This can be for a number of reasons.

Musical Sequences

This does not necessarily mean an old-fashioned song-and-dance sequence; it might be something as simple as a scene in a bar with a band onstage and people dancing to the beat, or cheerleaders dancing rhythmically at a football game. In either of these examples, decisions on how to deal with them should be made long before the shoot. Typically some type of playback is used, which requires careful planning and, typically, additional equipment.

Using playback ensures that the tempo will always remain consistent so that the same part of the song happens at the same time on every take. It also helps keep people in tune if you are recording a singer or other musical performers. Ultimately this will make editing picture much easier. If you do not use playback, picture editing becomes extremely difficult because every edit will also be a music edit and, without playback, tempo and pitch will drift from take to take (or even within takes), making it almost impossible to make an edit.

In order to do playback, music (or temp music) must be chosen (or at the very least choose a tempo and create a click track for dancers). If it is new music, or is to be a new performance, it must be pre-recorded. That music must be played back for the performers being filmed, but, if there is dialog or other music that you wish to record in the scene, the playback music must be kept separate. This necessitates in-ear monitoring for the performers, which not only means more equipment rented, but creates a much more complex job for the production sound crew. It is therefore common to have a second sound crew on the set for these scenes, to handle playback.

If it is a simple dance sequence, another way of dealing with it is to use a 'thumper' track, which is playback of a very low frequency thump instead of a typical click track. This can be played through speakers and filtered out using a high pass filter.

Music-driven Sequences

Some sequences cannot be edited without music, such as a music montage, so the editor will look for a piece to use over the scene.

Sequences that Benefit from Music

Overall pacing of a film is very reliant on music, so many picture editors will cut 'temp' music in necessary scenes to see if the overall pacing is working.

Test Screenings

This is probably the most significant reason for using temp music. Test screenings (or 'preview screenings') are screenings of the rough cut of the film for an invited audience of average movie-goers who are in the target demographic for the film. The studio and distributors consider these screenings to be extremely important.

They require, however, that people who are not used to seeing a work-in-progress judge the effectiveness of the film as a whole. As a result, editors try to 'finish' the film as much as possible, and one relatively simple way of doing this is to add temp music to any scene that might have it later on. This can either be beneficial or ultimately harmful to the film, if it is not done very carefully.

The Music Crew

There is a whole music crew that can provide support for the process. However, for many reasons, the music crew may not have been hired while the film is being cut. Following are some of the roles who may be able to help you.

Apple Loops

Soundtrack has a large collection of royalty free music beds in various styles that can be used as place holders or sometimes even as the final track. The tempos can be adjusted, along with the pitch. It's nice to have this tool in the toolbox.

Thumper Track

This is another item that can be created in Soundtrack and then exported to tape or a portable playback system for location shoots.

Temp Music

This is another great use of the music library included with Soundtrack.

The Music Supervisor

The job of the music supervisor is to oversee all elements of the music in the film. I highly recommend hiring the supervisor as soon as possible, especially if there is any music or musical sequences written into the script or that arise during filming. The music supervisor is usually paid a flat salary, so it makes sense to hire them as soon as possible. They can help you choose music that is both available and affordable (you'd be surprised how much music is unavailable, or which would cost seven figures or more for a single use).

One of the biggest mistakes that can be made with temp music is placing a song that you could never possibly obtain, then falling in love with it. The longer you hear that song with the film, the harder it will be for you to find a satisfying replacement that is both available and affordable. Remember that you may be watching your film with your temp music for months during the editorial process, and you may test screen it repeatedly to good response from an audience. A music supervisor can be very beneficial here because they can discourage you from placing inappropriate artists and suggest many alternatives.

The supervisor can also help you find a composer, budget all of your music, including the licensing of songs, plan your scoring session, and hire a music editor.

The Music Editor

The music editor has a complex job that is hard to describe in a single sentence. Generally the job covers several different categories, but the one that relates most to the picture editor is the editing of temp music. Depending on the budget, schedule, and preferences of the picture editor, the picture editor may do the first pass of editing temp music on the film.

Some editors would prefer not to deal with music at all, but it is now an expected part of the job. Other editors enjoy shaping the film through the use of music. However, if there are test screenings this may be too much work for the picture editor, who has many other things to deal with, so a music editor may be hired for this task. There are editors who specialize in temp tracks, and they may be able to 'feed' the picture editor with music to be used as they cut picture so that the process becomes interactive, or the editor may simply hand over cut sequences to the music editors for them to add music.

I should point out that some people (especially composers) think of temp music as a hindrance to the film and not a help. There is an element of truth to this. One problem is that people sometimes add a musical style that they could not possibly afford, such as using John Williams' orchestral music on a film that has a tiny budget. Since music is one of the last parts of the filmmaking process, it is not uncommon that, even on moderately budgeted films, there is very little money left for recording a score. It is important to keep this in mind. If you can only afford a synthesized score with a few live instruments, it is probably better to temp the film with similar music and not to use a large orchestra.

For this reason, it is beneficial to have members of your music crew assembled as early in the process as possible. Although some composers enjoy helping with temp music, many prefer to have nothing to do with that part of the process.

The Composer

Like the music supervisor, the composer is usually paid a flat creative fee (or is on a package deal), so it is best to hire them as soon as possible. Unfortunately, the composer is often hired very late in the process, which may limit their involvement. In addition, the composer usually likes to work with their specific music editor, so it may be to your benefit to hire the composer's music editor to do the temp music, to create a sense of consistency and continuity in the transition from temp music to final music. If you have not chosen a composer when you start temping, it is likely that you will have to hire two music editors.

I strongly recommend that you hire your composer by the time you have your first rough cut of the film. They will be tremendously helpful in the final stages of shaping the movie, and it will give them time to write the music well. Many features now have over an hour of original score music, and it is not feasible to think that a composer will write more than a few minutes of good material in a day. You should try to budget at least a month of time for the composer to work with the finished, locked picture, but in this day and age that hardly ever happens. It is not uncommon for a composer to have much less time to write a large orchestral score. This undoubtedly means the music will not be as good as it might have been, and might even necessitate the hiring of additional composers to complete all the music in time. Needless to say, this may result in a fractured, inconsistent score.

Sound Effects Editing

Sound effects are generally the last thing a picture editor does on a film, and only when necessary because the production

Royalty Free

Apple Loop music beds make a perfect tool to temp out a score because they have a good mix of quality and variety. If you find a combination of loops that really works, you can use it in the film without worrying about rights. The loops also contain a wide variety of quality that might match more closely to a low budget score.

sound is not usable or is nonexistent. They fall into three separate sub-categories:

- Background effects (ambiences);
- Synch effects (also called 'hard effects' or 'cut effects');
- Foley.

Background Effects (Ambiences)

Backgrounds are sounds which cover the length of a scene, without any specific synch relationship, and which are used to help establish location (and time) for the audience, as well as establishing mood for the scene. They are a subtle aural cue to the audience as to when a scene has changed. For this reason, the sound change should almost always match the picture change. If the picture change is a cut to a new location, backgrounds should be a hard cut on the exact frame of the picture cut. Occasionally people will put a short fade in to 'soften' the transition; this fade is normally very short, as little as one frame.

It is extremely rare to pre-lap or post-lap a background sound. Doing so breaks the reason for their existence: to explain scene changes to the audience. Transitions across scenes with a background sound will usually confuse the audience into thinking that they are still in the same location and time. If you wish to use a transitional sound, a specific featured synch sound effect (like a train whistle), a music cue, or dialog generally work better as transitions.

Common backgrounds include birds, wind, traffic, and crickets. Changing backgrounds is an excellent way of implying a scene change. Birds are a universal identifier for daytime. Crickets are a universal identifier for nighttime. If a time ellipse occurs as a dissolve from afternoon into night, typically the dissolve would be accompanied by a fade from birds to crickets to match the dissolve. If it is a short time ellipse, it is still best to change the backgrounds, even if it is in a very subtle way, such as switching from rush-hour traffic to light suburban traffic. If it is continuous time but a location change, such as interior to exterior, you may want to use the same backgrounds but simply shift the mix to feature different elements in different ways.

Another common background is 'walla.' This is similar to Group ADR except that it is deliberately recorded in such a way that there is no intelligible dialog. (Actors may speak gibberish instead of dialog.) There are two reasons for this. One is that you do not want the background chatter to be distracting by including real words. The second reason is that walla can be left in the foreign mixes without having to be replaced. Group ADR

Ambient Loops

Soundtrack ships with a collection of decent ambient audio files. It is not 100% comprehensive but there is enough there to get you started.

is used when you specifically want to hear real dialog instead of walla.

Sound effects are often your best dollar value in production. Remember that you can create a full 360-degree world with sound. Do not limit yourself to the obvious: that which you already see. Remember that surrounding any room, even if the windows are closed, there is always a full world outside. Be creative and think outside of the box literally.

Note that backgrounds are normally recorded in stereo or in multi-channel formats. This helps to give the illusion that the background sounds are surrounding the viewer. It also helps to keep the center channel reserved for dialog, so that the backgrounds are not muddying up the most important sound element.

Some background sounds will be intermittent and not really run the full length of the scene continuously. Examples of this would be an occasional crow caw or dog bark. It would be annoying for them to make noise through an entire scene, so an editor will cut them intermittently.

One important note: backgrounds are both very important and very difficult to do properly. Many filmmakers fall in love with the pristine, quiet sound of their production track, and are suddenly distracted by anything new that is added. In reality, these are very important sounds to have for creating a real world for the characters. Good backgrounds should make the audience feel like they are in the environment of the movie. Weak backgrounds will allow the production track to sound like it was recorded on a soundstage and will be counteractive to involving the audience. Poor choices for backgrounds would include 'room tone,' which is typically a fan or air-conditioner. These are the types of sounds (white noise) that most people find annoying. If they were to occur in the production sound, we would normally try to filter them out, so why would you want to add them back in? Occasionally it is necessary to add sounds simply to help smooth out the edits in the production dialog, and sometimes a fan can help that, but typically we try to find more creative elements that add something to the scene as well.

Finally, remember that sound can be very creative. Backgrounds should do more than just take up space on the soundtrack and fill in obvious holes. Good backgrounds will also strongly affect the mood of the scene, much the same way that music does. You can get away with a lot in sound design that you could never do visually. The audience will accept the 'wrong' sound at the right time, especially if it is mixed in a subliminal way and there are also reality-based sounds. For instance, in addition to a cold wind in an interior scene, you may also add distant wolf howls, even though

Surround Effects

Soundtrack ships with both stereo and surround sound effects. Some of them are really spectacular. If you are working in a surround audio room then try out some of the surround fireworks files. These are great to demo the capability of surround sound to potential clients.

there is no logical sense for them. Most audience members will not even notice them consciously, yet will be affected subconsciously.

Synch Effects (Also Called 'Hard Effects' or 'Cut Effects')

Synch effects are, as the name implies, edited into synch with something on camera. It may be something very obvious like a door close, or it may have an implied synch, such as a person turning his head to react to an off-camera door slam.

Sometimes there is confusion about what is a background sound and what is a synch effect. In some scenes, the same sound may be a background through much of the scene, become a synch effect, and then become a background again. For instance, the intermittent crow mentioned above would be a background until the editor uses a close-up of the crow cawing as a cutaway in the middle of the scene. For that shot (and only that shot) it would be split onto a synch effects track, and then back to a backgrounds track for the remainder of the scene. Even if a character simply looks up to react to a particularly loud squawk, that would be placed on the effects track instead of the backgrounds because of the implied synch relationship.

Both backgrounds and synch effects can come from a variety of sources. The easiest sourcing method would be to find the sounds in an existing sound effects library. However, there are several drawbacks to this. The first is that most good sound effects libraries are fairly expensive. Buying several large libraries can quickly add up to tens of thousands of dollars. An equally important drawback would be the lack of creativity in using library effects. All else being equal, most editors would prefer to record their own unique material rather than rely on library material. Editors quickly recognize library material. Even the average audience member may recognize over used sounds (albeit subconsciously), especially since many of these sounds have been in the libraries for four or more decades and have been used in thousands of television shows. (There is one wind that is still widely in use that was recorded in the 1930s.)

In order to record your own material, however, you will need time and money. On episodic television, these are very limited, so it is typical to use mostly library effects. Of course, it is possible to use library effects creatively, by combining or manipulating them in a way that makes them unrecognizable and original.

Recording sound effects, particularly elements such as vehicles or weapons, is very challenging. For sounds that may be difficult

Hard Effects

Look through the Soundtrack collection of sound effects in addition to other libraries. I am always surprised by sounds I find in the Soundtrack library that are perfect for specific uses. I have an additional library collection totaling over 250 gB, and the Soundtrack collection has sounds that are as good as those in any collection (although there is a wide range of quality).

to obtain or record, you may be forced to resort to a library. For simple backgrounds and sound effects (like doors), however, you may be able to quickly and easily record something unique for your film. On a big-budget feature, there may be a 'second unit' sound crew specifically for this purpose, who may get a month or more in the field recording elements for the film. However, this can also be expensive. Not only are you hiring a crew and renting their equipment, you are paying them for their time. If you have already invested in a library, you may be tempted to stick with those effects. Hopefully, though, you will have the time and money to record at least some original material. It makes a huge difference.

Sound effects may be recorded in mono, or occasionally in stereo or multi-channel. For sounds that take up a small physical space (like a door close), mono is usually fine. It can be panned in the mix if the door is on the left side of the screen. For sounds with a wide image (like a tank filling the screen), it is more typical to record in stereo, although matching the perspective of the shot may be difficult unless you bring a video monitor (or laptop) into the field to make sure you are matching any perspective change properly.

Foley

Some material is best suited to being recorded on a sound-stage while watching picture on a Foley stage (much like an ADR stage), so that Foley artists can perform the sounds. It is difficult to explain to beginners what should be recorded on a Foley stage and what is normally done in other ways. It all comes down to what is the best tool for the job, and how much money you can allocate to each method.

Foley artists are highly skilled specialists. Many of them have had training in dance or movement, and a surprising number of them are women. It's always interesting to see a 98-pound woman perform the footsteps for a bulky action hero. But it's all part of the magic of movies. Their work is such a specialty that they are very highly paid. In addition, a good Foley stage can be very expensive to rent. Foley artists generally have dozens or hundreds of pairs of shoes to choose from, and artists and stages generally have a mountain of props as well. Occasionally I see people trying to get their actors to perform their Foley. This is usually not the right choice and you should use specialists.

In a perfect world, you might be tempted to record everything in a Foley stage. This is prohibitively expensive, so you must decide which material benefits the most from being performed to picture.

Recording Foley

Soundtrack has a great set of audio recording tools that make it a perfect solution for recording Foley. If you need to record only a few items while working in Final Cut, it is possible to send just those selected areas to Soundtrack and in short order you have an audio file open, ready for recording with video attached. This requires only a couple of buttons to be pushed.

Footsteps

The Multipoint Video HUD (heads up display) makes synching sound effects easier than ever, but even it can't handle more than a couple of footsteps. And that's if you don't take into account the fact that the footsteps in the Soundtrack collection are mediocre at best.

The most obvious example would be footsteps. Imagine having to go to a sound library and edit every single footstep in a movie into synch, one step at a time. It would be extremely time-consuming for an editor (and time is money as well). So in the long run it becomes more effective to pay a Foley artist to perform them for you. A good Foley artist will get it perfect on the first take, frequently without even previewing the scene! In addition, library footsteps usually do not sound right. You generally have a small number of steps to choose from, and they begin to sound redundant.

The second element normally recorded in Foley would be props (short for properties), which means the same thing as in production: anything that is handled by the actors in the scene. Picking up a pile of papers and shuffling through them to find one page would create a unique sound that would be hard to find in a library and even harder to cut into synch. So again it is more effective to do this to picture in Foley.

Typically all footsteps and props are Foleyed throughout an entire film. The most obvious reason for this is that they will almost certainly be needed for the foreign mixes of the film, since the production track with English will need to be removed, along with everything that is tied to the dialog. Since the Foley needs to be done for the foreign mixes, it is generally done before the domestic mix so that the filmmakers have it if they decide to replace or augment the production sound. (You will also need the Foley if you have to use ADR in any scene.) Typically a full Foley track is a delivery requirement for distributors.

Foley can be quite creative. If you are doing an action film and you need fist-into-face punches or body falls, you would not record the real thing. In addition to hurting your Foley artists, you would not get very good sounds. So you are forced to be creative. You can also use the 'wrong' sound for the right moment in Foley, and get a more emotional reaction. You could use a ping-pong ball to create the footsteps for a comical character, or use a sledgehammer to create the footsteps for a superhuman villain.

Some elements are almost impossible to record in a Foley room. Weapons fire, or anything that is dangerous (lighting a fire or shooting off a fire extinguisher full of chemicals, for example) should be avoided and recorded in the field. However, gun handling, gun cocks, loading, and dry firing of weapons can be done in Foley. Another element generally not done in Foley would be doors. There is only one door in the stage and it's the door *to* the stage, and you don't want every door in the world to sound like that. Foley is almost always recorded in mono and panned in the mix (if there is time).

For all of these reasons, one of the first things that sound editors do is to create a spotting list of every sound element in the film and decide how it will be done, whether recorded in the field, recorded on a Foley stage, or found in a library. Some elements, such as vehicles or weapons, may need to be obtained before the recording session.

Some elements may be covered by more than one category in an attempt to make sure you have choices, or in the hope that the combined sounds will be better than the individual sounds. It's always easy to remove something if you don't like it, but just about the worst thing that can happen to a sound editor is showing up at a mix and realizing a sound was not covered, or the director rejecting a sound and you having nothing else to cover it. This can grind a mix to a halt, which is a disaster. The dub stage is expensive and is at the end of production when money is running out, and the movie will have a release date or air date that must be met, so pressure to finish on time is usually high. It pays to be organized from the start.

Due to changes in technologies, it has become more common to record Foley (and ADR) in the field. This may sound like an oxymoron, but it is now possible to bring a laptop with you to play back a QuickTime movie and record footsteps, props, or dialog that may be difficult or impossible to record on a stage. There can be both benefits and drawbacks to this. You are no longer in the pristine environment of the stage, so you may get unwanted background sounds. Yet, it may be impossible to get the sound quality that you want if you were recording indoors.

Field Recording

 Installing Soundtrack on a laptop makes a great tool for recording Foley and ADR in the field. Plus, you'll be able to do a quick edit to make sure the resulting recordings are up to par.

Re-Recording Mixing

The mix (or 'dub') of the film is when all of the individual tracks prepared by various types of sound and music editors arrive at a dub stage, and the mixers find the appropriate balances between all of the elements. Mixers control the volume level, panning between speakers, equalization, and use of reverberation to help place sounds in proper perspective with one another. They may also use dynamic range compression, delay, noise removal processing, and other signal processing to accomplish this task.

The final mix of the film is usually done by one to three specialists called re-recording mixers. For various reasons, the mixers are usually not any of the sound editors. Although this initially began as part of the Hollywood assembly-line process to streamline post-production (editors can turn over reel 1 of a film to the mixers, who can start mixing right away while the editors move on to preparing reel 2), there are other reasons for the mixers to be different people from the editors.

Effects in Soundtrack

Soundtrack has access to the world-class effects collection of Apple's Logic Studio. These effects include nearly every tool required in the mixing stage of your project. Of course, you can also work with effects made by other companies, as long as they are Audio Unit-compatible.

One reason is the highly specialized set of skills necessary to be a good re-recording mixer. Although editors also need many skills, the technical aspects of creating a good mix (compression, EQ, and noise removal, for example) are very demanding. In addition, mixers need to develop their ears very carefully to know when dialog is within acceptable level ranges and to hear other audible technical issues that can create problems when attempting to release or air a film.

Another reason is that it is often best for someone with no specific allegiance to any sound effects or music to come in and hear the mix elements 'blind,' that is, with no preconceived notion about what works best. A good mixer will bring new ideas to the table that no one else has thought of, even the sound editors.

Finally, especially with dialog, it is important to have new ears on the dubbing stage. The director has heard the dialog literally thousands of times from casting through shooting and editing. Even the sound editors may have heard it hundreds of times before the mix. A new mixer on the film will help protect the dialog for an audience who only gets one chance to hear and understand it.

In Hollywood, there have traditionally been three mixers who usually split the work as follows: dialog/ADR mixer, music mixer, and sound effects mixer (who usually also handles background sounds and Foley). This makes a lot of sense in some ways, as the sheer number of tracks allows a good split and each of these categories has its own specific needs in the mix. In a three-mixer dub, the dialog mixer is usually in charge and sits in the middle, as, by definition, dialog is the most important element when present. On some occasions, the mixers split the material differently, especially if the music mix is fairly simple, so that the music mixer is given additional faders, typically from background effects or Foley.

In recent years there has been a trend to move towards less mixers due to shrinking budgets. It is more common now, especially on television and smaller films, to see only two mixers on the stage. In this case, the dialog mixer also usually handles the music. This makes sense as typically you need to get the music out of the way of the dialog and, when the dialog stops, you want to hear the music come forward, so you are pushing one element up while the other goes down.

Outside of Hollywood, it is more common for one person to handle everything. This has almost always been true in New York, and sometimes in San Francisco. There is a certain logic to this, as usually it takes many passes to complete the mix regardless of how many mixers there are. Also, the head mixer usually manages

Warning

As a video editor considering the possibility of working on your own audio, you need to be careful that you keep fresh ears. You can do this by taking frequent breaks and by enlisting the help of others to listen in. You can also use reference tracks to help keep perspective. Keep other projects close by so you can compare what you are doing with them.

the other mixers anyway. There may be some drawbacks to working this way, however. It is always good to have extra sets of trained ears on the stage to help with creative ideas and to hear potential problems. It is also good to have an assistant, so that when one mixer gets busy trying to fix one element, the other mixer can continue moving forward or take a break. Mixing is a very long and tedious process, and having a second mixer really does make the day go by much more efficiently for many mixers.

It is also worth pointing out that a mix should happen on a dub stage and not in an editing room. An editing room is unlikely to have good acoustics and it probably does not have all of the gear necessary for a good mix. Most dub stages are multi-million dollar investments designed specifically for this purpose. Editing rooms typically have problems acoustically with flutter echoes or other reflected sound, and the small size of the room does not mimic what a real theater (or even a medium-sized living room) will sound like. Due to size constraints, editing rooms typically use near-field monitoring, which is unheard of in theatrical presentations and very rare even in the home environment. Intrusive noise is often a problem in editing rooms, from the noisy fans on computers to the sounds from other rooms in the building. Even worse, some editors mix on systems with very poor speakers. This makes it difficult to hear technical problems that may arise in the mix. The mix stage needs to be as pristine as a mastering facility for music recordings, as you are in fact making the audio master in this room.

As a result, using a dub stage is a very expensive process compared with editing. For this reason, it is always best to have everything as perfectly and thoroughly prepared as possible before coming to the stage. This means that as an editor you should insist that the creative forces hear and approve all of your material before coming to the stage. This is not always feasible due to their time constraints, but it is always the best preparation. A worst-case scenario (that is not that uncommon) is for a director or producer to show up at the dub stage never having heard anything and to be unhappy with almost every element from music to sound effects. This essentially stops the mix and forces the editors to start sound editing on the dub stage, which can be a phenomenal waste of money. Since the dub is one of the last processes done before releasing the film, it is also one of the most important and can therefore be very stressful, yet it is common that the producers are running out of money at this point, and they have an air date or release date that they are contractually obliged to meet. This can create very poor working environments. The best way to handle such pressure is to be prepared for the mix. If you are not over prepared, you are not prepared at all. It is always easier to drop something extra in the mix than it is to find new elements in the middle of a dub.

Regardless of how good your sounds are, if the tracks are not properly prepared for the stage, your mix may be impossible. Good editors know how to align tracks to make the mix as easy as possible for the mixers. (This is one reason why it pays for editors to have a little mixing experience.) Most importantly, tracks are organized by type of sound, with most similar sounds on the same track and the most disparate sound effects on separate tracks. However, the editors should always check with the mixers. Each mixer has his or her own preferences, including the maximum number of each type of track that they can physically handle on their console. Therefore it is sometimes necessary to share different types of sound effects on a single track. This can be acceptable as long as there is sufficient empty space between the elements, so that the mixer has time to change level or other processing without stopping. (Remember that dialog is never put on a sound effects or music track to prevent the possibility of English showing up in a foreign mix of the film.)

A good mix is like a performance art. In a perfect world, the mix would be a live play-through of the film with the mixer adjusting level, panning, EQ, reverb, delay, and compression all in real time. Of course, this is impossible, but for clients it would be ideal. Clients like to see the mix happening in as close to real time as possible, not only because the forward progress is immediately evident, but also, more importantly, because seeing and hearing the film in large sections makes it much easier to decide what is working both technically and creatively. The most difficult mixes are the ones that constantly stop for long periods and then restart, typically because the material was not prepared properly for the stage (elements are missing or wrong, or tracks are poorly laid out) or because no one ever approved the tracks before they came to the stage.

Of course, sometimes it is the mixer's fault when a mix goes poorly. Younger mixers who have learned to mix one track at a time by using a computer mouse are not at all prepared for what a real-world mix is like. Real mixers are capable of handling dozens of tracks at once in real (or near-real) time. Clients do not want to see a mixer volume-graphing. They can't hear what you are doing, and, since the movie has stopped playing, they assume that something is wrong and wonder why the mixer isn't mixing (in their view). They want to hear what you are doing in real time so that they can give you their feedback. To be a good re-recording mixer, one needs many hours of practice to develop both the technical skills and the ears to hear what is good, but one also needs to learn to deal with clients well. Once technical challenges become second nature, by far the most difficult part of the job is trying to make the clients happy, and this is often the breaking point for those people who are technically gifted but have not learned to collaborate well.

David Bondelevitch

David J. Bondelevitch, MPSE, CAS is an Emmy and MPSE Golden Reel Award-winning music and dialog editor, re-recording mixer, and Assistant Professor at the University of Colorado, Denver. He is a past president of the Motion Picture Sound Editors and current Vice President of the Cinema Audio Society. He studied composition at the Berklee College of Music and filmmaking at MIT and USC. He is also a member of the Academy of Television Arts and Sciences, the National Academy of Recording Arts & Sciences, the Motion Picture Editor's Guild, the American Federation of Musicians (Local 47), the Society of Composers and Lyricists, the Audio Engineering Society, the Society of Motion Picture and Television Engineers, and Broadcast Music, Inc.

He has been nominated for MPSE Golden Reel Awards 21 times. Credits include *Strangers with Candy, The Ten Commandments, The Hunley, Ruby's, Island Of The Sharks, A Separate Peace, Jeepers Creepers II, Black Knight, Passion of Mind, It Conquered Hollywood,* and *Stonebrook.*

Deliverables

Once the mix is complete, it is put into its final forms and the sessions are archived. I say forms, because rarely does a project end up in one final medium. These days movies are played in theaters, on television, on DVD, on the web, on iPods, and so on.

Often they are played in various languages, which requires a specific set of items, as mentioned above, primarily an M and E (music and effects only with no dialog). It is critical to have open communication with those on the receiving end of the project. They will tell you exactly what needs to be delivered and when it has to arrive by. This is a bad conversation to have once the project is complete; it should happen before you begin. This way you can plan for the deliverables early on in the process. Most big projects have this covered from day one, but things often morph as the project unfolds and it is important to ensure that someone stays updated on these details. See Chapter 10 for more information on exporting projects.

EXPECTATIONS OF THE VIDEO EDITOR

The expectations referred to in the title of this chapter include the group of transfer functions and Soundtrack installation items that an editor would need to know to get their Final Cut sequence into Soundtrack. This chapter covers a variety of those types of topics, starting with installation of Soundtrack Pro, covering the transfer of files from Final Cut Pro to Soundtrack Pro, and then on to a more abstract discussion of the audio tasks that you, as a video editor, may need to accomplish. The assumption is that you are working on either all or part of your project's audio in Soundtrack Pro and we are going to cover what needs to happen during the transfer of the files. After we cover the installation and transfer of files into Soundtrack Pro we'll transition into the next chapter, which covers the interface and basic editing features of Soundtrack. This means that, if you want to move right into the interface of Soundtrack and its tools, you should skip ahead to Chapter 4.

Installation

If you are like a lot of Final Cut Pro users who have been on the platform since early versions, you might need to pull out the installation discs to install the additional audio content for Soundtrack Pro. Many editors get to the point where they simply don't use the audio content often enough to justify a full installation. It will take some time and a sizeable chunk of space on the hard drive, but, if you need to work on audio for a project, it will likely be worth the investment. I'm not going to describe the installation process in detail here because I'm trusting that you know how to do it and that as a Final Cut Pro user you can find your way around a Mac. What I am going to do is explain what you'll need to know about the installation and then explore some of the items that are actually installed.

Install Location

When you install Soundtrack, either with the original Final Cut installation or at a later time, you are able to choose to install the additional audio content or to leave it out. The primary reason it is sometimes left uninstalled is that it takes up over 22 gB of space. You can always install the extra content at a later time by using the Final Cut Studio installation disc and choosing only the Audio Content portion. Aside from the Soundtrack Pro application, the following content is optional:

- Surround Impulse Response files;
- Sound effects;
- Music beds;
- Music loops.

I prefer to install all items on a separate hard drive along with my sound effects library and Logic Pro Studio content. This keeps all extra files in the same place and I can take the content with me when I am on the road using my laptop. While laptops drives are constantly getting bigger, using up so much space with extra content can be an inconvenience. You will also get better performance when using a separate drive. To install the files on a separate drive, click the Folder icon in the Location column of the Installation dialog.

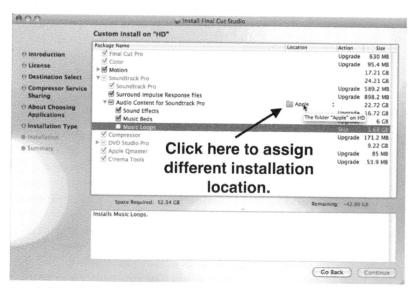

Figure 3-1 Installing audio content in a custom location.

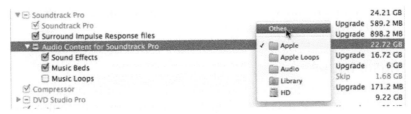

Figure 3-2 Choose the Other option.

In Figure 3-2 you can see what clicking on the Location drop-down menu looks like. If you want to place the files in a custom location, make sure the extra hard drive is connected and choose Other from the options. Navigate to the place you want to install the audio content and select it as the location. When you use Soundtrack with the drive attached you will have access to all of the content. When the drive is not connected, it will still show up in Soundtrack but will be highlighted in red to indicate that the files are not present. Simply hook in the drive and they will appear.

Next we will briefly cover what is in each installable option.

Surround Impulse Response Files

These files are part of the Space Designer reverb plug-in, which is used to create highly realistic acoustic space emulations such as the sound of a church, stage, or room. These are surround sound versions which can be used in the post process to create very realistic spaces in true surround. If you are working in surround, then these are a must have.

Sound Effects

The sound effects that ship with Soundtrack are pretty good. The collection includes everything from footsteps to gunshots, and explosions to ambient sound from various locations. While this collection is not enough to be a stand-alone sound effects library for large projects, it is enough to help out. I have used these sounds on numerous occasions when my 250 gB collection was lacking.

Music Beds

The music beds are a collection of music in varied styles and components. The collection houses fully completed pieces and also building block components that can be used to create new and original pieces of music. All music is royalty free; however, it is limited enough that some of the music will be easily recognizable to others that use the same library.

Music Loops

There is a smaller selection of music loops that is included primarily to provide access to 'legacy' content. These were used in earlier versions of Soundtrack and are probably the oldest set of music loops in the collection.

Dave's Video Editor Perspective

Temp Music Tracks

Working with a music composer is a process that every filmmaker goes through at some point, and it can be a rich and fulfilling experience if you know how to communicate your ideas. By creating a temp track, or scratch track, that represents the mood you hope the music will evoke you will be better able to tell your composer what you are going for. And frankly, the music content in Soundtrack is loads of fun to play with and can give you pretty complex music tracks if you spend enough time. Be aware, though, that there are thousands of loops and the tendency is to hear them all before you decide on which to use. (If you live with someone, wear headphones if you want to get along.)

Often, when you are editing, you need to have music to fill the dead spaces to see how the video is cutting together, and these tracks can really augment and inspire your editing process. The problem I have encountered is that once I get used to hearing the track I created using Soundtrack loops, the music the composer writes never seems to live up to what I've become accustomed to.

Sending Sequences to Soundtrack

One of the really powerful features of Final Cut Pro is the ability to send files and sequences directly to Soundtrack. This integration is a promise of potential collaboration that could be truly amazing. I have had enough experience with this feature, however, to know that it is not yet a perfect system. In fact, I will make some specific recommendations on how to use it and how to avoid some terrible time-wasting situations. I will also make a plea for future functionality and explain what it would take to make this tool unbeatable.

Explanation of Send to Soundtrack Options

There are three different Send to Soundtrack options. The first, Send to Soundtrack Pro Audio File Project, allows you to send an isolated clip (or clips) into Soundtrack for editing. Each clip is opened in an audio file project, which is similar to opening a video clip in its own preview window. You can look and edit, but can't layer it with other clips as you would in a sequence. When you save the file in Soundtrack, the clip is automatically updated on the originating sequence in Final Cut. If you resend the same clip back to Soundtrack, you can continue editing the file and have access to saved actions (rendered processing) that you may have previously completed in Soundtrack, which is similar to having access to the complete undo history. The clips are updated in Final Cut every time you save the project, thus providing a powerful way to edit clips in a dedicated audio editor without compromising sync and file locations. If you have your scratch and media locations set correctly in Soundtrack and in Final Cut, your files will remain in the desired locations. There is an explanation of the Soundtrack file locations below.

The second option, Send to Soundtrack Pro Multitrack Project, is to send an entire sequence into Soundtrack and edit/mix the sequence in a multitrack project. A multitrack project is very similar to the sequence functionality in Final Cut, but with a focus on audio editing and mixing. No matter what type of Send to Soundtrack you use, the video can be sent along, which makes the process of getting the files into Soundtrack very easy.

The third option, Send to Soundtrack Pro Script, uses Applescript technology to allow you to create presets that can then be efficiently applied to multiple clips on your Final Cut timeline. How to use the scripts will be introduced in this chapter even though some of the details of using Soundtrack won't make sense until later chapters.

Send to Soundtrack Pro Audio File Project

If you want to take advantage of the power of Soundtrack without transferring your entire project, then Send to Soundtrack Pro Audio File Project is the best option. It allows you to send a clip, or group of clips, into Soundtrack for basic editing without compromising synchronization. To send a file to Soundtrack, right-click on a highlighted clip, select Send To, and then choose Soundtrack Pro Audio File Project from the submenu (see Figure 3-3).

Immediately, a dialog will appear asking you to name the file and choose the export location, and giving you the option to Send only referenced media, which means that only the clip portion visible on the Final Cut timeline would be sent with handles on either side. I recommend leaving this unchecked because you never know when you might need to pull a portion of the file that

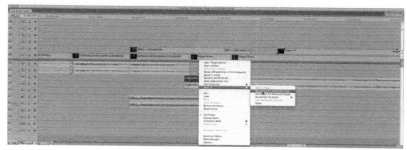

Figure 3-3 The Send to Audio File Project option.

isn't currently visible and it becomes hard to do once you send only the referenced media.

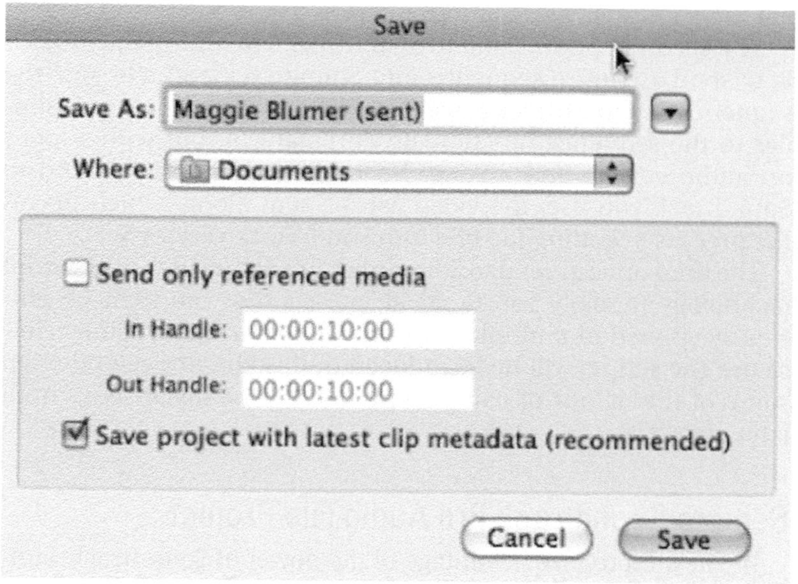

Save

Save As: Maggie Blumer (sent)

Where: Documents

☐ Send only referenced media

In Handle: 00:00:10:00

Out Handle: 00:00:10:00

☑ Save project with latest clip metadata (recommended)

Cancel   Save

Figure 3-4 The Send dialog.

The issue is that clips from the Final Cut timeline are converted to Soundtrack project files when they are sent to Soundtrack. They won't look or sound any different, but they reference a completely different file. After you add effects or change levels, you will need to save the file before it will reflect the changes in Final Cut. When you press Save, a dialog will typically appear (see Figure 3-5) the first time to ask if you would like to either reference the same files that the Final Cut sequence does, or create a copy. The dialog warns that, if you reference the audio, you will need to have the Final Cut project available at any time you wish to edit the Soundtrack project. The reason I prefer not to reference the audio is because it is nice to edit a separate copy of the files and it acts as a guard against accidental deletion or permanent alteration.

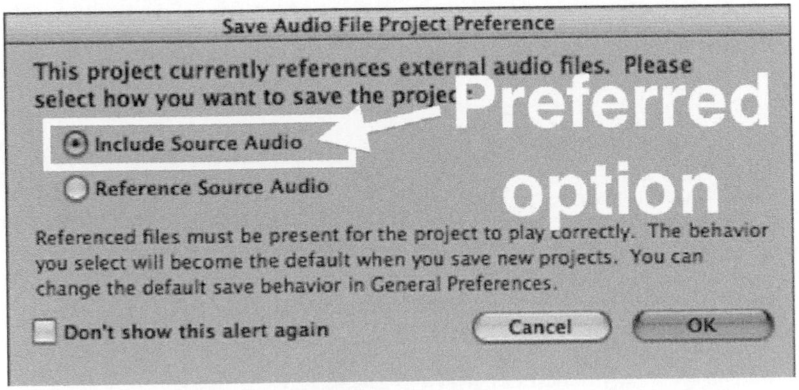

Figure 3-5 Choose Include Source Audio.

Another strength of adding effects using the Send feature in Final Cut is that all clips that were sent to Soundtrack individually for processing retain editability when the whole sequence is sent to Soundtrack as a multitrack project. This means that even though you may have sent a few files into Soundtrack for noise reduction, you will be able to look at, alter, or delete the noise reduction processes at any time. This may not seem like a big deal, but all audio filters in Final Cut are removed from the audio clips when the sequence is sent to Soundtrack. In fact, there are no transfer protocols (OMF [open media framework], AAF [advanced authoring format], etc.) that allow the Final Cut filters to transfer to any audio software system. If you want your audio processing to remain in place when the project is sent for audio editing and mixing, then using Send to Soundtrack for individual clips is a huge time saver and means all work you do on the audio is preserved for the future. Also, just as importantly, anything that is processed through Soundtrack may be reversed in the audio editing and mixing phase.

File Management

Much like Final Cut, Soundtrack relies on scratch locations for capturing and editing audio. You will set these by navigating to

Soundtrack Pro > Preferences > General. Near the bottom in the File Management section (see Figure 3-6) you will see two file management locations. The first, Scratch Location, is used when recording audio. The second, Edited Media Location, is used for storing files created through the editing process. I recommend choosing locations near your Final Cut project file locations.

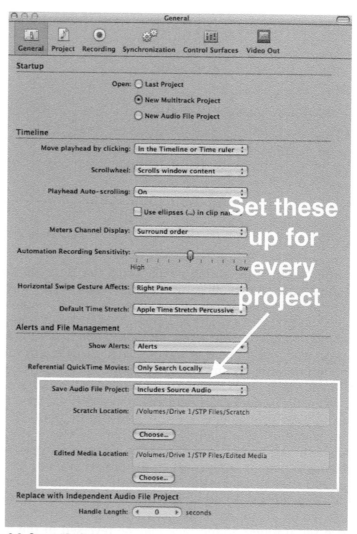

Figure 3-6 General Preferences.

One other thing that is important is the Save Audio File Project option. This is discussed early in the chapter in regard to sending individual files to Soundtrack. For that task, it is recommended that this option be set to Includes Source Audio to prevent accidental tampering with Final Cut files. While working with multitrack projects in Soundtrack, I recommend setting it to Reference Source Audio. After you have sent your sequence to Soundtrack and completed the initial save (discussed below), switch this option to Reference Source Audio. Otherwise, each edit you make

Dave's Video Editor Perspective

Setting Scratch Disks

In Final Cut it is essential that you set your scratch disks each time you start a project. If you are working on a computer that is shared with multiple users you should really check the scratch disk location each time to ensure that the settings are the same as previous sessions. It should become a habit that every time you launch Final Cut you check your scratch disk location. As you work on more and more projects you'll see that the number of media files associated with your projects gets larger and larger, and it is good practice to keep associated media files in the same folders in case there is any reason to locate, move, or delete a file. If you have media scattered all over your system on various drives and then try to move to another system, you may not have all the media files required to see your entire timeline. You will get a red dialog saying Media Off-line, and this is usually not good. Later, when the project is completed, you will want to back up the media, and keeping everything in one place will save time and energy trying to locate all of the associated media files. I always put the Waveform files and Thumbnail files in the same folder as well. Final Cut calls every Waveform and Thumbnail folder the same thing, so it will be better if you keep them in the same place for simplicity's sake.

It is also recommended that you set your capture scratch disk to be on a hard drive that does not also house the operating system (OS) and the Final Cut application. The computer will function more efficiently and you won't fill up your OS hard drive, thus degrading its performance. I would also recommend setting your auto save location to a hard drive that is different from where you are saving the project file. If you lose your project file because your hard drive has malfunctioned, you can always restore the edit session if you can find the auto save file associated with your edit, but obviously, if it's on the same hard drive, it too will be gone.

To complicate matters, Final Cut is set by default to open the last opened project when you launch the application. So, if someone else begins to edit on that computer and does not set the scratch disks, it will start putting media in the scratch disk folders you were using in your last edit. It then can get sticky if you, or the other person, decides to do some housecleaning and starts dumping files you don't recognize. I would therefore recommend going to **Final Cut Pro** > **User Preferences** and in the General tab deselecting Open last project on application launch. This way no one will accidentally start using your project's scratch folders.

Final Cut does have a Media Manage tool that is great for moving, copying, and consolidating all the media associated with your file, but if your project is very large this tool is not always flawless. It usually works pretty well, but you don't want to have to use it to clean up your media when you could have easily organized it before you started capturing it. Again, this is especially true when you have a system where there is more than one user.

So, setting your scratch disk in Soundtrack is equally as important as setting it in Final Cut, but there are fewer settings to consider. I would recommend that you put this folder in with your Final Cut scratch disk folder and call it STP_ProjectName_ Media, or something that clearly identifies its contents.

and file that you record will be saved in the Scratch and Edited Media Locations and also copied into the Soundtrack project file when you save the project. This redundancy can become quite confusing and is unnecessary. Also, it can be an efficiency killer because, after completing a large number of edits and file creations, Soundtrack will pause to copy all of the files and you will have to sit and wait. If you set this correctly, that will never happen.

Send to Soundtrack Pro Multitrack Project

Sending your sequence to Soundtrack is designed to be an easy process. The method of transferring is easy, the layouts are similar in both Final Cut and Soundtrack, the key commands are similar, and the overall feel is designed to be the same. If it weren't for the fact that Soundtrack needs to be an autonomous software package to have a chance at competing in the world of audio post-production, it would make more sense to simply incorporate all of the plug-ins and effects directly into Final Cut, and remove the hassle of having a separate application. At the present time, there are few video/audio platforms that are more closely integrated. If you opt out of using Final Cut filters for the Send to Soundtrack functionality, then nearly all audio prep work in Final Cut will transfer into the Soundtrack timeline.

Transfer Process

The easiest way to send your sequence to Soundtrack is to right-click on the sequence name in the Final Cut project Bin and choose **Send To** > **Soundtrack Pro Multitrack Project** (see Figure 3-7). A dialog appears that asks what to name the export, where to save it, whether or not you want to have it open immediately in Soundtrack, whether you would like a fully rendered video or just the base layer, and whether or not you want it saved with the latest clip metadata.

Aside from names and locations, the defaults for the options are usually perfect. The primary exception to this is when you want a different resolution video file from the sequence. In that case, you would turn off the video export and do it separately straight from the Final Cut sequence. This is a good idea when you want a smaller video for portability or simply because the original resolution is too big for your audio computer to handle. When you work on the same computer for audio and video, it will normally be able to handle the exact same video settings and you wouldn't need to export a separate version. As for having it open immediately in Soundtrack, this depends on why you are exporting. If you want to

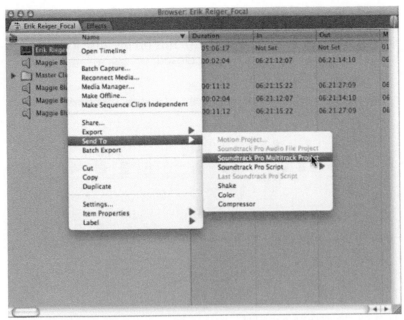

Figure 3-7 Send to Soundtrack Pro Multitrack Project.

Figure 3-8 Send to Soundtrack dialog.

get right to work then have it open right away. If you are exporting an updated sequence to begin the Conform process with an older Soundtrack file, then you would turn this off because it is easier to begin the Conform process with it closed.

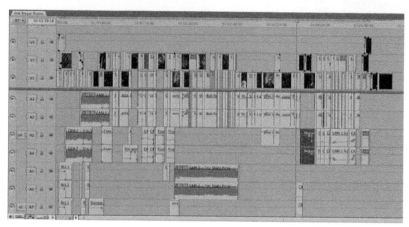

Figure 3-9 The sequence in Final Cut.

Once the Send function is complete and you have opened the project in Soundtrack, there are few things to remember.

- Opening a large project for the first time may take a few minutes because Soundtrack needs to build all of the graphic waveforms for the audio. Unlike Final Cut, Soundtrack cannot turn this feature off.
- Soundtrack and Final Cut handle audio playback in the same way using the system audio settings. If you hear sound in Final Cut, you shouldn't have to change anything when Soundtrack is loaded.
- Double-check your Scratch and Edited Media Locations (see Figure 3-6). It is highly recommended that these be located near or in your Final Cut project folders for organizational purposes.
- Set the Save Audio File Project option in the Preferences to References Source Audio (see Figure 3-6). This is important in terms of file management.
- If you chose not to export a video layer during the send process you will have to manually import the separately exported video. Otherwise, the video will automatically show up.

If the transfer is all happening on one computer and the project will not be copied to another for audio work, you should not

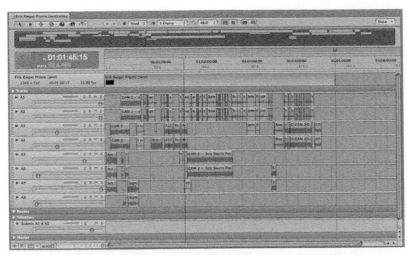

Figure 3-10 The sequence from Figure 3-9 in Soundtrack.

need to prepare the Final Cut sequence at all. If the project is quite large and you will be moving it to a new machine, performing a media manage might help out. The media manage will allow you to trim off excess files and create handles on the clips used in the timeline. This, combined with exporting a smaller video file outside the send process, will help keep the project sizes lower and more manageable. There are a few additional steps involved so it does take longer than the normal Send process; however, at least there is an option in such a situation.

Transfer Information

The Send to Soundtrack function is quite good at a number of things. The newly created Soundtrack multitrack session automatically matches the Final Cut sequence settings. The frame rate and audio sample rate will be identical and you should never have to worry about them. Of course, though, you should confirm that they are correct. Later in this chapter we will discuss the interface and you will see where this information is stored.

For all the audio information that is transferred, you should at least find your clips in the right place and at the correct time code locations. The Soundtrack project should be identical to the Final Cut sequence in almost every way. There are, however, a few things that do not transfer. This is important to know because it may change the way you work in Final Cut if you plan on moving into Soundtrack for the mix. The items that do not transfer are:

- Audio filters;
- Pan settings on stereo pairs;

- Audio fades (in and out) – this is not documented in the Final Cut manual;
- Exact audio levels (these are very close but not exact) – this is not documented in the Final Cut manual;
- Audio generators.

It would be nice if these items would all transfer correctly, but at least everything else does, though I would be hesitant to make any 100% assurances: all sessions should be examined after each transfer. With the latest versions of both Soundtrack and Final Cut, I have had very good experiences, far superior to using OMF or AAF. This is especially true when you consider some of the things that do transfer:

- Cross-fades;
- Nearly exact clip level (close enough to preserve the sound of the mix);
- All clips and clip histories processed using the Send to Soundtrack function;
- Video and sequence settings;
- Markers;
- Metadata;
- Enabled/disabled clip status.

Enough data transfers correctly that it is fine to use the Send to Soundtrack function. The issue of the levels being slightly different is a point of slight concern, but they are repeatable and in any case only slightly different to the original Final Cut levels. Part of the issue is in the graphic shape of the rubber banded levels. Final Cut draws with curves where Soundtrack draws with straight lines (see Figures 3-11 and 3-12).

Figure 3-11 Audio automation in Final Cut with curvy lines.

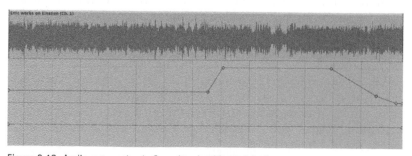

Figure 3-12 Audio automation in Soundtrack with straight lines.

While there is a slight difference in the levels, the majority of instances sound nearly identical. Normally, for an audio engineer, this would be a bust because the keyframes do not transfer exactly the same. However, the data transfers in the exact same way each time and this repeatability, even if slightly different to the original, is reassuring. It is the repeatability that makes it workable. Other clip levels that are adjustable in Final Cut without the use of keyframes are also a little off in Soundtrack. What should be a straight line in both programs often turns into a slight slope in Soundtrack. The difference is almost always inaudible because it ends up being less than a single decibel (a 3dB change is the normal minimum change required for the average listener to notice a difference). It is unnerving to look at the resulting project and see slopes in the audio level that weren't there in Final Cut, but it is rarely a problem that goes beyond resolvable. As stated earlier, all Soundtrack projects need to be examined after the transfer process.

There is another quirk regarding fades in the transfer. Cross-fades transfer with frame-accurate edges, while fades in and out of audio files don't transfer at all (see Figures 3-13 and 3-14). You might notice in Figure 3-13a and b that the cross-fades don't look exactly the same. The original Final Cut cross-fade is a little lopsided while the Soundtrack cross-fade is symmetrical. This is another example of data moving from Final Cut to Soundtrack almost exactly but without actually being identical.

Send to Soundtrack Pro Script

This is one area that we are going to explain in principle, but which to fully understand you will need to read further in the next few chapters. The concept is straightforward: take a set of effects in Soundtrack, create a script file based on the effects, use the script on a clip or set of clips in Final Cut Pro, and let Soundtrack do the work.

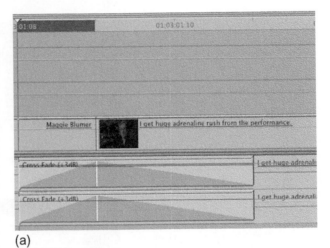
(a)

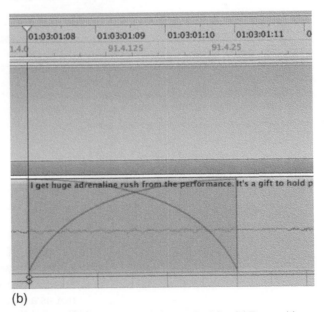
(b)

Figure 3-13 (a) The original cross-fade in Final Cut. (b) The resulting fade in Soundtrack.

(a)

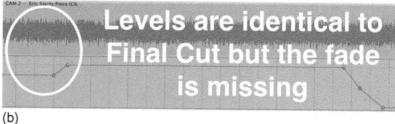

(b)

Figure 3-14 (a) The original fade in Final Cut. (b) The fade did not transfer to Soundtrack.

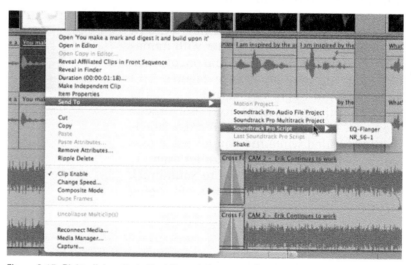

Figure 3-15 Right-click a clip in Final Cut to bring up the Send option.

The creation of a script typically begins in Final Cut and the process is as follows:

1. Send a clip into Soundtrack as an audio file project, but not as a multitrack project.
2. Process the clips with effects and processes.

3. Save the file as an AppleScript in the File menu. Make sure to save it in the default location so that it will show up in both the Soundtrack Script menu and as a right-click option in Final Cut.

The script saves the effects and processes as a list of what you did to the file. This list can be applied to other clips and/or groups of clips. Once you send a group of clips to a Soundtrack Pro script, they are opened in Soundtrack, processed, and then closed. If the clips have already been sent to Soundtrack, this will happen without a dialog, but, if they haven't been to Soundtrack yet, a dialog will appear warning you that the files will be altered permanently unless you permit them to be converted to Soundtrack project files. It is highly recommended that you say yes to this because if you don't the script will permanently alter the files.

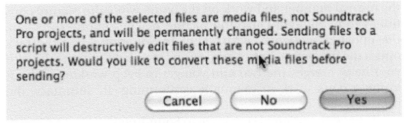

Figure 3-16 'Yes' is the recommended answer.

The Conform Process

Once you have a Soundtrack multitrack project you can begin editing and mixing. All too often your worst fears will be realized by a change in picture. No matter what anybody says, picture is only locked once it is put on tape for broadcast or on a disc for distribution. Many independent filmmakers are too afraid to move the mix into Soundtrack because they want to keep changing the picture while polishing the audio. Even harder is the time constraint often put on projects that really need more time to edit the picture, let alone mix the audio. The Conform function makes a bold promise to, in part, fix this dilemma by allowing the audio mix to begin in Soundtrack while the picture is still being cut. I performed a lot of tests in Soundtrack Pro 2 to near-success; however, there were aspects of the process that just didn't work correctly, for example files would end up missing or in the wrong place. Many times the cause of problems could be narrowed down to file types in Final Cut and not necessarily the Conform process itself. Either way, however, I made a number of project moves to compensate for picture changes by reading an EDL (edit decision list), cutting, sliding, and double-checking for mistakes, all without the help of the Conform tool because it wasn't 100% reliable.

Things have tightened up in Soundtrack Pro 3, or at least they seem to have tightened up because complex changes are translating better in the Conform process. Nevertheless, no matter how good it is, I still recommend only using this tool for basic changes. I also don't recommend working too much on audio until the final shots have been chosen because, if you do and things change, you will have wasted time and money. But when you have to work side by side with a picture edit, the Conform tool will help out.

The way it works is that you send a sequence to Soundtrack in the normal manner and work on the audio while the picture continues to be altered. Once the picture reaches another plateau, the updated sequence is also sent to Soundtrack. Soundtrack opens the projects together and compares the differences. It (with your help) merges the two and you get to keep working without losing a day's work in manually conforming. In summary, the process is:

1. Send the original sequence to Soundtrack.
2. Edit the audio and video projects separately.
3. Resend the updated Final Cut sequence to Soundtrack.
4. While the active audio project is open, click on the Conform tab in the lower pane (see Figure 3-17).
5. When you click on the Conform button, a dialog appears from where you can open the second project (see Figure 3-18).
6. A third and unsaved/untitled project is created which represents the combination of the previous two projects. The Conform tab now contains a list of all files, changes, and deletions with a section on the right where you can approve or reject items (see Figure 3-19). You can always approve all by selecting Command + A and then pressing Approve. Once you are finished checking each item and feel confident that everything is correct, press the Finish button at the bottom right of the Conform tab. At this point you should save the untitled project.

The global project view at the top of the Soundtrack interface is very helpful in locating the files in the list. When you click on one, it shows as a yellow block instead of a green block. This helps in the troubleshooting process while conforming.

Figure 3-17 The Conform tab.

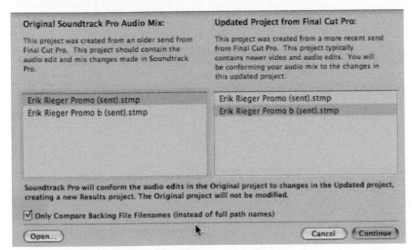

Figure 3-18 Choose Conform Project dialog.

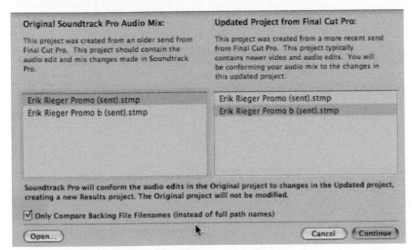

Figure 3-19 A long list of items to approve for the newly combined project.

Dave's Video Editor Perspective

The Conform Tool

Many filmmakers have small budgets and may not be able to hire the audio post personnel they'd really like to hire. But on occasion we will find the generous sound designer that will do your audio as a favor or for a small nominal fee. In those situations, you really have to provide picture lock and stick to it. If you don't, and you keep asking to make changes after the Sound Designer has put a fair bit of work into the edit, you may find your luck has run out and friendships are strained. Personally, I feel that Soundtrack provides an opportunity for a filmmaker to do much of the sweetening themselves.

I love the notion of the Conform tool because it allows me to make changes as I work through the fine cut. More times than not, after I think I am done with the edit I will find something that I want to cut out, and that change will impact on the work on the audio mix. For example, when I am doing the final color correction and I work through the timeline shot-by-shot, I often find a breath or an 'um' which I wish I had cut out. The color correction and final audio mix often happens around the same time, and for this reason I always find something because of the 'fine-tooth' nature of this 'combing.' If I were doing the audio and video by myself, the Conform tool would allow me to cut those two frames from the Final Cut timeline and it would automatically adjust the Soundtrack timeline. This is really exciting for the DIY filmmaker. You are free to change the cut as much as you want without worrying about creating more work for the audio post personnel.

The Conform tool gives the independent filmmaker hope and a reason to get better acquainted with Soundtrack. Or, if you are going to work with an audio engineer, it will also allow you to really work on the audio without worrying about locked picture until you are ready to send it away.

Other Thoughts on the Video Editor Role

As a transition into the next chapter, in which you'll have to put on the hat of audio editor, there are a few ideas I'd like to share. The first is that, as a video editor who will be working on audio, you'll need to advocate for both sides. This is very important in keeping things organized and efficient. An advocate for video might press for the following items:

- Audio of high enough quality to ensure the picture edit is making sense;
- Special sound effects to help with the edit;
- Music beds and temp tracks;
- A listening environment that is adequate to hear while you are editing.

On the other hand, an advocate for audio might seek the following items:

- A locked picture cut before a transfer occurs;
- Organized tracks from the Final Cut sequence;
- Minimal editing beyond what is required for the picture edit;

- Easily undoable audio processing (if any at all);
- The use of processes and audio editing that will transfer from Final Cut.

The primary point is that it is easy to get carried away when you know that you will be both editing the picture and mixing the audio. Instead of letting the lines between the roles become gray, you should pretend that someone else is completing the audio. In the first place, you never know if it will be someone else. Secondly, once you mix the phases there is a greater chance that things will become disorganized and this will inevitably cause problems later, at the expense of time and likely money.

Another thing to think about is your listening environment. There is a whole section devoted to this later in the book, but in the transition process from video editing to audio mixing it needs to be considered. Working on audio in a less than ideal location will prevent you from doing the best job possible, just like adjusting the visual spectrum of a shot using color without the correct monitor. Read the chapter on acoustics and get things set up before you begin working on the audio mix.

The last thing I want to recommend to you is the use of reference projects to help your ears to have a point of departure. If you have access to projects that have been commercially released to the same format as the project you are working on, then have them ready to play back at various points in the mixing process. This is a way to make sure you are on track and that you are achieving appropriate end results. Ears work best in a comparative manner, and they are very good at distinguishing between the quality of two projects. Listening to the reference will tell you almost immediately if you are on or off track.

4

BASIC AUDIO EDITING

Once you have installed Soundtrack and transferred your first project or file, the next step is to help you orient to the interface and general editing workflow. The best news is that many of the keyboard shortcuts and layout characteristics follow Final Cut. While there are things which are very different in terms of both design and functionality, there are enough similar items that you won't be completely lost.

Project Types

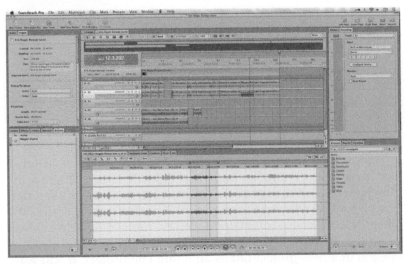

Figure 4-1 An Audio File project.

Before we even get to the interface, you need to know about the two different types of projects in Soundtrack. The first is the Audio File project, which allows you to open and edit a single file. There are no tracks to move clips around on and no mixer to adjust levels using faders. An Audio File project might consist of an AIFF audio file (see Chapter 10 for more on audio file types), Wave, or the .STAP file, which is proprietary to Soundtrack Pro. When you first save an Audio File project, you have the choice to save it as an Audio File project or as one of the other audio file types. The greatest benefit of saving it as an Audio File project is that all of the editing and processing added to the file is remembered in an Actions List that is saved with the file and can be recalled at a later time. The biggest problem is that the Audio File project can only be used by Soundtrack, Final Cut, and Logic Pro and not on other software platforms.

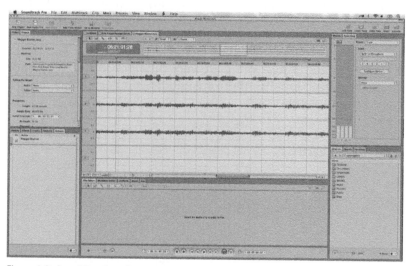

Figure 4-2 A multitrack project.

The second type of project is the multitrack project. This looks like what you are familiar with in Final Cut and resembles the Timeline view of a sequence. You can have multiple clips that can be moved all over the place. Multitrack projects and Audio File projects are also integrated together. You can double-click on a clip that is in the timeline of a multitrack project and it will be opened in a new project tab as an Audio File project. If you want to use an Audio File project on the timeline of a multitrack project, you need only drag and drop it in and it appears in exactly the same way as all of the other clips. The biggest difference in the way you will likely use these depends on which Send to Soundtrack function that you use. If you send a clip in Final Cut to Soundtrack, it will open as an Audio File project. If you send the entire sequence then it will open as a multitrack project. Over the course of a project, you will undoubtedly use both quite often.

General Interface

Soundtrack is designed with a simple default layout. It never takes more than a single mouse click or keyboard shortcut to access each tab, window, or specialized tool. In fact, the majority of the features can be accessed from the default single application window. Instead of using a system with various windows that are all disconnected, Soundtrack uses a single window that has a center section with three additional panes and a number of tabs in each pane.

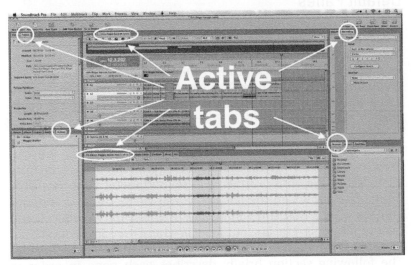

Figure 4-3 Active tabs in the default layout.

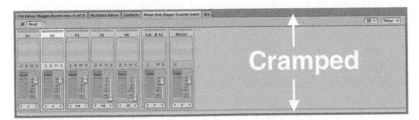

Figure 4-4 Cramped mixer tab.

One of the biggest issues with this system is screen space on a laptop system because using several of the important windows in a tab-style interface means that you will have very little room to work efficiently. The primary feature to help with this involves saved layouts. There are two that come preprogrammed in Soundtrack, but it is possible to save custom layouts. This is handy when setting up a custom workspace. A critical part of creating custom layouts is pulling tabs out of panes to make them free-floating windows. These can be expanded to full screen which allows detailed editing and mixing functionality. Once you create a custom layout, use the **Window** > **Save Layout** ... option to save the layout. One feature that is lacking here is the ability to recall layouts using keyboard shortcuts, beyond the two default layouts which are recalled using the function keys F1 and F2.

Default Panes

The center section of Soundtrack cannot be hidden or closed and represents the projects themselves. If you are working in an Audio File project, then the waveform is shown here. If you are working in a multitrack project, then the tracks containing the audio clips are shown here. You can have multiple projects open using multiple tabs. To switch between projects that are open, click on the tab of the project that you want to see.

The tools are visible immediately above this section. The panes to the right are typically more managerial in nature. You can browse your hard drives, search for Apple Loops, save favorite locations, meter your outputs, and set and meter your recording inputs. The panes on the left house the video, projects settings, and a few tabs that show information about tracks, effects, and restoration tools. The bottom pane is where the Mixer, Audio Bin, File Editor, Multitake Editor, and Conform tools are by default. The following section briefly describes each pane in order to provide you with enough information to navigate. Each section is described in a multitrack project context with the File Editor tab representing what the audio file project looks like because of their similarities.

As we go through the panes, the important areas will be emphasized and less time spent on areas that are of less consequence; while every area plays a role in Soundtrack, often there are two or three areas that do the exact same thing and it becomes messy if we spend the same amount of time explaining each one. The other thing to keep in mind is that I will be going through these panes and tabs based on the default window layout. In each pane there are various tabs which can be clicked-and-dragged to different tab areas, both within their original panes and onto other panes. You can also re-order tabs

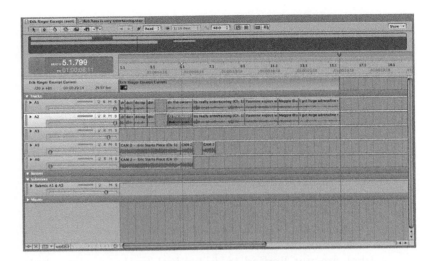

Figure 4-5 Center section with two open projects.

Dave's Video Editor Perspective

Cycle Region

The In and Out points on the Final Cut timeline constitute a good analogy of what cycle selection is in Soundtrack. With the timeline window active you create In points (I) and Out points (O) to insert precise locations on your timeline where you will be making an edit. Then, if you do an overwrite edit, it will only impact the portion of the timeline identified within the boundaries of those points. I also use these points on the timeline to activate other tools. For example, I might use the Blade tool to create an edit point. If snapping is active, the playhead will snap to these In and Out points and then I can take the Blade tool and cut the clip at these points if needed.

Figure 4-6 Center section items.

by clicking-and-dragging. One useful aspect of this is the ability to remove a tab from any pane so that it becomes free floating. Once the pane is free, it can be closed or expanded to full screen. To retrieve the default layout, press F1 on your keyboard.

The Center Section

The center section is the primary area in Soundtrack. The tracks can only be accessed in the center section. There is also a

Figure 4-7 Tools.

track for the video in this section. There is a ruler section (where you can set a cycle region for looping), a time code display, and above the ruler there is a global view that shows the entire project at a single glance. You can drag the box on the Global view to move the viewable area of the tracks below. Above the Global view is a group of important tools and other options.

The left set of items includes buttons for the primary editing tools (see Figure 4-7).

1. The Arrow tool lets you select clips and automation points, which you can then move around.
2. The Timeslice tool can make selections on the timeline that are not limited to individual tracks and/or whole clips. You can select contiguous portions of both clips and tracks and apply selection-specific processes. That means that you can select half of a clip with this tool and place an effect on it (similar to placing an audio filter on half a clip in Final Cut, which isn't possible without cutting the clip into parts).
3. The Blade tool cuts individual regions into smaller sections.
4. The Blade All tool cuts all regions across all of the tracks.
5. The Lift and Stamp tools store various pieces of information on a special clipboard that can be used to paste onto other clips.
6. The Scrub tool lets you click-hold-and-drag on clips in the timeline to hear the audio from the clip.
7. The first dropdown menu sets the automation mode (see Chapter 9 regarding mixing).
8. The Nudge menu lets you set the amount of nudge.
9. The Project Sample Rate menu lets you choose between the sample rates available. If you have a sequence from Final Cut, this is set for you and will match the Final Cut sequence sample rate.
10. The next two buttons determine how clips interact with each other. If the first is set, then clips will cross-fade when they are placed on each other. If the second option is set, overlapping files will cause the lowest file in the stack to be deleted. When you click-drag a file onto another file, the moving file takes precedence and the non-moving file loses whatever portion is overlapped.

11. The last set of options determines what happens to rubber-banded audio automation when clips are moved. In Soundtrack, automation rubber banding is attached to the track/timeline and not to the clips themselves. You can choose to have the automation move with clips that occupy the same track and timing by selecting the option here. You may need to toggle this quite often when editing because sometimes you may want the automation to slide with the clips, and at other times not.

The Video Tab

Figure 4-8 The video tab.

The video tab is the place where an imported video will play back. It can be quite small here, but in most cases that is okay because you will be working primarily on audio. You can choose the video zoom level using the dropdown menu. If you want to use an external monitor or an additional cinema display, there is a preference panel (Video Out) that provides these options.

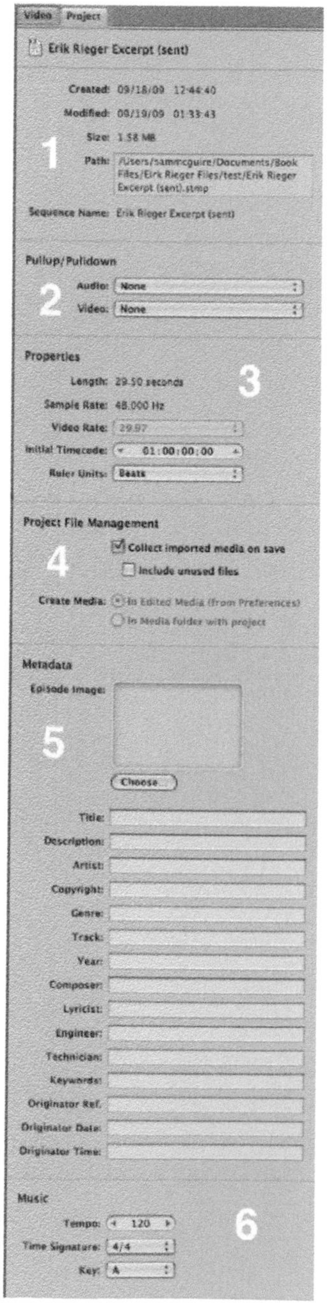

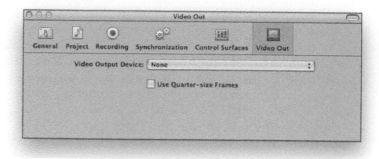

Figure 4-9 Video Out preferences.

You can choose any available device and also choose to make it quarter frame, which helps with larger files by making them play back at a lower resolution. I use a FireWire interface that has video outputs on it as the primary method of viewing video. The option shows up in Soundtrack as DV out FireWire (Digital Video Codec). The catch here is that the video will need to be converted to DV format for it to work. If you are using Soundtrack on the same computer as your original Final Cut session, you should be able to use the same interface (if any) that you were using in Final Cut. If you want to go full screen on your computer, the easiest way is to pull the Video tab off its pane and click the Expand button in the upper left corner.

The Project Tab

The Project tab is the place where you can view project settings and store metadata about the project. This tab is split into six sections.

1. The first section is a collection of information about the project file. This information is similar to that shown by pressing Command + I in the finder; it will show you the date created and modified, the size, and the file path. This can be useful when trying to find out if you are working on the correct version of your project.

2. The second section is the pull up/pull down section. This is a required function for all serious audio post-production software packages, but is not something that will normally be used in Soundtrack. For a good explanation of this concept see Tom Holman's book, *Sound for Film and Television* (Butterworth-Heinemann, 1997). The reason you will probably not use this feature is that it deals with audio that is connected with a film project that has been

Figure 4-10 The Project tab.

converted to video for an offline edit that will end up being broadcast. For major projects shot on film and going to a substantial broadcast, audio post is typically completed in Pro Tools or Nuendo. But, Soundtrack is ready for any task and would do just as good a job. It is safe to say that HD (high definition) video has changed much of the way the post process is completed for smaller projects and independent films.

3. The third area is called Properties and deals with additional attributes of the project. For sequences not originated in Final Cut or loaded with a video clip, you can independently set the time code rate. You can also set the initial project time code location and change the ruler units. The other data in this section are for information and cannot be altered.

4. The Project File Management section allows you to set whether or not imported files are collected into the project on the hard disc. I recommend turning this off in most cases, especially if you are in a closed environment and will not be taking your project to another computer. If you plan on changing systems, turning this on will ensure that you have all of your files. You can always turn this on later, following it with a save to pull all of your files into one place. The reason I recommend leaving this is off is to prevent large-scale duplications of imported files. This can really eat away at your storage space. The Create Media toggle determines whether or not any edited media is stored at the location set in the Preferences or in a folder created in the project directory. I leave this set to follow the Preferences because I am in the habit of setting the media and scratch locations at the beginning of each project. I could easily have gotten used to setting the media location to be with the project file.

5. The Metadata section follows standard media metadata conventions. This includes everything from an episode picture to the names of the various people who worked on the project.

6. The last section is to do with music and sets the initial tempo, time signature, and key.

Details

This tab changes its content based on the items that are in the current selection. It may reflect the entire project or a specific clip. When no clips are selected, you can numerically set the Cycle Region (loop feature) and Timeslice border values. If you

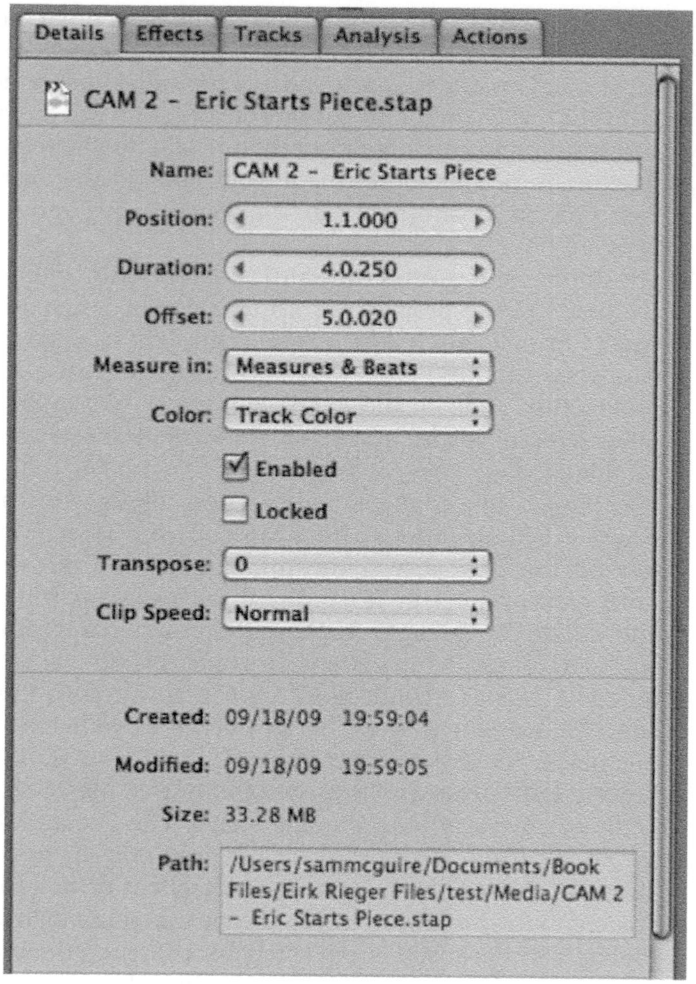

Figure 4-11 Portion of the details tab.

select a clip, a lot of information appears based on the selection. This metadata-style information includes:

- Name;
- Position;
- Duration;
- Offset;
- Measurement unit;
- Color;
- Enabled/disabled;
- Locked/unlocked;
- Transposition (for Apple Loops);

- Clips speed (for Apple Loops);
- General file information, properties, and metadata;
- Music information (Apple Loops information).

Effects

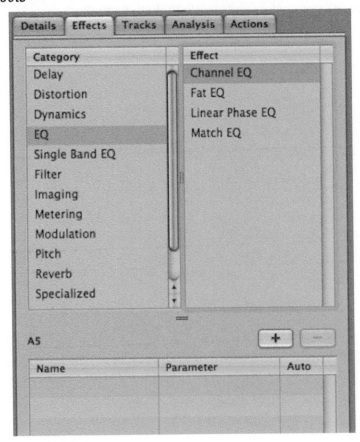

Figure 4-12 The Effects tab.

This is a tab where audio effects can be added to the various tracks. They are not added to individual clips, but to every clip that lives on the track. When you add an effect by selecting it and clicking the + button (or by double-clicking the effect) the effect will be placed on the track that is selected in the center section, which is why it is important to make sure you have the correct track selected in the first place. Once an effect is activated, it will appear in the effects list below the list of effects and the graphic interface of the effect will appear on the screen. The graphic interfaces for audio plug-ins have become a little out of control lately, with people tending to subconsciously think that a pretty plug-in also sounds pretty. Nothing could be further from the truth. Often a sleek interface is a cover-up for an average-sounding effect. In the effects list on the Effects tab, you can expand each plug-in's parameters and view/edit them textually.

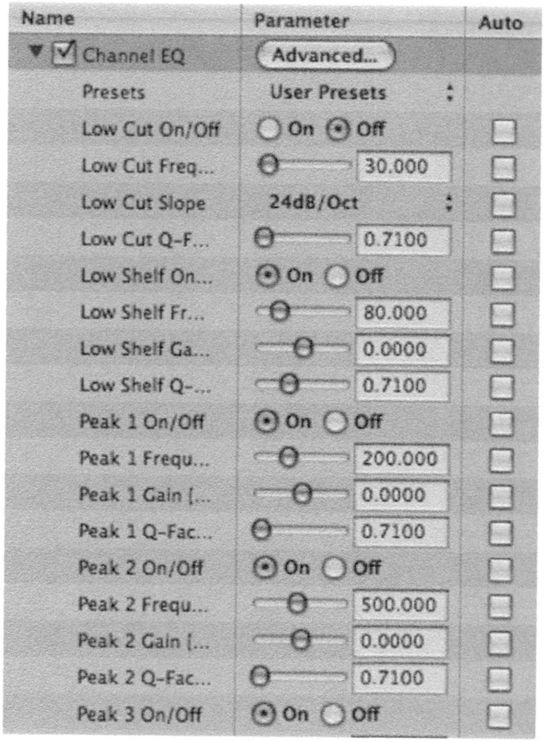

Figure 4-13 Effect parameters.

Clicking on the Advanced button will open the graphic interface and the check boxes on the right side of the list enable automation. This is one area in which the editor who is familiar with Final Cut will feel at home. A list of adjustable parameters is often much easier to use, but the graphic interfaces do offer advantages of their own (see Chapters 5–7).

Tracks

The Tracks tab is useful when you want to see an overview of all of the current tracks. While this is useful, if you need to do this with limited screen space, the Mixer tab in the bottom pane is

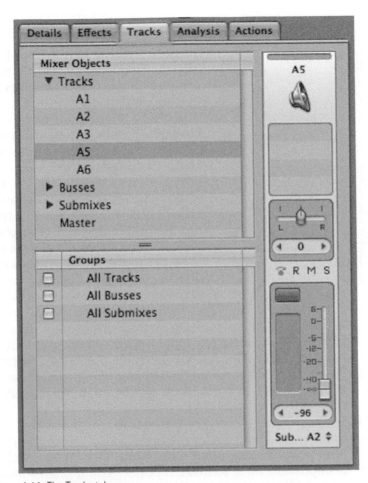

Figure 4-14 The Tracks tab.

much more useful and displays the same basic information. The only highlight of the Tracks tab is the ability to set various groups. In the Groups area, you can select all tracks and then, when you adjust a level or a pan, all tracks will change together. You can also select all tracks in the mixer by clicking on the first and then shift-clicking on the last to select all tracks. This forms a temporary group until the selection is released.

Analysis

The Analysis tab includes a set of helpful audio analysis and restoration tools. These tools include:

- Click/Pop – analyzes the audio signal looking for portions of the audio that experience a sharp rise and fall in level, creating a click or pop.

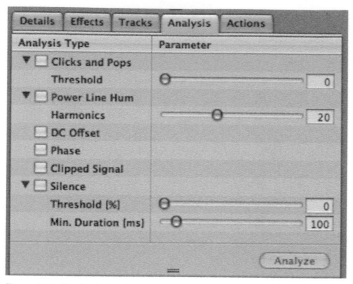

Figure 4-15 The Analysis tab.

Analysis tools demo.

- Power Line Hum – analyzes the audio signal looking for low frequencies that match power line hum. It also can remove the resonate frequencies or harmonics of the fundamental hum.
- DC Offset – analyzes the audio signal looking for DC offset, which is a very low frequency that pushes the audio off the center axis.
- Phase – analyzes the audio for phase problems. Phase problems almost always involve a stereo file, or a mono file that has been converted from a stereo file. It tests for potential problems in a stereo file that has channels that have consistently opposite waveforms. If one channel's waveform has peaks and valleys that are opposite to those of the other channel of the pair, the resulting audio if summed together would have partial or complete cancellation. For broadcast purposes, this could mean that dialog would disappear if heard through an older black and white mono television (they still exist!).
- Clipped Signal – analyzes the audio for portions that are too loud and that stay at the maximum level for a period of time. While Soundtrack offers to fix the clipped signal, it is impossible for it to make it perfect and it often sounds wrong. Clipping is most often caused in production when the sound is recorded to the camera with no dedicated sound person. If the levels are set too loud and no one notices, they will max out the microphone inputs and the signal will look like a straight line at the top of the scale. This often results in unusable audio.
- Silence – analyzes the audio for portions that are either completely silent or where the ambient noise falls below a set threshold. This is identified for informational purposes only.

The basic functionality of the Analysis tab is documented in Chapter 13 as well as on the DVD. Use the analysis tools sparingly because too much processing will likely damage your audio worse than the original problems.

Actions

This is an interesting portion of Soundtrack because it represents a major difference in thinking between video editors and 'traditional' audio editors. The Actions List keeps track of all effects applied to clips on the timeline. You can rearrange the effects in the list, edit the parameters, and deactivate them without deleting them. Most video editors immediately feel at home with this functionality because it mirrors what is possible in Final Cut. Audio engineers who are used to working in programs such as Pro Tools are often surprised by the functionality and are inevitably envious. Pro Tools doesn't have a feature like the Actions List. You can process clips in Pro Tools, but you cannot access a detailed history and make changes after the fact without going through a lot of trouble. The Actions List also keeps track of edits and almost every 'action' taken on the selected clip.

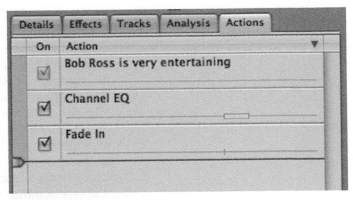

Figure 4-16 Actions tab.

In addition to the obvious strengths of the Actions List, you can also do a few other really useful things. If you Control + click on an action in the list a dialog appears offering additional options, as follows:

- Edit the settings of the action.
- Re-select the portion of the clip affected by the action (the first selection of the action that took place with the original processing).
- Change the portion of the audio in the action by selecting a different portion of the clip and choosing the Set Selection for … option. The action is reprocessed using the new selection instead of the old one. This is useful if you are using noise reduction and are just reducing a portion of a clip's noise. Once you process the audio file, you may find that you did not have enough of the file selected. Instead of starting over, go to the Actions List for the clip and, after making a larger selection of the clip, Control + click the action and choose Set Selection for … The larger selection will now include the noise reduction.
- Delete the action.
- Flatten audible actions. This is similar to flattening in Photoshop; all actions that are active will be rendered into

the file itself. This is useful because then the file can be pulled into other programs without having to worry about the Soundtrack session format.

- Flatten all actions, which renders all audible actions into the file and removes the inactive ones from the list.
- Play without actions. This allows you to hear the original file with no actions active. This is a great way to hear how much you have done to the audio file.
- Play all actions. This re-activates all actions.
- A/B the last two actions in the list. A/B is a reference to comparing two effects to see which one works best for the task at hand. The A/B option only works when there is more than one effect, and it allows you to compare the last two in the list.

When you are working with an audio file project you can use real-time effects just as with a multitrack project. In order to save the file, these effects need to be converted to actions using the Render to Action option in the Process menu. If you try to save without rendering, a dialog appears warning that the effect will not be heard. The Actions tab is also explained in Chapter 13.

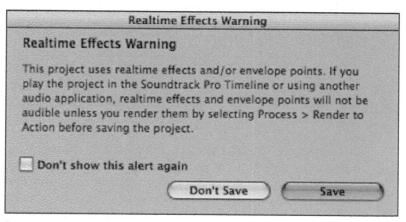

Figure 4-17 The Warning dialog.

The Bottom Pane

By default, there are five tabs in the bottom pane. These five require a bit more room horizontally than the rest, so it makes perfect sense to include them here.

File Editor

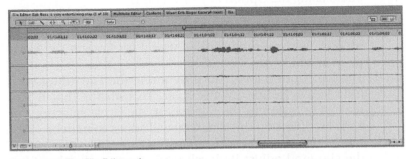

Figure 4-18 The File Editor tab.

The File Editor enables the editing of audio files in the context of the multitrack project. It shows you the file that is currently selected on the timeline above. This is similar in function to opening an audio clip as an audio file project. The File Editor has several flexible tools.

Figure 4-19 The File Editor tools.

1. The Arrow tool is the same tool as used in the timeline and in Final Cut. It selects things.
2. The Frequency Selection tool is used in conjunction with the Spectrum view, as described below.
3. The Pencil tool provides editing capabilities when zoomed in closer to the audio data. The File Editor allows you to zoom in on the audio until you can see each sample. In most post-production audio sessions, the audio sample rate will be 48 000 Hz. This means that there are 48 000 pieces of audio data each second. With the Pencil tool, you can zoom in until you are working with 1/48 000 of a second and draw new curves. This is useful for fixing clicks and pops.
4. The Audio Stretch tool is a personal favorite. You can use this to expand or compress audio timing without changing the file's pitch. See Chapter 13 for a detailed explanation of how to do this.

5. The Zoom tool allows you to zoom in to and out from the audio using the Option key as a modifier.
6. The Scrub tool lets you click-and-drag on the audio to hear how it sounds. The speed of the sound varies depending on how fast you drag. This is useful for finding the exact point at which you wish to edit.
7. The Link button links the selection in the File Editor with the Cycle selection on the ruler. This means that if you make a selection in the File Editor, the Cycle selection (In and Out points on the timeline) will adjust to match.
8. The Solo button and accompanying fader allow you to solo the clip (and adjust its level) while muting all other files. This gives you some sonic privacy while editing.

Dave's Video Editor Perspective

Sub-Frame Editing

For some new video editors it is not obvious why you might choose to do your audio editing in any application other than Final Cut. What may not be understood, however, is that Final Cut works at the frame level, meaning that you can only zoom into your timeline or audio waveform to a single frame. That may be okay for some situations, but it will be limiting at points when you need to do more precise fine-tuning. Some may be thinking that they don't see when they could possibly need more precision than a 30th of a second; however, when you start to hear clicks and pops or you cannot find the clean-out point of a sentence, you will fully understand the power of being able to get in to an audio clip at 48 000 samples per second. This is a fine-tuning capability that just does not exist in Final Cut Pro. Further, it is a good example of what an audio engineer can actually do for your sound that may not be obvious to the video editor/filmmaker.

Figure 4-20 Additional tools.

The buttons on the right side of the File Editor tab do two things. The first button takes any selection you have in the editor and pastes a copy at the current playhead position on the timeline, but only on the selected track. This is very useful for copying sound effects to new locations without messing with the old location. It is also very efficient because you can select only the portion of the sound you want to copy to the new location by simply selecting the segment, lining up the playhead, and pressing this button. The other two buttons switch the view of the File Editor between Waveform view and Frequency Spectrum view.

Frequency Spectrum View
For those of you new to audio, this view can be very intimidating. There is a practical look at using it in Chapter 13, but I want to take some time to explain it in greater detail here.

The Waveform and Frequency Spectrum views display similar file information. Instead of displaying the audio as amplitude (level) on the vertical scale and time on the horizontal scale like the Waveform view, the Spectrum view shows time horizontally, frequency on the vertical scale, and the amplitude (level) using various color schemes. The primary difference between the two views is that Spectrum is the only view that shows frequency. The real power of the Spectrum view is that you can edit the spectrum using the Frequency Selection tool. This tool is able to select rectangle-shaped portions of the Spectrum view and either delete, change gain using the Process menu option, or copy/paste data. It can be used to select portions of noise or rumble and then simply delete them. There is a demonstration of this on the DVD and a sample file you can work with while watching the examples. You can right-click on the Spectrum view to open a dialog which allows you to customize the view settings. These options are outside the scope of this book, but are briefly demonstrated on the DVD.

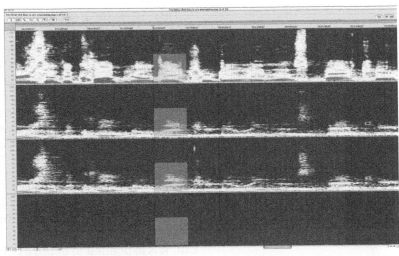

Figure 4-21 Frequency Spectrum view.

The Frequency Spectrum view explained.

The Multitake Editor

Figure 4-22 The Multitake Editor.

This is a tool used primarily for editing recorded ADR. Chapter 13 includes sections on both recording ADR and using the Multitake Editor. The basic premise of the Multitake Editor is that, if you loop record an audio file in Soundtrack using the Cycle selection on the ruler, the files will all be stored in a single clip that can be edited after the fact. The files appear as lanes and, once you split them into sections using the Blade tool, you can use the Arrow tool to pick between the different takes. Any portion that is selected will be automatically placed on the top level so you can hear it when it plays. This is an efficient tool that make editing ADR very easy.

Conform

The Conform functionality in Soundtrack is used to transfer sessions and updated sessions between Soundtrack and Final Cut. It is explained in detail in Chapter 3.

The Mixer

The Mixer is at the heart of audio routing in Soundtrack. You can mix levels, add track-based effects, and see the entire project at a glance. Most video editors stay clear of the Mixer and opt for a more Final Cut Pro-style experience. The Mixer can definitely be confusing when it is used for the first time, but it offers a lot of flexibility. See Chapter 9 for an in-depth exploration of the Mixer and the final mix stage of the project.

The Bin

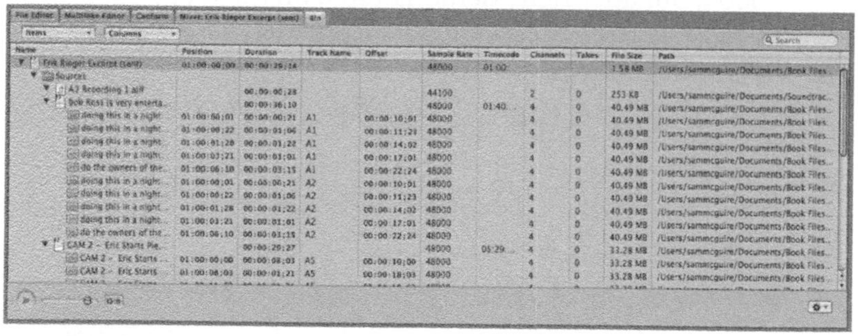

Figure 4-23 The Bin.

The Bin is the file management portion of Soundtrack. All open projects appear in the Bin along with all files that are a part of the open projects. You can see all of the available data about each project and file, including:
- Name;
- Position;

- Duration;
- Track name;
- Offset;
- Sample rate;
- Time code;
- Channels;
- Takes;
- File size;
- Path;
- Annotation;
- Author;
- Copyright;
- Tempo;
- Time signature;
- Key;
- Scale;
- Looping;
- Beats;
- Instrument;
- Genre;
- Hint quality;
- Project;
- Scene;
- Take;
- Tape;
- Circled;
- Ch. Index;
- Ch. Name;
- Note.

You may notice a wide range of metadata items available, including the newly integrated iXML standard. The Bin provides search capabilities as well as full integration with the timeline. You can Control + click on any file and choose from the following items:

- Show in Finder – useful when tracking down files.
- Reveal in Browser – shows the file in the Soundtrack browser.
- Replace selected clips with ... – switches one file for another.
- Open in Editor – opens the file in an audio file project.
- Reconnect – lets you reconnect media that has lost its reference.
- Remove Unused – useful for cleaning up the Bin.
- Spot to Playhead – places the selected clip on the timeline at the playhead on the selected track.

Figure 4-24 Bin view options.

- Spot to Timeline … – places the clip on the selected track at a specific time code reference set, in a dialog that appears once you choose this option.
- Show in Timeline – moves the view of the timeline to show you the clip's current location.
- Rename – renames clips.

The Bin shows four types of items: files, clips, markers, and podcasts. These four items can be toggled between visible and invisible, thus enabling you to keep the Bin visually organized.

The Right Pane

The right pane has five tabs that focus around either project metering or file browsing.

Meters

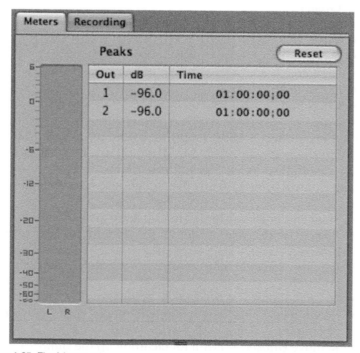

Figure 4-25 The Meters tab.

The Meters tab shows you the levels of the outputs of Soundtrack. The meters themselves span the entire range of audio (−infinity to +6). While you should check this to keep an eye on general levels, it is recommended that a separate and more detailed level meter be placed on your master track. This is critical when working on projects destined for broadcast, because the specific levels are critical. This tab also shows the highest peak level, the amount of the level, and the time it was reached. This is useful information when trying to discover problems. You can reset the peak data using the Reset button.

Recording

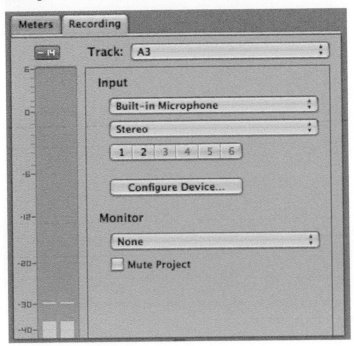

Figure 4-26 The Recording tab.

The Recording tab provides access to the audio inputs to Soundtrack. It has level meters showing how loud the input signal is, and has the ability to set the input information for each track. See Chapter 13 for a step-by-step explanation of how to record audio. There are many different audio interfaces and video interfaces that handle audio, and so you may have to refer to the manufacturer's documentation to get things set up with OSX, but, once you do, it is almost guaranteed to work with Soundtrack.

Browser

The browser is your link to the Finder. Here, you can view your volumes and network locations. The button on the top right can be switched between your computer and your home directory. The popup menu in the bottom right corner provides several options for placing files from the Finder into your project. These closely resemble the options in the Bin.

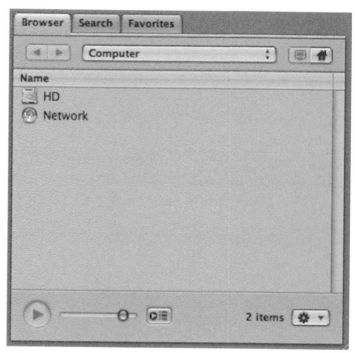

Figure 4-27 The Browser tab.

Search

The Search tab is in the Apple Loops browser. You can find Apple Loops here to use in your project. Due to the complex nature of music, it is way outside the scope of this book to explain how to create musical arrangements and temp music tracks. What I have done is to create a couple of DVD demos to help you to become oriented with this complex portion of Soundtrack. See also Chapter 13 for information on the search functionality of the Search tab.

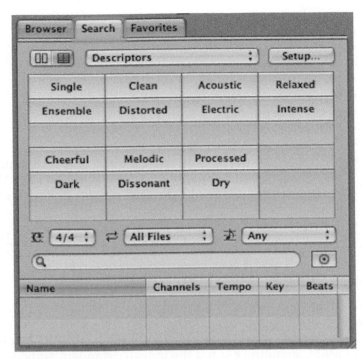

Figure 4-28 The Search tab.

Apple Loops explained.

Favorites

This tab is a place to set favorite locations so that you can easily find files. The way to create a favorite is to use the browser, Control + clicking a file, and choosing Add to Favorites.

Transport

Figure 4-29 The transport.

The transport is a permanent part of the Soundtrack interface and cannot be removed. It offers a number of useful options, including:

- A master level control (linked to the master level in the timeline and mixer);
- A Sum to Mono button (this has been fixed since Soundtrack Pro 2, in which it caused speaker and ear damage);

- Timecode entry for playhead position;
- Record button;
- Play from Beginning button;
- Rewind to Beginning button;
- Previous Frame button;
- Play button;
- Next Frame button;
- Fast forward to end;
- Cycle activate;
- MIDI sync, to sync Soundtrack to a MIDI time code source for transport control or another synchronization task. The preferences for this are in the Preferences window under Synchronization;
- Time code selection length.

Audio Editing

Now that we have made it through the interface, it is time to look at the editing process. Editing audio is most likely the biggest part of what you will be using Soundtrack for. All personal biases aside, Soundtrack is not the industry standard audio mixing tool. You will not see it being used in the majority of audio post-production facilities for mixing purposes. In fact, since you cannot buy it by itself, Apple has set it up as an appendage to its other Pro applications: Logic and Final Cut. That being said, Soundtrack is an excellent audio editor. It is better at audio editing than the more-used Logic Pro 9, which is why it is bundled with Logic and is fully integrated into it as a closer than typical external audio editor. You can select a region in Logic, press a key command, quickly begin editing the file in Soundtrack, press Save (nothing else is required), and the file is updated on the Logic timeline with the normal metadata and Actions List items saved as part of the file. Why create such close integration if Soundtrack is not better at editing than Logic? I can say that, as a result of personal experience, I wish Logic had the editing capabilities of Soundtrack. If it did, I would use Logic for everything! If Pro Tools had the same capabilities as Soundtrack, I would switch back to Pro Tools. As it stands, I use Soundtrack, Nuendo, and Sonar because they all have very advanced and similar clip-based editing capabilities that lend themselves well to post-production editing. Of those three, Nuendo has the best mixing capabilities, with Sonar and Soundtrack taking a back seat; *but*, Pro Tools is still used the most and has excellent mixing capabilities.

The Basics

The good news is that editing in Soundtrack is very similar to editing in Final Cut. In order to explain the editing process in as efficient a way possible, I have broken it down into various tasks. On the companion DVD there is an example session with about 30 seconds of material. The following tasks are designed so that you can load the example session and follow along.

Project file.

The Process Menu

The Process menu is the primary place to add effects directly to the clips. The menu is split into seven sections, each with a different focus. Let's go over a task from each section.

Process > Effects > EQ > Channel EQ

You will need to select an entire clip on the timeline, a portion of a clip using the Timeslice tool, or any portion of a file in the File Editor tab. Selecting a clip only processes the visible section of the file and not the handles under the edges. If you look at Figure 4-31, you will see the portion of the file in the File Editor that is visible as it is highlighted. The gray bar at the top that looks like a connected pair of markers indicates the specific clip boundaries. If you look to the left, you will see a group of other gray bars. These represent other clips on the timeline that share the same root file, but different clip definitions. This is a powerful way to see the entire file.

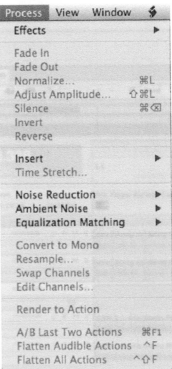

Figure 4-30 The Process menu.

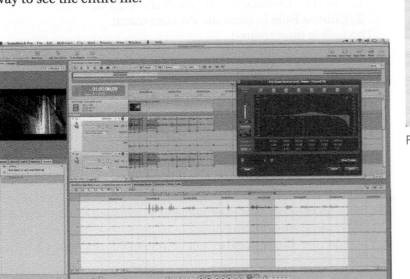

Figure 4-31 Processing with EQ.

If you process a single clip on the timeline, only the portion selected will be changed. If you open the File Editor and choose the entire file, you can process everything. This is useful because you can add the same effect to all clips from the same camera angle, even if it is cut up all over the place.

Once you have set the EQ to alter the sound, press Apply. This adds an action to the Actions List and changes the selected portion of the file. You can always edit the EQ settings by double-clicking the action item.

Process > Fade In

The next section in the Process menu (see Figure 4-30) contains some basic editing options, including:

- Fade In – creates a fade across the entire selection;
- Fade Out – creates a fade across the entire selection;
- Normalize ... – raises the volume of the clip to a set level;
- Adjust Amplitude ... – raises the volume of the clip by a set amount;
- Silence – replaces the selection with silence;
- Invert – inverts the waveform of the selection (changes phase by 180 degrees);
- Reverse – reverses the direction of the selection.

These options alter the file non-destructively, and each can be changed or deleted in the Actions List. For example, if I wanted to create a short fade at the beginning of a file to help it enter without a click or pop, I would use the following steps:

1. Use the Timeslice tool to select the edge of a clip;
2. Choose Fade In from the Process menu.

The fade is then created.

Of all of the options in this section, the fades are the ones that have a preferred alternate method of implementation. You can use the Arrow tool on the timeline to create fades on the edges of clips by hovering in the upper left/right corner of the clips and then click-dragging into the clip. This creates a fade with similar results to the Process menu fade. The reason that you might want to use the Process menu fade is that it can fade any portion of an audio clip, including portions not on the edge of a clip. Using clip fade on the timeline only fades the audio in that specific clip, while a Process menu fade is applied to all clips sharing the root file. Let's go through that process as well because it demonstrates several nice editing functions.

1. Use the Blade tool to cut a piece off the end of a clip (Figure 4-32a).
2. Use the Arrow tool while pressing the Option key to click-and-drag a copy of the clip. Now there should be two copies of the small clip (Figure 4-32b).

(a)

(b)

(c)

(d)

Figure 4-32 Example: using a Process menu fade.

3. Use the Timeslice tool to select the edge of only one of the clips (Figure 4-32c).
4. Use the Fade In option from the Process menu to make the clip fade in.
5. Notice that both clips fade in in exactly the same way (Figure 4-32d).

If you have a bunch of clips that share the same source file and you want to process them all, it is very easy to do. If you have a bunch of clips that share the same source file but you are not sure where they are on the timeline or you don't want to process them all in the same way, then you should use process effects sparingly or tell Soundtrack to make the clips independent.

Dave's Video Editor Perspective

Adding Fades with the Arrow Tool

I am a pretty careful editor and try to do as much of my fine-tuning in Final Cut as possible, because it's the software I am most familiar with. Also, I want to minimize the busy work I have my audio engineer doing. So, I listen carefully to all my edits when I am fine-tuning and approaching picture lock. I add many cross-fades to my timeline to reduce the harsh edits. I am applying a recurring effect, and therefore I have created a 'favorite' audio dissolve of two frames so I can quickly apply dissolves with a keyboard shortcut. However, I like options. There are times I prefer to work in the timeline because Final Cut has a very intuitive timeline. That being said, the one thing that I envy from the Soundtrack interface is the ability to add fades using the Arrow tool. If I could click and drag to create fades in Final Cut, it would give me another option to speed up my process of editing.

New File from Selection

To take a clip and make it independent from all other clips on the timeline, all you need to do is select the clip and choose **File > New > File From Selection**. The clip's audio is copied into a new audio file and saved in your Edited Media Location, as set in the Preferences. This new clip will retain the actions in the Actions List, but will be independent.

Process menu > Insert > Silence

This is one way to create audio content without recording. If I have a file that is too short to fill a gap in the audio, I add extra time using the Insert function and then use the Add Ambient Noise function to make it sound natural. The easiest way to create a new blank file is to create a new audio file project in the File menu and then use the Insert Silence function from the Process menu to give the file some length. One other option is to import an audio file and then delete its contents. The main reason for doing this, if it is done at all, is that the Add Ambient Noise function only works on pre-existing audio files.

Noise Reduction, Ambient Noise, and Equalization Matching

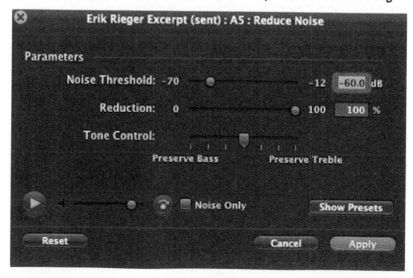

Figure 4-33 The Noise Reduction dialog.

Noise reduction, ambient noise, and equalization matching are explained in Chapter 13. They work much like all of the other Process menu items but are more specialized. Over the course of a large project I used to use them rarely. With Soundtrack 3 I am using them more often, especially since the Noise Reduction tool has gotten a lot better. The noise print used in the process has a higher resolution and so it does a better job pulling out the noise. The Ambient Noise tool is one that I have always had a hard time with because there are no parameters. Normally I use another track with a piece of ambient noise on it that I can copy and paste, cross-fade, and process to fit correctly. The Ambient Noise tool takes a sample and adds it in, but there is no guarantee that it will sound right. I still avoid this tool most of the time, but have used it occasionally with success when I had a really consistent and long piece of ambient noise. Equalization matching is another really great idea that I only rarely use because spectrum matching is something that takes a good ear and is not an automatic process. When I do use it, it gets me to a good starting point and I use an equalizer to finish the job. See Chapters 6 and 13 for more on this.

Dave's Video Editor Perspective

Finding Ambient Noise

If you can hear the absence of sound in your edit, it is probably a bad edit. You need to fill that spot with ambient sound or room tone. As a video editor and a filmmaker I have had numerous occasions when I needed to add some ambient noise to a track, to either hide something or fill in a dead spot on my timeline. What I've found is that recording room tone tends to be something a film crew neglects to acquire. So, what do we do as editors? We waste time trying to locate a dead space between words. We look at audio waveforms, we scan through the media, and sometimes we can find something usable. However, more often than not, we find something that has a background sound in it so, when we need several instances of the sound to make it long enough to fill the blank spot, you can actually hear that ambient sound looping and it may sound awkward and/or unrealistic. It's a waste of time and can be very frustrating, and it often provides unsatisfactory results. Please, take the time and make the effort to record room tone. It will save you time and money in the editing room. As a video editor, you want to be focused on storytelling and natural progression. When you are wasting time looking for room tone, you are taken out of the process. Soundtrack can help alleviate this problem, but you'll do it better if you get the room tone on location.

Process > Edit Channels

This section of the Process menu is grayed out most of the time and usually only applies to audio file projects. If you want to work on files that need channel re-ordering, double-click the file to open it as an audio file project. In Figure 4-31 you'll notice that the clip on the timeline looks like a mono file, but in the File Editor it has four channels, three with audio. That is because the original footage came from a source with four audio channels and all four were captured into Final Cut. At some point, the other channels were either split out to other tracks or deleted from the sequence. The File Editor looks at the original file and not just what is visible on the timeline. Once I double-click the file and open it as an audio file project, I can go to **Process > Edit Channels**. The reason for doing this would be to switch between microphones on a clip or to fix a clip that was somehow re-ordered somewhere else (such as QuickTime, where you can re-order audio tracks in the Properties dialog).

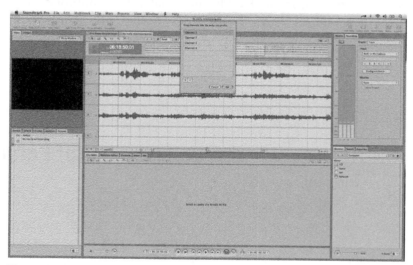

Figure 4-34 Edit channels.

In the dialog that appears, you can re-order the channels, delete a channel, and add channels. Another thing to consider while working on multichannel files in either the File Editor or in an audio file project is that you can select channels independently using the Command key.

Other Items

The rest of the Process menu was explained above in regard to the Actions List. One thing I like about the Process menu is that I have rarely ever wished there were more I could do. The system has been well thought-out and is fairly well implemented. Of all of the options, my only comment is that Add Ambient Noise should not have to have audio present to work and should be able to create extra portions of files, but since I use it so little it is probably not a big issue.

Editing in the Timeline and Using Menu Options

The timeline is an important part of the editing process. This is where the clips live and you can use a lot of different tools to achieve your editing objectives. The one thing we are not going to cover here is automation, because it is covered in Chapter 9.

The Selection Tool (Arrow)

The Arrow tool is all-purpose. Even though the tool is technically called the Selection tool, I prefer Arrow, because the keyboard shortcut is A and that helps me remember how to access it in the easiest way. With this tool you can select files and move them around, but it also does a lot more and can be used in the following ways:

- Click in the upper corner to add fade to the edges of clips;
- Click at the side of the clip to trim clips' edges;
- Hold shift while trimming to limit trimming to the edges of other files
- Hold Command + Option while dragging the file to slip the contents of an audio file;
- Hold Shift while dragging clips onto other clips to maintain the same time code position – make sure you press Shift before dragging because it will keep the time position only after it is pressed;
- Use in conjunction with the Multipoint video HUD (see Chapter 13);
- Use in conjunction with the Snap feature.

Snapping

Let's explore the snap options in the timeline. You can turn snap on or off by navigating to **View** > **Snap** and you can set the snap grid in **View** > **Snap To**. The Snap option is important when lining things up on the timeline. You can snap to ruler settings, other items on the timeline (edits), and markers. One important distinction to be made concerns the overall project time base. Soundtrack projects can be measured either in seconds (time code) or beats (musical measurements). This is determined in the Project tab by choosing either Seconds or Beats from the Ruler Units menu. Unless you are working on a musical project, I recommend leaving this as seconds. Either way, the snap options change depending on the project time base. When snap is active, you can always hold the Command key to bypass its effects. You can also activate the snap by pressing the Command key.

Dave's Video Editor Perspective

Snapping

Something I do often in Final Cut is toggle snapping on and off. The shortcut is the N key (the same as in Soundtrack). Sometimes snapping is a hindrance and at other times it is a necessity, and because it varies from moment to moment I am constantly turning snapping on and off. The novice editor often will make the mistake of trying to drag the playhead to the edit point on the timeline to add media to this point, or to make some adjustment. The problem with eyeballing it is that if you've expanded or reduced the size of your timeline (something else we do frequently when editing) you may be off by several frames and not know it because the timeline is compressed to show the whole edit across the entire window. Then you make the edit, and unknowingly you have a flash frame that you'll have to fix later. The canvas window will show you a little icon to let you know when you are on the edit line, but, if your snapping is off, you may have to scrub back and forth trying to find that point. Snapping is great for making the timeline snap to the edit point and should be a part of your workflow. At other times you might need to drag the playhead through your timeline to find spots in your edit that are not on an edit point, and the snapping will prevent you from finding that spot. Here you would need to deactivate snapping by hitting the N key. The name of the game is efficiency and accuracy so that you can be creative and inventive.

The View Menu

The View menu is a good place to become acquainted with the different zooming capabilities. Having a good grasp of the various zooming options is critical to editing and, for beginners, it is almost as important as actually listening to the sound. Using visual cues can be a useful crutch when in a situation when there isn't a good listening environment or there is loud background noise. The one thing that can never be replaced by careful listening is the blending of ambient noise from mismatched tracks. One zoom in particular is an eye opener for most video editors who are working on their own audio, and that is the Waveform Zoom In/Out. This makes the waveform graphic bigger just as a level boost would, but without the boost. Zooming in like this allows you to see what is in the softer portions of the sound. I don't recommend using this all of the time, but it can help you catch any issues that might be living in the softer sections of your sound. There are also many other zoom features that let you do everything from zooming on a selection to changing the track height.

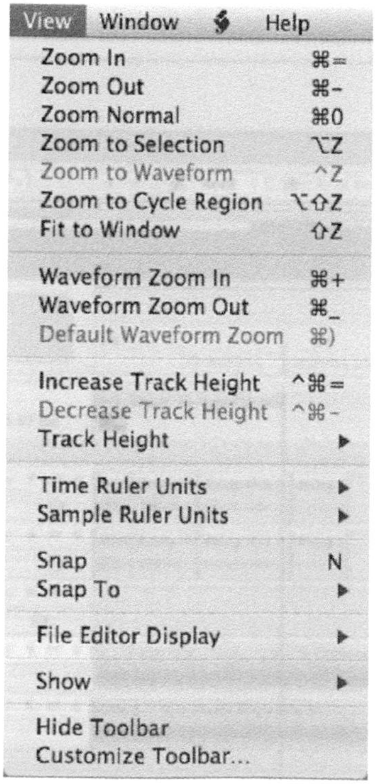

Figure 4-35 The View menu.

Figure 4-36 Low waveform zoom.

Figure 4-37 High waveform zoom.

Dave's Video Editor Perspective

Waveform

Final Cut Pro has a Waveform view that I use often. One example of how I use it is when I need to identify a clean edit of a word or sentence. It is not uncommon for the subject on camera to speak fast and to move on to another thought without taking a breath. It may be difficult to find that edit point if you are simply trying to stop the playhead at that point or scrub one frame at a time to find the correct spot. I've found that if I open the audio in the viewer, by double-clicking an audio clip on the timeline, I can then zoom in and find the spot a little more easily. Also, once you double-click a clip on the timeline, it will open up a version of the clip that is associated with the clip in the timeline, and not the browser. This will be indicated by the sprocket holes that you'll see right below the preview image in that window. They are telling you that, if you make any changes in the viewer window now, your timeline will be affected. So, if you make a new Out point or In point in the viewer window, it will update that edit point in the timeline. Also, once you've got that waveform window open, you'll see a red line. This line represents your volume level. It's much bigger than it is on the timeline so, if you are making level adjustments with the rubber band feature, you'll have a large window to work with. There is also a pan line that will allow you to visually make alterations with the Pen tool just as you do with the volume level line.

Another waveform tool in Final Cut that can be helpful is the ability to see the waveform in the timeline window. If you go to User Preferences > Timeline Options you can enable Show Audio Waveforms. This will create a visual waveform on your timeline that may help you to see the audio and thus assist in identifying important parts of your sound. There are certainly times when I will turn this function on, but I find it bothersome to leave it on all the time. The problem with leaving it on is that every time you resize the timeline or move the playhead to a part of the timeline outside the current view it takes a few seconds to redraw those waveforms, and requires that you wait until it is finished before you can continue editing. It gets bothersome, so I turn it off once I've used it to locate the audio I was looking for.

Markers

Markers are often used as a tool to make the editing process more efficient. Scoring markers, which are a source of information about, for example, specific areas in which the edit might require attention, transfer from Final Cut. These cannot be deleted in Soundtrack, but Soundtrack has the ability to create it own markers. The available types of markers include time markers (green), beat markers (purple), and an end-of-project marker (red). Each marker is assigned to a frame number, but the time and beat markers can be assigned a region length. When a marker is selected, the Details tab in the left pane shows the properties for the marker and you can add a duration. Once a duration has been set, you can adjust the length on the ruler above the timeline and moving

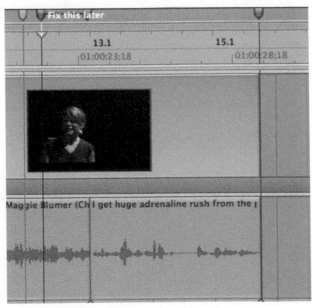

Figure 4-38 Markers.

Scoring with markers.

the marker's handles will snap to an active snap setting. Also in the Details tab, you can type a name for the marker. This makes markers a great tool for making notes, setting locators on sections that need work, keeping track of picture items that need sound effects, and any other documentation needs that you might have. Markers are also useful for adjusting the tempo of a project to fit the needs of an Apple Loop. See the DVD for an example of how this works.

Clip	Mark	Process	View	Window	🔊	Help

Channel Select ▶
Recording Take

Lock Clip ^⌥B
Disable Clip ^B
Color ▶

Split S
Join ⌥S
Create Envelope Points at Clip Edges ⇧⌘E

Trim In Point to Playhead D
Trim Out Point to Playhead G

Crossfade ⌘F
Fade In to Playhead ⌥D
Fade Out from Playhead ⌥G

Transpose ▶
Speed ▶

Spot to Playhead ⌘\
Spot to Timeline... ⌘I

Select All Occurrences of Yasmine enjoys work Track 1
Reconnect...

Open in Editor
Add to Favorites
Add to Bin ⌘B
Reveal in Browser
Reveal in Finder

Convert to Multitake Clip
Replace with Independent Audio File Project ⌥⌘I

Figure 4-39 The Clip menu.

The Clip Menu

The Clip menu has a number of options that affect the editing process on the timeline. Also, note that Control + clicking on a clip in the timeline will bring up a nearly identical set of options. Following are the items that are in the Clip menu:

- Channel select – allows you to switch the currently visible audio file channel with others in the audio clip. If you have an audio file with four channels and only one is being used, you can switch with any of the four.
- Recording Take – allows you to switch between takes loop-recorded using a cycle region (see Chapter 13).
- Lock Clip – locks the clip to prevent further editing /moving.
- Disable Clip – turns the clip off and prevents it from playing.
- Color – lets you change the color of the clip, which is useful for organizational purposes.
- Split – lets you split the currently selected clip and also lets you split a clip into three sections when using the Timeslice tool and creating a selection on a clip. The clip is split at the edges of the selection.
- Join – connects two pieces of a clip that were separated, but not two unrelated clips.
- Create Envelope Points as Clip Edges – Envelopes is the Soundtrack equivalent of audio level key frames (rubber banding) in Final Cut (see Chapter 9 for more on automation).
- Trim and Fade options – these next few options allow you to trim and fade the edges of clips up to the point where the playhead is.

- Transpose and Speed – these options only work with Apple Loop files.
- Spot – these options are explained above in the File Editor section.
- Select All Occurrences of … – is a way to select all other clips that share the exact same root file.
- Reconnect … – allows you to reconnect lost media.
- Open in Editor through Reveal in Finder – these are self explanatory.
- Convert to Multitake Clip – converts the clip into a multi-take clip that can be edited using the Multitake Editor (see Chapter 13).
- Replace with Independent Audio File Project – this is another option for making a shared clip a new file for individual editing.

When right-clicking, there is a very nice feature called Replace with Related File. This provides a list of other files with similar names that can be used to replace the currently selected file.

The Edit Menu

The last area we are going to cover in this chapter is the Edit menu, but you should already be familiar with most of these options from Final Cut. Video editors are usually masters of the ripple cut. Since the video is hopefully locked (at least it won't be changed during the audio editing by the audio editor) you won't have to use ripple deletes very often. When I record a non-sync voiceover, I may use the ripple delete when tidying up the audio. However, the most interesting option in the entire menu is the Adjust Selection to Zero Crossing. One reason why audio edits often have pops is because an edit point may have taken place while the waveform is in the middle of a curve. When that is pushed up against another clip, the waveforms may be totally different and the speakers simply cannot handle the sudden change from one to the other. One typical way to fix this is to use a cross-fade, which transitions the files together and thus the jump is smoothed over. Another way is to make edits at a place where the waveform crosses the center axis. If both audio files are cut like this, when they are pushed together there is no sudden jump. Sometimes, when the audio content is still extremely different, there might still be a cross-fade required.

Adjust Selection to Zero Crossing takes any selection you make in the File Editor tab and adjusts the edges to line up with zero crossing points. In most cases, changing the selection to hit zero crossings happens at a sub-frame point and will not throw off the sync, but it can remove a moment of audio and thus leave a gap

Figure 4-40 The Edit menu.

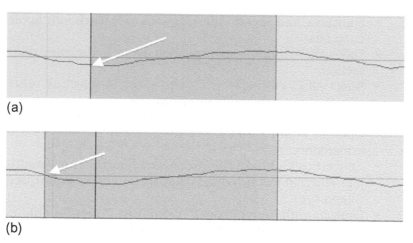

(a)

(b)

Figure 4-41 (a) Selection at non-zero crossing. (b) Selection moved to zero crossing.

Heads up display (HUD) demo.

in the ambient noise. Most often, a cross-fade is the best answer to clips and pops.

Heads Up Displays

The heads up displays (HUDs) are a useful feature in Soundtrack that I use in every project. Information about these is located in Chapter 13; however, because they are useful for editing, I wanted to give them a mention and indicate that there is a short demo on the DVD.

Summary

The tools of editing that are available in Soundtrack have been explained in this chapter, along with some common techniques. For further explanation of the process of editing in a variety of audio situations, see the audio post-production section in Chapter 2, in which David Bondelevitch does a great job of explaining the overall process. Now you can take the tools explained in this chapter and the following chapters and begin the editing process. For better or worse, audio editing is often just as time-consuming as the picture edit, and the problems encountered are often even worse. Soundtrack is able to help with many of them, and mastering these editing tools will give you the best shot at success.

5

INTRODUCTION TO DYNAMICS

In order to fully understand the dynamic plug-ins in Soundtrack, we are going to explore them in two stages. In this chapter we will introduce each dynamics plug-in and in the next chapter we will get under the hood and grapple with level standards. While understanding how to use your tools is of the utmost importance, the foundation for Soundtrack's dynamics capabilities starts with understanding general concepts and exploring the functionality of each specific plug-in.

Defining Dynamics

Think of dynamics as the audio level of your project. In fact, you may think 'audio level' in your head whenever the term 'dynamics' is written on the page. The reason that I have not simply used 'audio level' is that it is important that you begin to think more like an audio engineer. The type of project you are working on will define what you should do with your dynamics (audio levels). If you are preparing audio for broadcast, the resulting dynamics will be very consistent and you will not have a lot of loud and soft sections. When viewers watch the end product on a television, the dialog needs to be at a level that can easily be understood. If you are preparing audio for a feature film, there is a lot more room for   exibility in your dynamics usage because the audience will be in a controlled environment and you can use a greater variety of sound levels. Dialog in a feature film can be both quite soft and extremely loud without being a problem.

Dynamics Processors

Soundtrack offers a number of processors, which are used to manipulate the dynamics of sound. Most of them operate in a similar manner, which is nice when trying to master them. In fact, there are a few concepts that are key to understanding most of the plug-ins, so they are presented here as an overview.

Dynamics Concepts

The concepts listed here are not necessarily complex but are not usually explained on the interfaces of the tools themselves. While this section will not cover every single standard feature, it does cover the most obvious ones.

Ratio

Figure 5-1 Ratio.

The ratio parameter describes the difference in level between the input and output audio levels for one section of the dynamics processor. The ratio setting is typically measured in dBFS, which stands for Decibels Full Scale. This is the standard digital audio metering system, which uses 0 as the very loudest the audio can get. It is the unit of measurement that Soundtrack uses. So, if the ratio is set to 5:1, for every 5 dB that enter over the set threshold (see below), the audio level is turned down so that only 1 dB passes through. You could also make the same adjustment using automation or rubber banding, but the ratio allows for levels to be more precisely controlled. Still using a 5:1 ratio, if the audio that enters is measured at 15 dBs, then the output will be reduced to 3 dBs. You can calculate it by dividing the input audio level by the first number in the ratio: $15 \div 5 = 3$, which means that we are turning the level down by 12 dB. In other words, a 5:1 ratio is quite steep. A ratio such as 20:1 is considered a brick wall and has the ability to remove all dynamic variance in the audio signal.

Threshold

Figure 5-2 Threshold.

The threshold sets the level at which the dynamics processor will be activated. A threshold can either be a ceiling that must be passed over or a oor that must be passed under. If the threshold is set to −24 dBFS and it is a ceiling, then the audio must be louder than −24 dBFS in order for the processor to be activated. If the threshold is a oor, then the audio must be below −24 dBFS in order for the processor to be activated. The type of threshold is specific to the processor you are using and will be described on an individual basis later in this chapter.

Attack and Release Times

Once a threshold is crossed, there is a period of time before the full strength of the processor is in place. This is called the 'attack

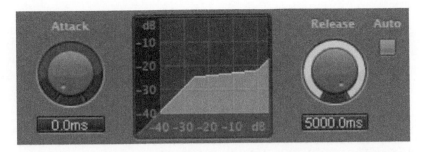

Figure 5-3 Attack and release.

time.' While it is not possible to have an instantaneous attack, it is possible to have an extremely short time, less than a single millisecond. The longer the attack time, the longer the transition will be into full dynamic alteration. The release time determines how quickly the compressed audio transitions back to its natural state.

The Knee

The shape of the knee affects the transition of the dynamic change when the level crosses the threshold and passes through the attack time. A hard knee creates a linear transition that sharply moves into active dynamic changes, while a softer knee offers a non-linear fade through the attack phase.

Figure 5-4 The knee.

Figure 5-5 The entire compressor.

Soundtrack's Dynamics Processors

Now that some of the basic principles of dynamics processors have been covered, it is time to look at the specific dynamics processors available in Soundtrack. The available tools form a comprehensive dynamics tool kit that has every area covered in a myriad of ways. The four types of dynamics tools are compressors, limiters, expanders, and gates.

The Compressor

The compressor is probably the most used dynamics tool. Just as the name implies, a compressor squishes or compresses the dynamic range and makes it less 'dynamic.' Once the range is compressed, the entire sound can be turned up even louder than before because the result has more headroom. Of course, it can also be left at a lower level with a certain amount of perceived loudness gain. In other words, even though the level hasn't been turned up overall, a compressor can make the audio seem louder. The dynamics are altered by turning down the louder peaks while leaving the tails of the sounds at the same level.

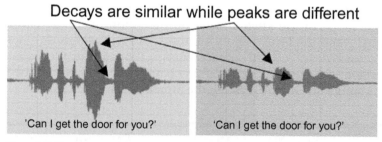

Figure 5-6 Uncompressed versus compressed audio.

Threshold

The threshold sets the level that the audio must go above to turn on the compression. If you pull the threshold down too low, you run the risk of pulling up any ambient noise. This happens when the compressor is reducing the dynamic range and then raising the overall level. Ideally, you will set the threshold so that the compressor is only active while the audio input is receiving the loudest sound and becomes inactive when the sound is only ambience and background noise. This way, the softer sounds will remain unaltered.

In addition to the basic threshold, there is an additional switch that changes the fundamental way in which the threshold analyzes the audio input. The two choices are Peak and RMS, which stands for root mean square. When set to Peak, the compressor looks at the very loudest peaks of the audio and uses them to determine when the threshold is crossed. When set to RMS, the compressor

Compression demo.

looks at the equivalent of an average of the audio signal to determine the threshold. The result is a snappier response when set to Peak and a slower response when set to RMS.

Noise pulled up close to volume of dialog

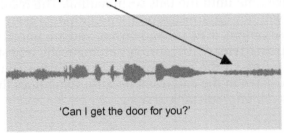

'Can I get the door for you?'

Figure 5-7 Threshold set too low.

Gain

Another thing to watch out for is the Gain control, especially Auto Gain. The compressor is most often used to compress the dynamic range in order to make more room so that the audio can be turned up even louder without clipping. Many compressors have auto gain makeup controls, which allow the compressor to always have a loud output, even when you are really cranking down with the threshold and ratio. With sounds such as sound effects and dialog, you do not want to push it as loud as it can get, so you should turn off the Auto Gain and adjust the gain manually. This gives you the most exible control over the newly compressed audio.

Attack/Release Times

If the attack time is set very short, you run the risk of blunting the start of any audio that has a sharp attack, such as words with T sounds or sound effects such as a door closing. If we compare the two waveforms in Figure 5-8, we see that both are compressed. The first is compressed with an attack of 0 ms and the second is compressed with an attack time of 100 ms. Notice the spike at the beginning of the second file. The attack time allows the attack through before the compression is fully activated. The first clamps down on the sound before the initial spike makes it through. The end result is inevitably duller-sounding, and should only be sought when the original attack is not wanted.

The release time involves the same concept, but takes place when the threshold is crossed and the compressor lets go of the

Figure 5-8 Comparison of waveforms.

audio. A longer release time can bring up ambience that is present in the sound, but a very short release can sometimes be audible as the sound springs back to its original level. To find an appropriate release time, set a very long release time and then listen to the tail ends of sounds. If the ambient oor seems to get louder, try a shorter release time and/or a higher threshold. Shorten the release time until the tails seem natural. The resulting release time will not be a distraction. An additional feature is the Auto Release button. This is handy when you are not sure about the appropriate release, because it automatically adjusts the release time to match the audio passing through the compressor. Be sure to listen to the end result because sometimes the auto feature gives you unpredictable results.

Ratio

If you need a sound to fit into a specific volume range, such as dialog for broadcast, the ratio is one parameter that is important to adjust. The problem is that compressors often bring up the ambient noise when they are set to bring the overall sound into a very specific range. It is possible to avoid this, but extra care must be taken not to pull the threshold in the audio range below the desired sound. Ultimately, use the ratio to adjust the amount of audible change in the dynamic range. If you want a mild change that is transparent, use a lower ratio. If you want a highly controlled range, use a much higher ratio.

The Knee

The knee parameter provides additional control over the transition levels as the compressor kicks into action. A low knee setting creates a linear transition – one in which the ratio is taken at face value. If there is a 3:1 ratio, then for every 3 dB over the threshold, only one gets through. The higher the knee setting, the less linear the transition is, creating a smoother transition. If you want absolute control, a linear knee is suggested. If you are looking for softer and more transparent compression, try a higher knee setting. A softer knee provides a slightly more organic result.

Circuit Type

The Soundtrack compressor offers a special feature. Through the history of hardware compressors there have been a number of methods for reducing the dynamic range. The Circuit Type dropdown menu allows you to pick from six different types, and these are modeled after hardware types. It is impossible to describe each different type because the general results are still quite close. However, you should experiment with these to see which gives you the results you are looking for.

The Limiter

The compressor also has a limiter built in. The section immediately following describes the limiter plug-in and contains explanations and descriptions. The reason it is included with the compressor is to provide additional exibility and efficiency – it's nice to have an additional ceiling on your compressor to make sure the gain never reaches distortion.

The Limiter Plug-in

Limiters are very similar to compressors. In fact, most of the dynamics tools are similar, so you may notice these descriptions getting progressively shorter. One of the primary differences is that limiters do not have an adjustable ratio. Instead, they are set to the highest possible ratio and are designed to perfectly prevent sound from passing above an adjustable loudness level. Limiters also don't have a parameter called a threshold. Instead, a limiter has an output level. The idea is that nothing should be able to leave the limiter at a level louder than the output level. Basically, the output level is the same parameter as the threshold on a compressor. Interestingly enough, instead of pulling the threshold into the audio when you use a limiter, you will push the audio up against the output level of the limiter. In the case of the limiter in Soundtrack, the output level can be lowered to only −10 dB. However, the gain fader adjusts the input level up to +20 dB. That is plenty of adjustment within which to push even softer signals up against the output level.

The other three parameters on the limiter are the Lookahead, Release, and Softknee.

Figure 5-9 The limiter.

Lookahead

The Lookahead feature allows the limiter to take extra time while analyzing the signal. Using the Lookahead feature is useful when the waveform is complex with a lot of sudden peaks, because it allows the limiter to see them coming and react appropriately.

Release

The release parameter is conceptually the same as the release on the compressor. When the audio falls below the output level, the limiter continues to work for a specified amount of time. This helps to make the transition from limiting to not limiting much smoother.

Softknee

Normally, a limiter acts as an unbreakable ceiling, preventing the audio from going past a specific level. When the Softknee function is turned on, the limiter ramps into action, creating a smoother result. Using a softknee is better for things that have a little wiggle room in terms of dynamics, and that you want to keep sounding natural. If you need the sound to be limited to a specific level and never budge, then turn off the softknee. One of the main reasons a limiter is used as opposed to a compressor is that the limiter is really good at setting a specific output level while leaving the softer parts alone.

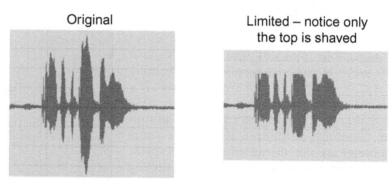

Figure 5-10 Before and after limiting.

The Expander

Expanders are not going to be hard to understand after looking at compressors and limiters. In the simplest of descriptions, a limiter is the opposite of a compressor. Instead of making the dynamic range smaller, an expander specializes in making the dynamic range wider.

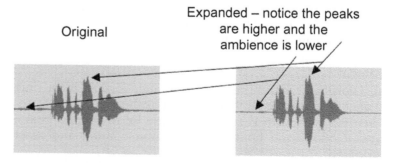

Figure 5-11 Before and after expansion.

The primary difference is the ratio parameter. Instead of going from 1:1 and up, the parameter is 1:1 and below. The expander doesn't really make the louds louder and the softs softer in one step; it in fact brings the softs that are below the threshold down and then brings up the overall gain. The end result is a wider dynamic range.

Figure 5-12 The expander.

The Noise Gate

The noise gate is a potentially dangerous tool. It is designed to be an automatic mute control. When the input sound falls below the set threshold, it is turned off. It can also be turned down instead of off, but the potential problem is focused around the material being gated. If you are trying to gate something like dialog with noise that is audible while the dialog is present, then the gate will often accentuate the fact that there is noise. If you are gating sound effects or other material that will be mixed into a bed of other sounds, then the gate might work fine. Instead of using a gate, you can always edit the files by cutting out the noise and using fades. The noise gate is an automated method of doing just that.

Figure 5-13 The gate.

Reduction

There are several parameters that are different from the other previously discussed tools. The first is the Reduction slider. This tells the gate how much to remove when the sound input falls below the threshold. When it is set to −100 dB, expect all sound to be removed when the input level is below the threshold. The threshold on a gate sets the point the sound must break through in order to open the gate.

Attack, Hold, and Release

The attack and release parameters are the same as above, with the addition of the hold, which keeps the gate working for a set period of time after the threshold is re-crossed. The point of this is to retain the natural decay of the sound even if it is below the threshold. An example of this would be reverb decay on a sound. If the hold and release are set short, the natural decay is cut off.

Hysteresis

The gate in Soundtrack has a specialized function called 'hysteresis.' This sets a range around the threshold to prevent the gate from opening and closing in rapid succession. This is a typical problem with gates that have to be set at a threshold that is similar to both the material you want to gate and the material you want to keep. In other words, the noise is very similar in level to the rest of the audio and a gate may be hard pressed to know which is which. If the gate did not have this function, then you would have to edit the noise out manually.

Side Chain

The Side Chain function allows you to alter the way in which the gate looks at the signal that is triggering the threshold. You can make the gate look at only the higher frequencies of the incoming signal by using the High and Low Cut filters. To hear what you are doing you can press the Monitor button. This lets you hear exactly what you are using to trigger the gate. Using a gate and side chain controls requires a lot of tweaking and adjusting to get the gate just right. Plus, you will need to listen through the whole thing every time you make a change to ensure you have the right gate settings. In the end, more often than not it is better to do the same thing by cutting manually and not using a gate at all.

Advanced Dynamics Plug-ins

The compressor, limiter, expander, and gate are the primary dynamics tools you will use in the realm of audio post. However, there are several other tools that Soundtrack offers which take the concepts listed above to new heights and which have very special applications.

The Adaptive Limiter

The adaptive limiter is very similar to the traditional limiter. Instead of using a linear wall to stop the sound from passing a specific level, the adaptive limiter models an analog amplifier. It rounds out the peaks and the results are based on the input signal. Different material will be affected differently as it passes through. The key to setting the three parameters is quite simple. Set the input scale so the audio input is as close to 0 on the left meter as possible without clipping. Next, set the out ceiling to somewhere between −2 and 0. Lastly, turn up the gain to a level of pushing that sound right to you. It is highly recommended that you place a gain plug-in immediately after the adaptive limiter on your channel strip to control the level of the resulting audio. The adaptive limiter can create a dangerously loud signal.

Figure 5-14 The adaptive limiter.

The Multipressor

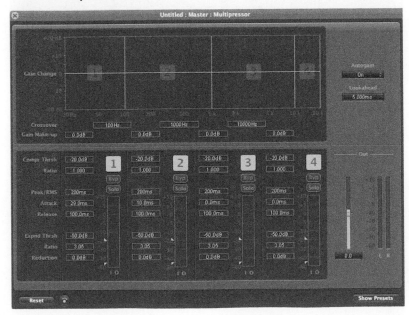

Figure 5-15 The multipressor.

The multipressor is a conglomeration of most of the different dynamics plug-ins. It is a combination of an expander, a compressor, and a limiter. The primary difference is that the audio input is split into four different frequency bands, and each band is processed separately. This is a great way to control the dynamic range of specific parts of the audio while leaving other parts alone. It is common to compress the bass frequencies while leaving the rest untouched. One powerful aspect of the multipressor is that the most used parameters can all be controlled graphically. The frequency bands can be changed as well as the compressor/expander parameters. This means that you can make changes quickly and efficiently even though there are a lot of different things to set. I highly recommend using the band Solo buttons to hear the specific bands you are working with separately from the entire audio track. This plug-in is one of the rare ones in that it allows such intricate monitoring of audio processing.

The Surround Compressor

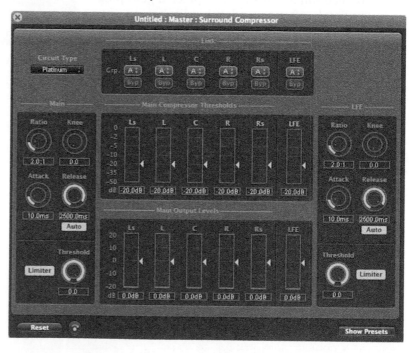

Figure 5-16 The surround compressor.

The surround compressor is another example of a specialized plug-in that is really just an expanded version of one of the basic plug-ins. In this case it is just a surround version of the compressor.

It is a useful tool for when you need to compress a surround stem, surround submix, or the entire surround output. Refer to the compressor explanation above for details on the inner workings of the surround compressor.

The Enveloper

Figure 5-17 The enveloper.

The enveloper is a unique dynamics processor. In a nutshell, it gives you the ability to boost and cut the attacks and releases of your audio's peaks. This is useful to punch up the attacks of sounds or pull down ambience as a sound is ending. The specific settings on the enveloper are fairly straightforward. The left half represents the attack and the right half represents the release. To boost or cut either side, adjust the sliders up or down. The time knob allows you to adjust the length of the change as the transients come and go. The threshold should typically be left at −100 dB because that keeps the enveloper constantly working. However, you may need to change this when seeking specific results with audio that has a narrow dynamic range.

General Application of Dynamics

In this last section of the chapter, the tools described above are looked at in a more practical light. Knowing what each does is important, but knowing when to use them is even more so. This section is split into three areas that reinforce a practical approach: audio preparation, micro-dynamics, and general dynamics.

Audio Preparation

Before you even use a dynamics plug-in, the audio can be prepared to make the process as seamless as possible. The preparation phase includes setting independent clip loudness and manual editing.

Clip Loudness

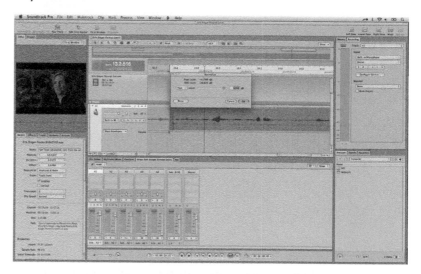

Figure 5-18 Normalization.

There are two general ways to adjust independent clip volume. One is to change the actual clip level and the other is to automate the volume of the track on which the clip resides. In Figure 5-18 you can see both of these methods at work. The volume lane area demonstrates drawn in automation that is changing the level of the track above it. The window that is displayed above the clips is a non-automated volume change that is being applied to the Scottish bagpipe loop. It has it's current level listed and allows you to change the level to any you choose.

The reason for leveling the clips is to help optimize the dynamics tools' effectiveness. Problems occur when audio clips of varying levels enter a dynamics tool. You can set a compressor to work on all of the levels, but the audio that is more compressed may sound distorted and/or worse than the audio that is better optimized. One of the goals of altering the clip levels is to create a set of audio files that are all of a similar level.

Manual Editing

Another part of the preparation phase is to edit out any audio that will inappropriately trigger or affect a plug-in's efficiency. If you are working with dialog, for example, a cough or extra breaths may inappropriately trigger a compressor and result in an uneven sound. To avoid this, manually edit out such sounds.

Micro-dynamics

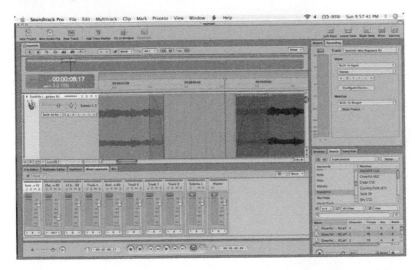

Figure 5-19 An audio file that has been edited to remove an unwanted section. This helps prepare the files for dynamics processing.

Micro-dynamics are defined as clip- and track-specific dynamics; the next section, general dynamics, refers to dynamics placed on submixes and master tracks. Micro-dynamics help to sculpt rough edges and individual sounds, while general dynamics finish off the project and level the overall sounds all together.

Clip Dynamics

One thing to remember about post audio is that you'll be working with a lot of different audio elements. It is impossible to assign each element to its own track, so you will inevitably be placing unrelated sounds on the same tracks. One way to deal with this is to process the dynamics directly to each clip. In Soundtrack, you can process clips and then tweak them using the Actions List.

In Figure 5-20 you can see the Process menu structure in Soundtrack Pro. You select the audio file you want to process and then choose the tool you want to use. Once you apply the effect, you can add more and then later make adjustments using the Actions menu. The really efficient thing about this is that you can

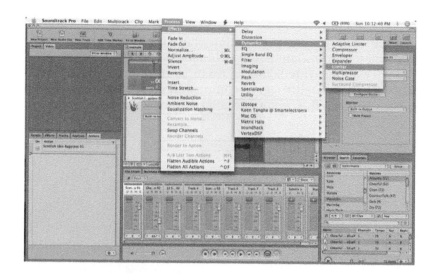

Figure 5-20 Accessing the limiter in the Process menu.

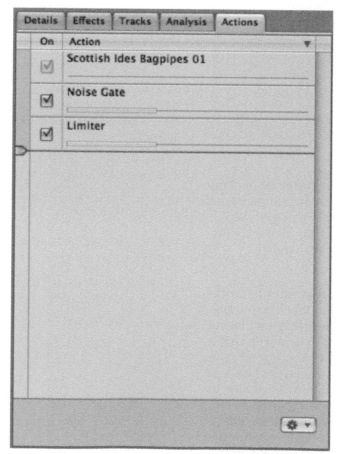

Figure 5-21 The Action List.

adjust any of the items in the Actions List and the changes will automatically ripple through the other effects. Additionally, you can change the order and the change will be rippled as well. Best of all, this list is stored with the audio clip and Soundtrack never forgets what you have done to each and every clip.

Track Dynamics

If you have a track with all related items, such as dialog, then you may consider placing a real-time dynamics effect on the track. This will affect everything on the track. This only works if the track is appropriately prepared (see audio preparation, above). As an additional level of control, you can automate the inserts and change things at different points on your timeline.

In Figure 5-22 you can see automation curves for the compressor that is inserted in the first track. This is an extremely flexible way to control your dynamics tools, but you will need to stay organized with what you are doing because automating plug-ins often removes the ability to tweak the effects on their graphic user interfaces.

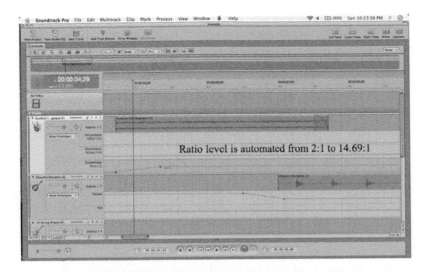

Figure 5-22 Automating the ratio level.

General Dynamics

This is the final layer of dynamics control. If you take care of the preparation and micro-dynamics appropriately, the final layers of dynamics will be much easier to set in place. The two places this applies are on submixes and master tracks.

Submixes

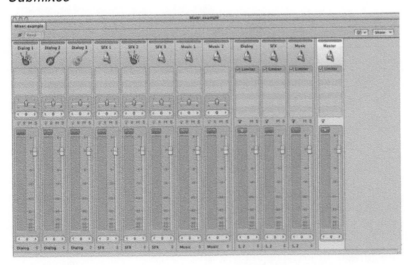

Figure 5-23 Mixer with submixes.

A submix is an audio funnel. You might send all of your dialog tracks through a submix track. You might send all of the sound effects from a scene through a submix. You will definitely want to send all of your music through a submix. By that point you will probably have leveled out and prepared all of the individual clips and tracks. Once that is done, you will be able to set overall levels for each of the specific submixes. If the goal is to prepare for broadcast, then the submix is where you will set the overall dialog levels to keep them to station standards. It is possible to do such a detailed job at the micro level that setting the general level on the submix might not be required. However, it is never a problem to set up a limiter on the submix as a safeguard against clipping and distortion.

Master Tracks

The master track is the final pipeline for the audio of your project. The primary goal of using dynamics tools at this phase of the project is usually to set the output to a specific loudness range. Using a limiter to set the output ceiling is standard. However, it is not recommended that too much limiting is used here. Make the project sound good and let the delivery format define what you do, but remember that the master track is the best place to affect the project as a whole.

6

DYNAMICS STANDARDS

Chapter 5 explored the dynamics tool-set specific to Soundtrack. It covered what the tools are and how to use them, and talked about some generalized methods of implementation. In this chapter we are going to explore some of the specifics dealing with meeting the volume level standards for a variety of projects. This chapter could easily have been located immediately after the chapter on mixing (Chapter 9), but I think it is important to start working towards the appropriate end result very early in the process. If you were to wait until after the mix was complete to figure out how loud everything needs to be, you would probably have to redo the mix anyway.

Soundtrack as the Right Tool for the Job

I am going to be 100% honest about how well I think Soundtrack is suited to each of the following scenarios, which might affect how you approach them as a video editor trying to work on the audio portion of a project. Let's focus on four different project types and explore what you should expect and how well Soundtrack is able to handle the different scenarios.

Theatrical Mixing

To mix for a theatrical release, you need a very specific set of tools and you have to be in a specific type of room. Because of the size of movie theaters, you simply can't mix in a small audio control room and expect it to translate well to the big screen. That's why theatrical projects are mixed in theater-sized mix rooms. These rooms cost a lot and the equipment is typically state-of-the-art. With so much money on the line, the equipment and software have to be the best and most efficient, and also have to be compatible with the highest number of other potential mixing/editing spaces. This almost immediately rules out Soundtrack as a competitor for such mixing spaces because it is not widely used and does not have the high-end feature set that systems like Pro Tools and Nuendo offer. That's okay, though, because Soundtrack really shines as an audio editor and as a mixer for smaller projects. I have used Soundtrack in a small mix theater, but only for small projects that were easier to accomplish as a send from Final Cut, or to edit replaced dialog long before a final mix.

Speaking in over simplified terms, theatrical mixing uses a calibrated system to ensure the levels transition correctly from any mix room to any theater (as long as both use the correct calibration methods). To calibrate a mix stage (theater for mixing) you use a level reading of −85 dB with pink noise at a −20 dBFS calibration level. The room is also checked for frequency consistency. You want a room that is flat or, in other words, doesn't raise or lower frequencies in the sound. For rooms that are not perfect, you can use corrective equalizers to make the room sound flat. One software package, Nuendo, has corrective features built in and can be used to compensate for room problems. Soundtrack has nothing to help with this process.

If you are prepping materials in Soundtrack that will be used as a part of a theatrical release, you will want to use the same −85 dB calibration. This way, your work will have a similar level to the rest of the project. It should be noted that, in comparison with the loudness that most audio systems are capable of, the resulting sound coming out of a −85 dB calibrated system will seem low. Separate releases for DVD and the web need to be mixed differently.

The nice thing about mixing at the calibrated level is that once the system is calibrated you only need to worry about how it sounds to your ear. You can set levels low for quiet scenes and, if you can hear what is going on, it should transfer to the theater experience.

Official stance: Soundtrack is not the right tool for theatrical mixing.

Broadcast Mixing

The major difference between theatrical mixing and mixing for television is that the dynamic range in mixing for television has to be a lot more controlled. Instead of setting up a calibrated room (although these are still typically calibrated to −79 dB with pink noise at −20 dBFS) in which you can mix with whatever levels work for the scene, in television things have to be monitored much more closely. While the rooms are still calibrated to make sure you are hearing exactly what is there, it is the level meter that is watched to make sure nothing goes over the specified limit. Instead of having a big room that is designed especially for mixing, you need to have expensive level meters that tell you every detail about the loudness of your signal. It is easier to complete a mix for broadcast on a set of headphones, if you put everything at the appropriate levels, than to achieve the same for a theatrical release.

One of the most important parts of working in broadcast is communication with the receiving end of the final mix. You should know what they expect long before you start the mix. As an example of this, I have a couple of excerpts from the submission document that PBS uses. The Program Operations Office of PBS informed me that I was welcome to print a small portion of their submission document but I should keep in mind that parts of it are going through major updates due to the switch to digital broadcasts. While this is an exciting time for the end consumer, the practical implementation of format standards is like walking through quicksand. You are going to need to keep up to date or you may be submitting something that is no longer the ideal standard. If you don't meet the requirements, many local stations will still play it but it could be brutally abused by the station's broadcast equipment, which has to make the audio fit into the standard no matter what you submitted. Other stations might not play it at all.

So what are the current PBS submission requirements? The entire document is freely available on PBS.org so I won't repeat too much of the information, but I do think you'll see the essence of the process by looking through a couple of the settings.

This is an example of the specifics involved. What this portion of the document is establishing are the average levels of the program material. The material can vary over a total of 8 dB, which is not that much. Specific sections can go louder, but not louder than an average of -17 dBFS. The math behind all of this is explainable, but not really helpful. What is much more helpful is a practical explanation of how you might see this information in Soundtrack. Soundtrack has a useful metering plug-in, but if you are doing really serious metering you should probably buy a third party solution, like the Broadcast bundle from Waves or a hardware metering solution from Dolby.

3.1.2 Programs are to have average loudness levels that fall between -28 dBFS and -20 dBFS during the majority of a program as measured on a digital meter calibrated to the RMS/VU ballistic. Average loudness should not go above -17 dBFS at any point during the program.

(PBS, 2007. Technical Operating Specifications – Submission. PDF version downloaded September 27, 2009).

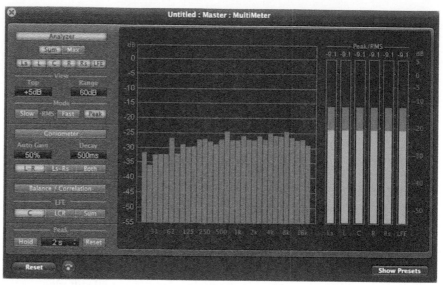

Figure 6-1 The multimeter.

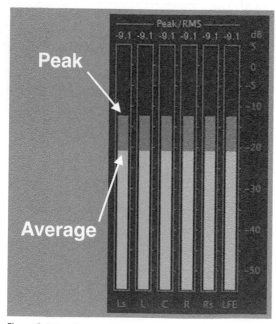

Figure 6-2 Levels.

To access the metering plug-in in Soundtrack (called the multimeter), choose the multimeter effect from the Metering category. You should place this on the master track, which you can access by clicking the master track on the timeline and then choosing the Effects tab in the left pane. The interface of this plug-in has two primary sections: an analyzer and a goniometer. The analyzer displays the audio levels as both peak and average readings along with a spectrum display that shows the different frequencies. The goniometer displays phase relationships. For this part of the discussion, you'll be using the analyzer and you'll be watching the levels on the right.

You will also need to watch the meters in the Meters tab in the right pane because, while these provide less information, they do provide peak information for specific time locations. You'll be able to see the exact location of the loudest peak.

A serious weakness of the Multimeter tool is that you never have the ability to know the exact average

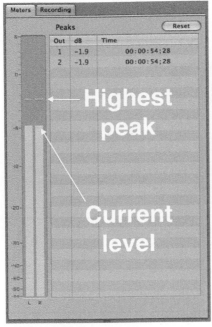

Figure 6-3 The Meters tab.

Figure 6-4 RMS limiting.

(RMS) reading. Every meter view displays the peak reading, but none of them display the average reading. It is possible to tell approximately where the average is, but when I have had to use this tool I have had to rely on compression to make sure the average never crosses the −17 dBFS average maximum reading. The Soundtrack compression effect allows you to set the threshold using an RMS reading instead of a peak reading. Setting it to −17 dbFS in conjunction with a maximum ratio setting turns the plug-in into an average level limiter, preventing the average from getting louder than the set threshold.

Don't just set this and forget about it, because you'll need to make sure you are not limiting too much just to meet the requirements. You also need to make it sound good.

3.1.3 Programs are permitted to have audio levels that regularly peak near but not above the following limits using a digital peak meter: SD: −10 dBFS HD: −3 dBFS.

(PBS, 2007. Technical Operating Specifications – Submission. PDF version downloaded September 27, 2009).

Figure 6-5 Peak limiting.

3.1.4 Programs must be mixed using dialog level LAeq metering or subsequent ATSC standard method. They must have dialog levels with a value of −24 dBFS ±2 dB. Programs may have peak music or effects levels up to the level limits specified in 3.1.3 during moments of dramatic impact, as long as dialog levels are maintained as specified.

(PBS, 2007. Technical Operating Specifications – Submission. PDF version downloaded September 27, 2009).

This item indicates the highest peak values that are acceptable. For standard definition (SD) broadcast it is −10 dBFS; for high definition (HD) it is −3 dBFS. This is where I would use a limiter to cap out the highest peak level possible.

One thing you may have noticed immediately is that the limiter has an output range of 0 dBFS to −10 dBFS. This makes the limiter a perfect fit for these submission guidelines. However, once you have the limiter in place, you can also insert a gain plug-in after it in the chain to adjust the overall output level. In this way you could limit to −10 and then turn down the gain on the gain plug-in by any dB amount (for example, −3 to achieve a combined maximum level of −13 dBFS).

This section refers to controlling the dialog levels. The specific metering standards that are documented here (LAeq and ATSC) refer to specialized systems of metering that have stringent metering designs and implementation. While the Soundtrack meters don't meet these requirements, you can still place the dialog in the general ballpark. The problem is that in broadcast there is usually very little room for ballparking when you are trying to pass the quality check done by the broadcast facility. What you need is a meter that is Leq(A) (called LAeq in the PBS document) certified, such as the Dolby LM100 loudness meter. Then you have to mix the dialog all by itself while watching the Dolby unit and making sure your dialog never crosses −24 dBFS (with a range of 2 dBFS on either side). The few shows I have mixed for PBS have not been completed with an official unit, but I was careful to control the dialog and get it close enough that it wasn't rejected. I used the multimeter and the compressor using an RMS setting. Once the dialog is leveled, you can add any sound effects and music. If you are planning on doing a lot of broadcast mixing, you'll need to get the right metering tools. This is an area outside of Soundtrack's software capabilities so I am going to finish up by pointing you to the web. Do a search for 'Leq(A) metering' and you'll find many resources, especially forums which will help you figure out what you need and how you can achieve the required settings.

One additional note about this is that there are some software tools which you can use but that are not as efficient as using a 'real-time' box. One such tool is the AudioLeak application from Channel D. This has an analysis mode that can analyze files or a 'live' audio input. There is a free version (limited) and a pro version. The free version has enough features to help you meet the requirements for a submission. At least it's nice to know there are some options available.

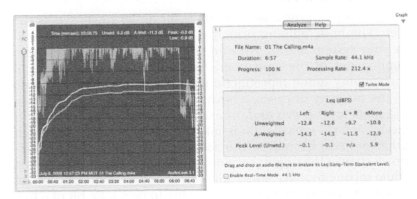

Figure 6-6 AudioLeak analysis of Leq(A).

Official stance: Soundtrack can be used for broadcast mixing when used with third party solutions.

Mixing for DVD

The good news for DVD mixing is that there is a wide range of levels that end up on DVD. Recently, the levels have been going up and up. DVDs, and now Blu-ray discs, are starting to sound as loud as CDs. In the world of music, there has been a loudness war taking place because producers and record labels feel they have to constantly compete with the loudness of every other CD, which means that music is getting grotesquely loud. This is now happening with the audio on visual media. Much like mixing for television, you will still work on a calibrated system but it will typically be in a 'home theater'-type setup to ensure the result translates well to that environment. Since most DVDs are using AC-3 schemes, you should at least be familiar with Dialnorm (a setting used to ensure programs have consistent levels with each other; measured via Leq(A), as described above), which uses a tag encoded when the AC-3 file is created to tell the stereo receiver how loud to play back the mix. There is more on this in Chapter 10 in regard to Apple's Compressor app, which can create AC-3 files and set the Dialnorm setting. I almost always leave this set to −31 so that the mix I create is played back at the same level with no adjustments being made during playback.

Official stance: Since the accepted standards are less strict, you can comfortably use Soundtrack for DVD/Blu-ray creation. You can export straight to AC-3 from Soundtrack, but not to the HD audio formats available for Blu-ray.

Mixing for the Web

If there was ever a new territory for audio mixing, it is the web. The basic guiding principle is to mix everything as loud as your system allows. No one seems to think that the audio coming out of the consumer's computer may be capable of high quality sound reproduction, and unfortunately this is true in the majority of cases. I have mixed a number of high profile spots for the web and, in each case, I was asked to make it louder. What I typically do is mix the spots so that they match other projects hosted on the same website. This involves getting a copy of the original or doing a lot of comparative listening while mixing to make sure the levels are consistent. Until more standards are put in place, this is going to be a little bit of a free for all.

Official stance: Soundtrack is the perfect tool for mixing audio for the web.

The Goniometer and Correlation Meter

These meters inform you about the phase of your audio. Phase is still commonly checked for broadcast television these days, it being one of several places where you might still find a mono playback medium (a black and white television). While this is becoming less and less frequent, it is always a good idea to check the mono-compatibility of your audio. This means finding out what would happen if your audio tracks were to all be sent to a single speaker. If your audio has a positive correlation, then you would still hear everything. If your audio has a negative correlation, then some parts of the sound would be canceled out because the waveforms are moving in opposite directions and, when mixed together, the opposite parts are reduced to nothing just like adding together 3 and -3.

A mono file has a correlation of $+1$ and looks like a vertical line on the goniometer (see Figure 6-7).

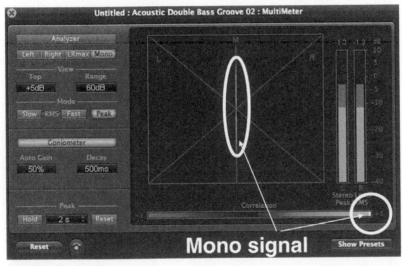

Figure 6-7 A mono file.

With a mono file it is impossible to have a mono-compatibility issue. When you have a stereo file that doesn't have compatibility issues, it will read between 0 and $+1$ on the correlation meter (see Figure 6-8).

With a file that has a problem, the correlation value will be a negative number (see Figure 6-9).

Of course, it is the sound that matters most, so I recommend pushing the Sum to Mono button on the transport to hear what summing to mono sounds like for your project. If it sounds fine, then you don't likely have a mono-compatibility problem.

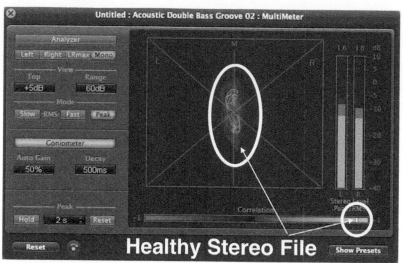

Figure 6-8 A stereo file.

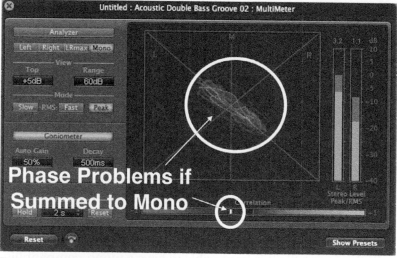

Figure 6-9 Negative correlation value.

Figure 6-10 Sum to Mono button.

Other Thoughts

While this is not the end word in the discussion of setting levels, the primary goal has been to demonstrate the wide variety of issues that exist and the attention to detail required when mixing for a variety of formats. One thing that is not covered here is the actual setup of the speakers in your room. See Chapter 11 for information about acoustics and hints for creating the best acoustic space possible. If nothing else, this chapter has likely helped you to realize the importance of having a good relationship with a professionally designed post-audio facility.

7

SPECTRAL TOOLS

Now that we have made it through dynamics, it is time to explore the spectral tools in Soundtrack Pro. 'Spectral' refers to the tools that affect the audio spectrum. If you need to make changes to a sound to make it 'brighter' or cut out some of the 'mud,' these are the tools that will make this possible. Additionally, you will be able to match production dialog with looped dialog and create special effects like the 'telephone' effect.

Equalizers

The evolution of the modern equalizer began at the dawn of the telephone. When running telephone lines over long distances, the audio signal would not be able to maintain full quality. An equalizer was used to restore the conversations to a more natural sound, or to 'equalize' the highs and lows of the sound. Modern equalizers are used as surgical tools to either drastically change the audio or to accomplish subtle clean-ups and improve the sound. Besides covering the basics of how an equalizer works in this chapter, we'll also cover typical ways of using them.

Dave's Video Editor Perspective

Equalizers

For those of you who have used the equalizers in Final Cut, there are several that might be a good introduction to those in Soundtrack. Their interfaces may be a bit less intimidating since they are only a series of sliders instead of the stylized interfaces you'll usually find in Soundtrack. Getting familiar with what the various frequency adjustments do will make the transition easier, and it is in your best interest to do so. In Figure 7-1 you'll see there are three simple sliders. By making adjustments you'll hear the effect your adjustments are having.

Figure 7-1 The AUParametricEQ.

If you have access to an audio device that has equalization adjustments, playing around with the settings will make you better able to transition to the software interfaces in Final Cut Studio. These adjustments are obvious to audio experts, but as a new video editor you will need to train your ear a bit to understand the frequencies you are working on and the impact your adjustments can make.

When working on the video edit and not really addressing the sound quality yet, I will sometimes make minor adjustments to the audio to see if they result in a decent enough quality to include in my edit. For example, if I am hearing a hum, I will see if I can reduce it easily, and in these instances the simple equalizers are quick and straightforward. If I know I might be working with an audio engineer later in the project, I might remove the equalizer filter that I applied, knowing that the tools in Soundtrack may provide better quality than what I can get in Final Cut.

Equalization demo.

Filters

The equalizers in Soundtrack Pro are called parametric equalizers. They have a variety of parameters that can be tweaked to control the available bands. A band is another term for a set of controls that affect one adjustable frequency. These bands can also be called filters, which can be confusing at first because all audio effects in Final Cut are called filters. In Soundtrack, what Final Cut calls filters are called effects, and the term filters refers only to individual bands on equalizers. I think this will all make more sense in the context of the primary equalizer available in Soundtrack Pro, called the Channel EQ. This equalizer has eight different bands. It has two pass filters, two shelf filters, and four peak filters. Each has a different role, but all allow you to control the levels of different frequencies.

High Pass/Low Pass Filters

We are going to spend a little extra time explaining the pass filters because, once you have a grasp on what they do, the rest

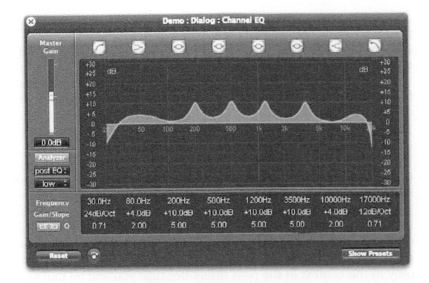

Figure 7-2 The eight-band Channel EQ.

will be more manageable. The high pass filter is the left most filter on the equalizer and in Figure 7-3 it is highlighted in the white
rectangle.

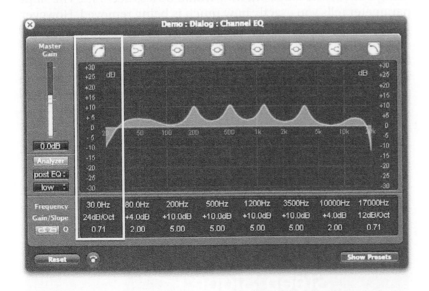

Figure 7-3 High pass filter.

As the name suggests, the higher frequencies of the sound pass
through unaffected, while the lower frequencies are reduced.
This is immediately useful as a means to remove unwanted low
frequency rumble that might exist in your audio due to traffic,

air-conditioning units, or noisy microphone handling. The low pass filter is the opposite and removes high frequencies while letting the lows pass. This is useful for removing high frequency hiss and noise from your audio.

There are several settings available for tweaking on the pass filters. The first is the frequency setting. This parameter gives you control over how much of the high/low content is removed. The available range covers the entire range of the equalizer (20–20 000 Hz). The next adjustable parameter is the slope setting. This determines how steep the filter is. The slope is measured in decibels per octave, which makes sense if you know what decibels and octaves are. An octave is more widely understood because it is a musical term; it represents two pitches that have a 2:1 ratio. Each pitch, no matter the octave, has the same letter label: an A is an A in any octave. In terms of frequency, one pitch in an octave is either twice or half of the amount of the other. This is important only in the context of the pass filters because you will be making the slope either very steep by turning up the number of decibels that are pulled down per octave, or you will be making the slope gentle by turning the number of decibels down. Confused? I think the terms gentle slope or steep slope would be more practical than using a dB/octave label, but they would be less accurate. The slope parameter tells you exactly how much is being removed. However, what you need to know is that a gentle slope sounds more musical and has more transparent results. The steeper slopes remove more of the low frequencies and allow for higher-precision changes. The default setting works best in most cases and should only be changed if it is not doing an adequate job. The changes you should

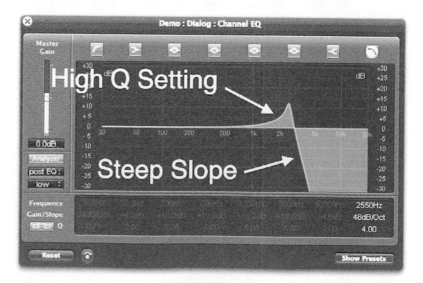

Figure 7-4 Low pass filter.

make at that point will be based on trial and error because so much depends on the specific audio you are equalizing.

The last parameter that is adjustable is the Q setting. As a side note, the Q setting is deactivated when the slope is set to 6 dB/octave. The Q adjusts the bandwidth of the slope at lower values, but at higher values in the pass filters it introduces a resonant frequency. This frequency is represented graphically on the equalizer and at higher levels can be easily heard. This is a feature that carries over from the analog equalizers used before the computer age. I rarely suggest using a Q setting above 1.5 on a pass filter because it will draw attention to itself. The one example of where I use this is when I use a low pass filter to remove some high frequency noise but also want to boost a little right around the diction frequencies of the voice. I would use a relatively steep slope and higher Q setting to cut the high frequencies where the noise is but still boost some of the frequencies where the voice is. You might ask me to give you specific parameter settings, but I can't because every sound is different and a specific number might not work in your individual case. The key is to slowly adjust the frequency parameter until it sounds right. In a little bit I am going to provide some tips on how to do this, so keep on reading.

High/Low Shelving Filters

Next are the shelving filters. They are similar to the pass filters but can boost or cut high/low frequencies through the range of audio. The Q setting on these filters sets the slope of the filter and there is a gain parameter that determines the overall boost or reduction of the shelf.

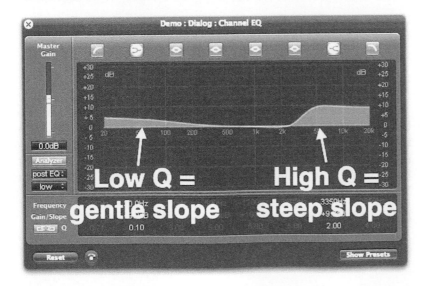

Figure 7-5 Shelving filters.

You might use a shelving filter to lower the low or high portions of the spectrum, from a specific frequency through the end of the range, instead of using a pass filter to completely remove it all.

Bell Filters

The four bell filters in the middle of the equalizer are perhaps the most surgical filters of all. You can set the frequency, the gain, and the Q just like with the previous filters, but the Q sets the width of the bell-like shape of the filter and can produce very wide or narrow results.

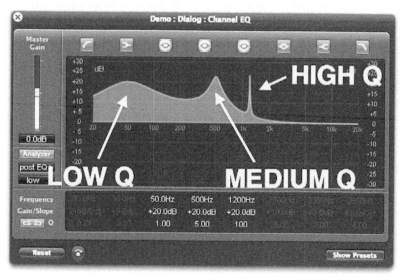

Figure 7-6 Bell filters.

The Analyzer

The channel equalizer and the linear phase equalizer use the same interface and both have a built-in analyzer. This is an invaluable tool especially for those who may be working in a non-ideal listening environment. It will show you your sound right underneath your equalizer curve. There are several items you can adjust that will help you to optimize the effectiveness of this tool.

Analyze Activate

To activate the analyzer, press the button labeled Analyze. This activates the analyzer and switches the scale on the right side of the equalizer to a 0 through −60 dB scale instead of 0 through ±30 dB, which represents the boost or cut of the filters. You can click on the 0 to −60 scale and drag vertically to change the range with maximum range bookends of +20 to −100, but only a total range of 60 dB can be visible at one time. When you are not using the analyzer I recommend turning it off or closing the plug-in window. Both will conserve CPU resources.

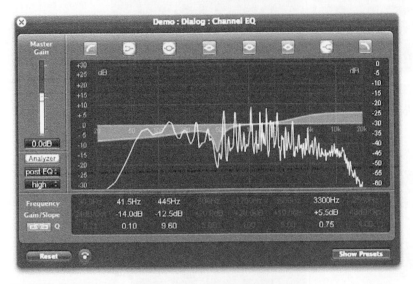

Figure 7-7 The analyzer in action.

Post/Pre EQ

The post/pre toggle option is a powerful metering tool. When set to Post, the analyzer waveform re ects the added boosts and cuts affected by the various filters. If you want to compare the source waveform with the newly equalized waveform, you can switch between Pre and Post. This is useful when troubleshooting filter changes.

Resolution

The option below the Pre/Post menu allows you to change the resolution of the waveform. For a very detailed representation use the higher resolution setting, but note that it uses a lot of CPU power to do this. If you need to have a number of equalizers open at the same time, all using the analyzer, you might have to use lower resolution settings.

Dave's Video Editor Perspective

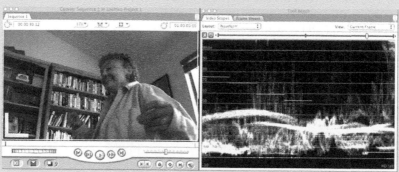

Figure 7-8 The waveform monitor.

Figure 7-9 The vectorscope.

Analysis Tools

The video editor may be familiar with tools like the waveform monitor and the vectorscope (see Figures 7-8 and 7-9). These tools allow you to see the brightness (waveform) and the color information (vectorscope) of the video image. The more you use these tools the better you will be able to identify the portions of the image and what levels those components might be at. You can then make adjustments to make the image more appealing and 'broadcast-friendly.' If you look at the waveform monitor, the portions of the scope that are near the top represent the brightest part of the frame. Seeing this information is useful when adjusting either on the set or during post-production. When using the vectorscope you are evaluating the saturation level of the colors in your shot. The further out the blob goes, the richer the color. If it is too far out, the colors might start to bleed and become ugly, and video noise may be introduced into your image. If the image is de-saturated, meaning all color information is removed or reduced, the blob will disappear or shrink (see Figure 7-10).

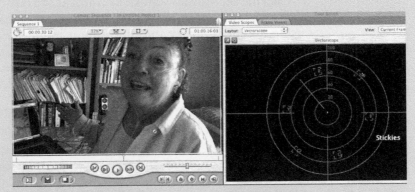

Figure 7-10 De-saturate vector.

If we consider these tools in the video world, we have the aural equivalent of the analysis feature in the equalizers and the spectral viewer in the File Editor. It takes a degree of practice in each of these situations to recognize the visual components as well as the various frequencies, but it is worth the time investment to work with these tools so that you can see as well as hear the areas that may need adjusting.

The Interface

Besides the master gain, which allows the entire output to be raised or lowered, there are a few really efficient design features on the channel and linear phase equalizers. You can double-click on the parameter numbers to open a text entry window. This is the easiest way to enter specific numerical changes. You can also click-hold-and-drag on these numbers to change them. The easiest way to make changes, though, is to click on the curves in the graphical display and pull the different filter curves around. Each filter has a different color and when you hover over a specific filter it comes into focus and you can drag it around. The node point that exists on each line can be used to adjust the Q settings. In this way you can easily adjust all eight bands in a short period of time. The shapes at the top of the equalizer that represent each filter can be used to bypass each filter. Using them allows you to quickly hear the effect of each filter by turning it on and off in succession.

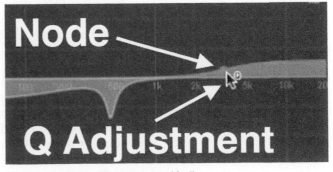

Figure 7-11 Making adjustments graphically.

Presets

Clicking on the Show Presets button at the bottom of the interface displays a number of useful equalizer presets. If you are using an equalizer for the first time it might be a good idea to start with a preset to give you some ideas. Then you can tweak it and make adjustments as needed for your specific situation.

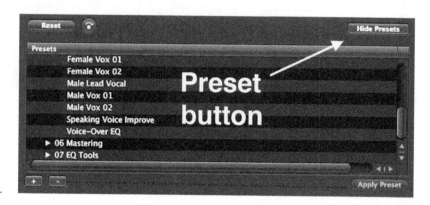

Figure 7-12 Presets.

Channel Equalizer vs. Linear Phase Equalizer

The channel and linear phase equalizers look identical, and in fact their interfaces are the same. While there is a big difference between the two under the hood, it will take some time of using them to hear the difference. The channel equalizer is a traditional digital equalizer that works based on the same principles as analog equalizers. The linear phase equalizer is a relatively new digital equalizer that provides pristine results that are nearly transparent. There are two sides to the issue of which you should use: the channel equalizer uses less CPU resources yet adds a little more 'character' to the sound, whereas the linear phase equalizer taxes the CPU quite a bit more but the resulting sound is noticeably more natural when in use. The best part is that you can share presets between the two.

The Fat Equalizer

The other equalizer available in Soundtrack is called the Fat EQ. The filters and band options are all very similar to the equalizers listed above, without some of the handier interface options such as the analyzer and the graphical tweaking of parameters. The sound is different and so it is nice to have as a tool in the toolbox; however, I have never used this equalizer on a project.

Figure 7-13 The fat equalizer.

Single Band Filters

There is a whole plug-in category devoted to single band equalizers. Think of these as the individual bands taken from the other equalizers. They are great when all you need is a simple fix. If all you need is a high pass filter then you might not need to use the full channel equalizer, but if you want to keep your options open then use the full channel equalizer.

Using the Equalizers

In this section we are going to focus on how to use the equalizers. By this point you should be beginning to put the pieces together and you should be chomping at the bit to apply all of this information. Equalizers are powerful tools, but don't be fooled into thinking that they are simple. Mastering the art of equalization will take some time because it is your ears that need to develop. This section is designed to help propel you into proficiency a little early.

The three main uses of equalizers are:

- To remove parts of a sound. Highs = noise or hiss; Mids = ringing, boxiness or mud; Lows = rumble or boominess.

- To boost parts of a sound. Highs = brighten up or add clarity; Mids = character or thickness; Lows = accentuate bass.
- As an effect. High pass + low pass = telephone effect; Subtract with high shelf = add distance.

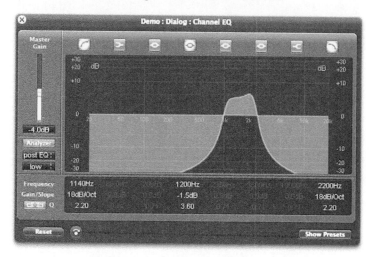

Figure 7-14 The telephone filter preset.

Following is a top ten list of uses with explanations.

Reducing Rumble

You can use a high pass filter to reduce rumble in your audio. Adjust the frequency until the rumble is no longer audible. If you reach that point but the other parts of the audio are affected, use a steeper slope to allow you to remove more of the rumble while isolating the audio you want to keep.

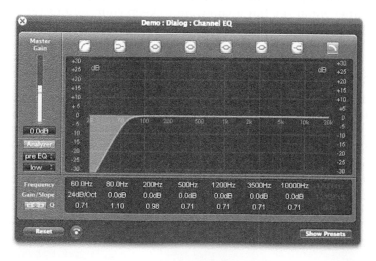

Figure 7-15 Reduce rumble.

Dave's Video Editor Perspective

Dealing with Rumble

It happens more than we like, no matter how carefully we try to minimize sound unwelcome to the edit: an air-conditioner in the room or sounds of wind or traffic that exist on your audio track are distracting to the viewer. I've had shots that used a decent lavaliere microphone that had a windscreen, but which still had some wind noise that sounded like a consistent low frequency rumble. In this situation, I applied the AUGraphicEQ and minimized the low frequencies. I kept moving down the stack of frequencies until it sounded like I was depredating the sound of the voices. While I was in this tool I may have boosted some of the voice frequencies to make the voice brighter (see Figure 7-16).

Also, be sure when you are recording sound in the field that your audio cables do not cross over your power cables because this may introduce a 60-cycle hum into your audio. This can be reduced, but you'd be better off not having to do so. If you do have this hum, there is a tool to help remove it in Final Cut called 'hum remover'. By default it comes up as 60 Hz since this is the most common problem. You can, however, use this tool to reduce any frequency of hum (see Figure 7-17).

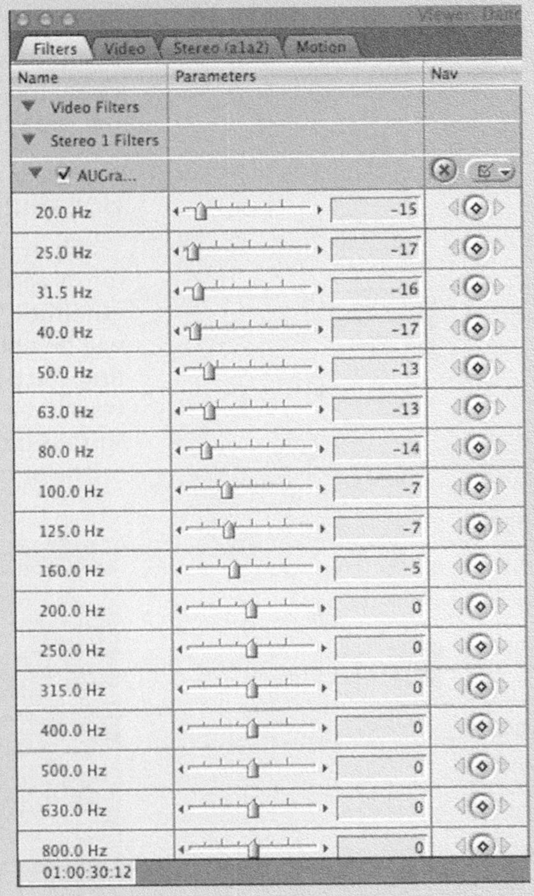

Figure 7-16 Adjusting for rumble.

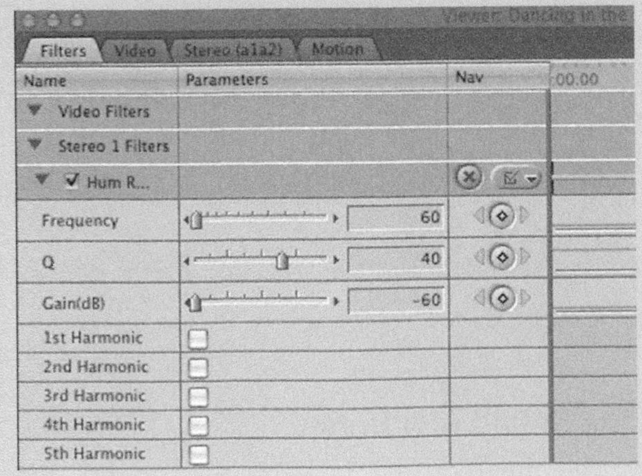

Figure 7-17 Hum remover.

Reducing Hissing Noise

Using a low pass filter to help reduce hissing noise is very effective but, if overdone, could make the audio sound dull and lifeless. Adjust the frequency until the noise is removed. If the other parts of the audio are being affected then try a shelving filter to reduce the noise without pulling it out completely. If the low pass filter is close, then pull it in but turn up the resonant frequency to boost the sound immediately preceding the noise you are removing.

Boosting Diction

When there is dialog that is hard to hear, you can use a bell filter to accentuate the speaking voice. Each voice is a little different, but if you use a high Q setting and boost by about 20 dB you will be able to sweep through the different frequencies until you find the portion of the dialog that really adds to its clarity. Once you find a good spot, pull down the gain and widen the Q until it sounds more natural. Doing too much can make the dialog sound brittle or hollow, so be cautious and don't overdo it.

Figure 7-18 Finding the right frequency.

Removing the Sound of a Room

Sometimes you are required to work with audio that was recorded in a small-sounding room. While it is very hard to make it sound different, one thing you can do is to filter out some of the sound of the room modes. A room mode is the resonance of a room caused by sound reflections in the room itself. Using the same technique outlined above, by boosting a narrow band of equalization (see Figure 7-12), you can find room modes by listening for uneven responses to a frequency sweep through the whole range. When you find a frequency that really pops out at you, remove it by pulling the band into the negative gain range and widening the Q setting. Do this for as many as you find, but be careful not to go too far overboard because doing so will eat into the sound you want to keep. The key is to take a few places in small doses while leaving the parts of the audio that you want to preserve in good condition.

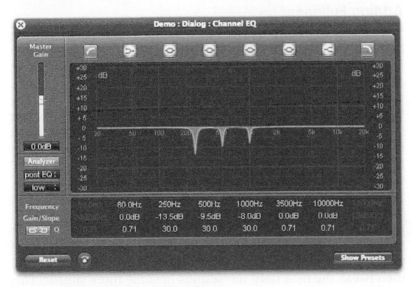

Figure 7-19 Removing the sound of a small room.

Carving the Music to Make Room for Other Audio

If you have a music track that you are layering with dialog, it can help to cut some frequencies to make room for the frequencies of the dialog. The important frequencies involved with the speaking range are typically between 1000 and 4000 Hz. Make some cuts in that area with a low Q setting and a small amount of gain reduction to create the smallest of changes to the music track. This small change can make a big difference without affecting the music too much.

The Telephone Effect

I'm using one of the most clichéd of effects here to give you the principle upon which you can create a lot of different effects. Use a high pass and low pass filter to progressively narrow how much audio is passing through. Technically this is the same as what a lot of programs call a band pass filter. Instead of letting highs or low pass through, a band in the middle is created and passes through. The reason this works as a telephone effect is that traditional analog telephones have a limited frequency response that is void of highs and lows – just like a band pass. If you want to create the sound of a megaphone or cell phone, the principle is the same.

Adding Fullness

If you have a sound that sounds hollow, it may be possible to add some fullness. The only caveat is that an equalizer cannot boost any frequencies that do not exist in the original. If you boost in a certain area but nothing changes, then the chances are that the original sound just didn't have any of that frequency; you can't boost what isn't there. Boosting frequencies is a terrific way to alter a sound because it can really help to make it larger than life. On the other hand, if you want to make something sound improved, it is usually better to cut away muddy or unwanted frequencies.

Matching Another Sound

We are almost at the point where we can talk about using the match EQ plug-in. However, you can reproduce its effects manually as well. All you need to do is listen closely to one file and then tweak the next until the sounds become more similar. This is useful for matching sound effects from different libraries, or dialog from different takes. It is tricky, but possible. When you are attempting this, you should do a lot of sweeping with high Q settings and high gain. This will help to inform your ear about the sound you are trying to match. Ultimately, there are a lot of things that go into matching the sound of two different files, but equalization is a huge part of it.

Helping a Sound Effect to Fit Properly

Here's a crash course on sound properties. High frequencies do not travel as far in the air as low frequencies. Case and point: a subwoofer in a car as it approaches. What do you hear first? All of the low (and often annoying) sub-tones. If you want an effect to sit better in a mix, then this is one principle to keep in mind. Ask yourself how far away the sound is. If it is a little way off then turning down the high frequencies will help it to sound more natural. Another principle: sound bounces off hard surfaces (especially the high frequencies). If you are putting a sound effect into a cement room, there will be more high frequencies than if you are putting the sound into a closet full of clothes. In other words, pay close attention to the environment and try to make sense of which frequencies would really exist and which would be lost.

Using the Analyzer Tool

The Analyzer tool is a little bit of a crutch. It's slightly akin to using audio to help you make picture edits (which I have seen done on occasion). However, if you are new to equalization, I think a crutch is the perfect solution. Use it to see what your audio is doing. If you see a spike on a certain frequency, then that is a good place to start looking for a problem. Using the analyzer will also help you to identify ranges that are common for different types of audio. Think of it as a training exercise. Once you have a better grasp on the overall range, turn it off and equalize things by ear alone. Eventually it will be second nature to fix a spectral issue with no problem at all.

Dave's Video Editor Perspective

Matching Shots and 'Sonic Fingerprinting'

When trying to match the sounds of shots cut together the video editor will have to do the audio equivalent of using the color correction tools available. For the sake of simplicity I will talk about the Three-Way Color Corrector tool instead of the powerful Color application that ships with Final Cut Studio. The Three-Way Color Corrector effect is a very useful tool

that I use all the time. If you are cutting together several shots, they may have different color balances which can be distracting to your edit, so to make the transition from shot to shot invisible you need to make adjustments to the hues. In the Three-Way Color Corrector window you'll see the Match Hue button (see Figure 7-20).

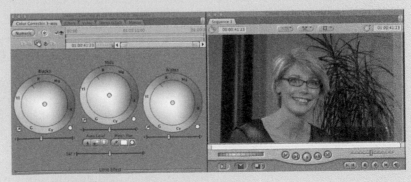

Figure 7-20 Matching hue.

You can select a color with the eyedropper and then apply that hue to subsequent shots. This often requires further tweaking and you must be looking at your external monitor as well as the scopes inside Final Cut (see Figure 7-21)

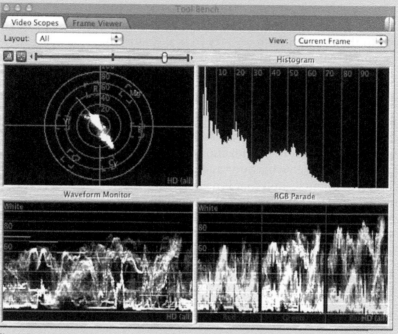

Figure 7-21 The scopes.

In Final Cut you can compare shots side by side to see how the color is matching up. This is analogous to sonic fingerprinting, which is used to make audio edits invisible. This process usually takes place near the completion phase of your edit. You shouldn't waste too much time color correcting or audio matching until you have achieved picture lock because there is always the possibility that the shots you are working with may not make it to your final cut.

Matching the Sound of Audio Clips

The Match EQ concept is similar to the quest for the Holy Grail. The idea is to use a single plug-in to analyze the sound of one file, create a sonic mold from it, and then stamp it onto other audio files. Equalizers have existed for years, and there are third party tools that do this, but Soundtrack Pro is among a small group of programs that has attempted to integrate sonic fingerprinting into an easily usable and powerful audio editing tool. It is not perfect because equalization is highly subjective and what may seem good mathematically to a piece of software might not make sonic sense to a human editor.

There are two incarnations of sonic fingerprinting, which we will now explore. These are the Match EQ plug-in and the Sound Palette Lift Equalization Print. Both accomplish similar end goals, but the Lift Equalization Print is a much simpler iteration and therefore it will probably be the one you use most often. Match EQ is a much more complicated tool that provides similar results to the Lift tool but requires a lot more work to get there. It is more powerful and more exible, but it is better suited to matching mixed music tracks and analyzing tracks that are playing in real time. The end results have strong similarities, so I am opting out of a written explanation of Match EQ in return for an explanation on the DVD. The Lift Equalization tool is explained here, along with a general idea of how you can and can't use sonic fingerprinting.

Match EQ Demo.

The Lift Equalization Tool

The Lift Equalization tool is part of the Sound Palette system in Soundtrack Pro. The easiest way to access this window is to switch to the Lift tool from the toolbar.

Figure 7-22 The Lift tool.

The Lift tool is used to collect equalization prints from audio clips that you click on. When you switch to the Lift tool, the Sound Palette is automatically opened.

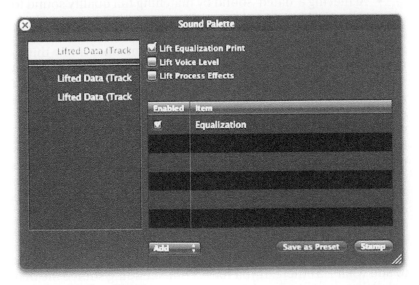

Figure 7-23 The Sound Palette.

The Sound Palette handles three tasks: Lift Equalization Print, Lift Voice Level, and Lift Process Effects. It can do all three simultaneously if you have each box checked. Be careful to deselect the items you do not want to copy because you can easily mess clips up by accidentally lifting and stamping process effects when all you wanted to lift and stamp was an equalization print. Once you have the Lift tool selected, you can click on any audio clip or any portion of an audio clip using the Timeslice tool. Once you select a clip, the Lift tool automatically switches to the Stamp tool. You can use this to stamp any clip with the selected items in the Enabled Item list in the Sound Palette. You can easily switch back to the Lift tool by pressing and holding the Option key.

What Can/Can't the Matching Process Accomplish?

This is a specialized tool that you may not have a need for in everyday use. However, there may come a time when it would really help you and unless you understand it you probably won't even know where to look to get started. The following is a short list of potential uses:

- Matching production dialog with re-recorded dialog (ADR);
- Matching sound effects with each other;
- Matching music tracks with each other;
- Creative sound design (matching a line of dialog to a thunder sound);
- Achieving a 'dated' sound by matching full quality sound to the sound from an old recording.

The equalization matching process changes the sonic characteristics of audio, but it's important to remember a few things that it doesn't do. It cannot change the volume levels of the clips so it may be best to match the levels of the clips in advance of matching the equalization. However, matching the levels of the clips may cause other problems such as messing up the ambient noise levels in the clips you are changing. The equalization matching process also doesn't tailor itself to individual portions of the files. It takes an average equalization print from the entire clip and then applies that average reading to the stamped files. This means that if the low rumble of a sound that you really like only lasts for a short portion of the file, it may not transfer to the sound effect you are stamping. The low frequencies would have to be a substantial part of the file to affect the average equalization print. The last thing the equalization print isn't able to do is to add what isn't there. If you have a full-sounding source file that you want to transfer to a thin-sounding file, it may not be possible if the destination file doesn't have frequencies to boost. The equalization matching tool will try, but it can only work with the frequencies that are there.

SubBass

Let's look at one other important spectral tool in Soundtrack Pro. Unfortunately, this is an example of how Apple has great ideas but sometimes creates a complex and hard-to-understand system of implementation. They really should have taken the 'Garageband' approach with this and kept the controls simple to understand and use.

Explanation of SubBass

SubBass is a subharmonic synthesizer. It takes sound, analyzes it, and then creates additional low frequencies that match the original. You might be asking how this differs from boosting low frequencies with an equalizer, and the difference is that it can add low frequencies when they aren't there. This has a number of great applications in the post-production realm because it can repair damaged audio and/or be used to create subwoofer rocking sound effects. The main problem with this plug-in is that it has a complex set of controls. What I recommend instead of trying to use them, because they are so abysmal, is starting with a preset and then tweaking only a couple of the parameters. The primary issue is that SubBass is designed to be used primarily with musical material, which is why the various settings are designed as they are. Once you have chosen a preset, adjust the Dry and Wet parameters. The dry signal is the original audio, and the wet is the new low frequency sound. Err on the side of not using too much low frequency sound because too much is always distracting and possibly even dangerous. If you are not using speakers that can reproduce low frequencies, you may have a hard time hearing what the SubBass plug-in is doing. You will probably need a subwoofer.

Figure 7-24 SubBass.

SubBass Warning

There needs to be a warning included with this section because the SubBass plug-in can be dangerous to your equipment and ears. If your speakers cannot handle large amounts of low frequencies then turning up the Wet parameter has the potential to damage them. Do not push the Wet level too much. If you do have a speaker system that can handle large amounts of low frequencies, then turning up the SubBass can damage your ears. Either way, be very careful!

Using SubBass

SubBass would typically either be used as an effect on a track dedicated to the LFE (low frequency effects) channel or as a process effect for specific sound effects. It is a great tool to use to beef up explosion sounds and other loud sound effects. It can be used to add emphasis to more ordinary sounds like footsteps and door sounds. If you have a production sound that is hollow-sounding, you might try using this tool to add back some roundness. Unfortunately, the controls make achieving some of these results hard because they are very non-intuitive. Even though I have scoured the manual and used it many times, I have found that the center and bandwidth settings have no colloquial equivalents. Or rather, I could explain exactly what each does but it would only be even more confusing. The original instructions stand: use a preset and adjust the Dry/Wet parameters, don't use too much, and be very careful not to damage anything!

8

TIME EFFECTS

Time effects are an important part of the post-production process. The primary time-based effect is the reverb effect, which is used to mimic the sounds of various locations and rooms. Other effects, such as the Delay Designer, are sometimes used to create special effects and are powerful in their own right; however, they are used less in day-to-day post-production tasks.

Reverb

There are three reverbs available in Soundtrack Pro 3. The simplest is the Soundtrack Pro Reverb, which provides the simplest interface and also the lowest amount of flexibility. It works well in small doses and doesn't require a lot of system resources. Next is the PlatinumVerb, which is similar to the Soundtrack Pro Reverb but with a lot more adjustable parameters and some really great tools. The last reverb is among a new trend of specialized reverbs that more accurately mimic real acoustic spaces and is called Space Designer. Before we jump into the specific plug-ins, let's spend a few moments exploring the history of reverbs.

A Brief History of Reverbs

Even though the term 'reverb' has not necessarily been the primary term used throughout the history of the effect, I am going to use it in each case for consistency. Reverb refers to the reflections of sound off the various surfaces in a physical space. These reflections bounce around and then decay into silence over time. If you have ever been in a gymnasium or large church, you have experienced a location with a long reverb time. However, even your living room has reverb; it is just a very short and dry reverb so it is not as noticeable. That being said, if you were to close your eyes and walk around your house you would probably be able to identify the various rooms by how your voice sounds in each space.

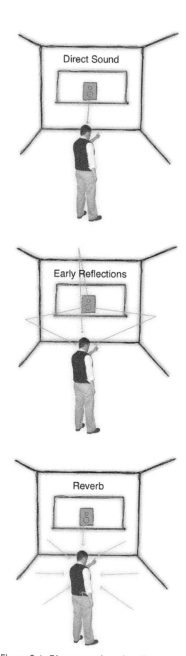

Figure 8-1 Direct sound, early reflections, and reverb.

Chambers

The first reverb emulators were actually specially designed echo chambers that had a speaker on one end and a microphone on the other. The sound was fed to the speaker and then recorded through the microphone. It was very simple in concept, yet it took up a lot of room. I wouldn't really call this an emulator, though, because the reverb was very real and not simulated via an effects unit or computer.

Plates

An early reverb emulator design was a large steel plate encased in a wooden box. These units were around four feet high, one foot wide, and 15 feet long. While smaller than a chamber, they were still large by today's standards. The sound was sent to a device that worked like a speaker and was attached to the middle of the plate. Microphone-like devices were attached to each side and captured the sound after it moved through the plate. Both chamber and plates created reverb-like sounds but could not easily be changed to mimic a specific location; therefore, they didn't really make good tools for matching looped dialog to production dialog. Spring reverbs, popular in guitar amps, work on the same principle as plate reverbs but on a much smaller, and lower quality, scale.

Digital Reverbs

Once digital audio started to become more commonplace, it became easier to create effects that used delays to create reverb. In an actual space, reverb unfolds in a semi-predictable manner.

The original sound reaches your ears, then early reflections arrive after bouncing off nearby objects and surfaces. Then, the sound fills the space and arrives at lower levels from all directions. Once that happens, it quickly begins to die out. A digital effect can mimic this by using a series of repeated delays at various levels to create a reverb-like sound. The more layers of delay, the denser the reverb. The more complex the delay system, the more realistic the result. The Soundtrack Pro Reverb and the PlatinumVerb work on this type of system. They are decent reverbs that work well in a variety of situations, which we'll get to in a little bit.

Convolution Reverbs

This type of reverb is on the newer end of reverb history. It uses impulse responses (IRs) from actual places to create reverb. These IRs are usually created in one of two ways, the first being through an actual impulse in a particular space. Either a starter gun being fired or a balloon popping do the trick, but a full-range sound (covering all the frequencies from low to high) is needed to create an accurate impulse. This impulse can be used directly in a convolution reverb to simulate the reverb for the original acoustic space.

The second method is to broadcast a sweeping sine wave through the audible range of sound and record how it sounds in the physical space. The way to do this is to place a speaker in the room, attached to a computer that plays a sine wave sweeping through the audio range (this sounds like a tone that starts really low and slowly rises until it is higher than you can hear). To record the sine sweep, you'll need a microphone that is also hooked up to your computer. You can subsequently take the original sine wave sweep and the recorded sine wave and use them to create an impulse using a deconvolver. The deconvolver analyzes the differences between the two signals and converts the results into an impulse that contains enough information to recreate the sound of the room. The good news is that Soundtrack comes with a convolution reverb plug-in and an impulse response utility that allows you to create impulses for use. The reverb is called Space Designer and is one of the more powerful tools in Soundtrack Pro.

Soundtrack Pro Reverb

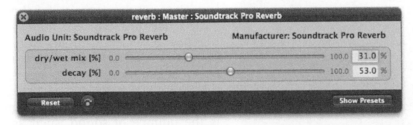

Figure 8-2 The Soundtrack Pro Reverb interface.

As you can see from the interface, this reverb is very simple. You only have two sliders: one to adjust the mix of the reverb and one to adjust the decay of the reverb. While the interface is simple, these two sliders are important to master because they appear on all of the various reverb plug-ins. The dry/wet mix percentage refers to how much original (unprocessed signal) should be mixed with the reverb signal. Typical levels are usually around 30% or lower. The decay determines the length of the reverb signal. Again, smaller amounts are typical. In both cases, you may find reasons to use larger settings to create special effects, but then again you would probably be using a different plug-in to do so. One problem I have with this plug-in is that it uses percentages instead of specific values. I always like to know the actual length of the decay in milliseconds and seconds and not in percentages.

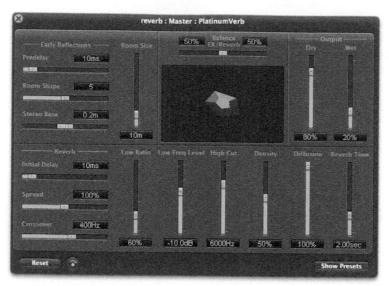

Figure 8-3 The PlatinumVerb interface.

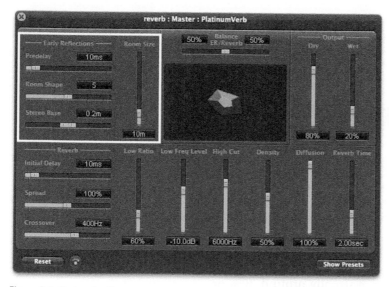

Figure 8-4 Early reflections.

PlatinumVerb

With this reverb, we have a powerful tool with which to create a variety of reverb sounds. Let us look at the reasons we might be using a reverb in the first place. Often, it would be to create the sound of a specific location to match on-screen dialog. This effect can be achieved with the PlatinumVerb plug-in, but the plug-in is still more often used for music production. It is a rather pleasant-sounding reverb with a smooth decay. To the professional's ears, it sounds like a nice digital reverb, but nothing extraordinary.

The Early Reflections Section

The Early Reflections section is used to set the predelay for the early reflections, which is a delay that pushes back the initial reverb sound. At high settings, this can easily separate the reverb completely from the dry original. The effect that this is good at creating is the bounce of sound, such as a gunshot or other loud sound, off a distant wall. The sheer distance is much easier for the ear to understand when the reverb follows the dry sound after a short pause. These settings only apply to the early reflections, which are the reflections that happen first as sound bounces off the surfaces which are nearest.

The Room Shape setting allows you to change the general shape of the virtual room. You can see this reflected in the graphic in the center of the plug-in. The more complex the shape, the more complex the reverb. Sometimes, a nice simple shape creates a reverb that will remain in the background and not draw attention to itself.

The Stereo Base defines the wideness of the reverb, with higher settings creating a very wide sound and lower numbers creating a mono reverb. This is based on virtual microphone placements in the room, with higher settings representing microphones that are further apart. Since this reverb is not a perfect model of a virtual space, the concept is rather more hypothetical in nature.

The Room Size slider changes the size of the virtual room. In conjunction with the decay time, you can create some very interesting sounds. For instance, if you set a very short reverb decay but a very large room size, it will make the processed sound larger without placing it in a large room. This, as you might imagine, can be confusing for the ear and is typically done for specific reasons like making footsteps seem larger than life or creating a dark effect on someone's voice.

The Reverb Section

Once we are past the early reflections, we enter the Reverb area, which is what describes the sound when it is no longer bouncing off nearby objects but has bounced in so many places that it begins to fill the space and comes from all directions. Just like in the Early Reflections section, there is a delay setting for this portion of the reverb which is used to put a brief pause between the early reflections and the reverb, but I rarely adjust this parameter beyond whichever preset I am using. However, if the predelay and reverb sounds are blending together too much, you might try extending this setting to help with separation.

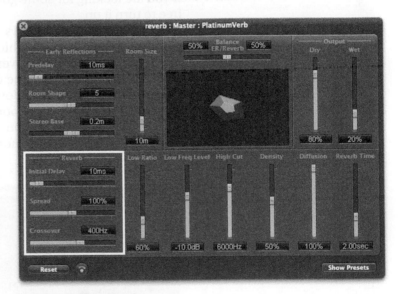

Figure 8-5 The Reverb section.

The Spread setting is similar to the Stereo Base of the early reflections. Use it to widen the reverb or to make it narrower. Crossover is a parameter of the reverb that causes more confusion but offers more excitement. It allows you to split the reverb into two bands for slightly separate processing. The crossover determines the frequency split point and the Ratio slider immediately to its right determines what happens with each band. At 100% the bands are equal in length. With settings below 100%, the low frequency band (as determined by the Crossover slider) is shorter. When above 100%, the low frequencies are longer than the high frequencies. My first question was 'why?' This appeared to be a confusing set of parameters that would only make things harder. What I realized is that the parameters make a couple of specific things really easy to do. The first is to create reverb that sounds like it is coming from a distance. Think about any action movie in which you hear explosions from a distance. Most of what you hear is the low frequencies. With this Crossover slider, you can set the frequency to be somewhere around 200 Hz and then set the ratio to over 100%, and as a result the low frequencies will ring out longer than the high frequencies. This creates a very realistic effect of things happening further away.

The Low Frequency Level slider allows you to turn up or down the low frequency band as defined by the Crossover slider. If the reverb is too muddy, this would be a perfect slider to turn down. If you are looking for some good low frequency rumble, then feel free to turn it up.

The High Cut slider allows you to reduce the higher frequencies. It is a low pass filter which cuts all sound above the set frequency. If you want the reverb to sound like it is in a normal carpeted room, cutting some of the higher frequencies will help. Leaving all frequencies untouched gives an effect that sounds closer to a metal or stone room. If, following the example in the crossover section above, you would like to create the sound of distant rumbling, then cut more of the high frequencies.

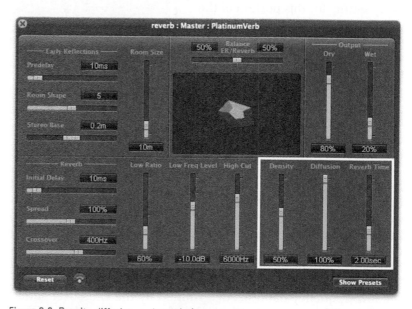

Figure 8-6 Density, diffusion, and reverb time.

The last three sliders are very important because they do a lot to determine the sound of the overall reverb. Adjusting the density of the reverb increases the number of reflections. Typically, you will want to set this higher to create more realistic and complex reverbs, but sometimes you may want to lower it to create a simpler reverb. The diffusion is defaulted to 100% and I rarely change it. The diffusion affects the consistency of the reverb and low settings result in grainy and unusable reverb sounds. Turning the diffusion down to a low setting gives a great place to explore for special effects. The reverb time determines how long the reverb should last. This is an area that will require a good ear and a good monitoring system because too much reverb tail really affects how the reverb sounds and either makes it muddy (with too much) or unnoticeable (with too little). Finding a good balance is critical to achieving usable sounds. See the section after we explore Sound Designer (see page 162) for tips on getting good reverb settings for different applications.

Master Controls

You can control the mix of early reflections and reverb using the slider at the top. The overall dry/wet signal can also be controlled by using the sliders on the right.

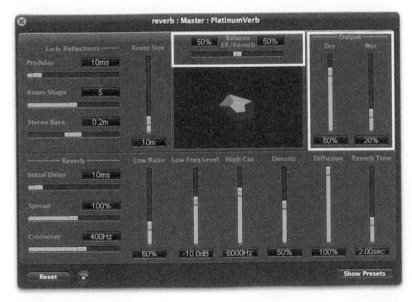

Figure 8-7 Master controls.

These two areas are important because they allow you to control what actually leaves the reverb effect. The first slider, which controls the balance between the early reflections and the reverb, allows you to create a space that is heavier on the early reflections. The end result would be a much smaller space that doesn't sound as natural. If you want a reverb sound that is the most natural, leaving the slider in the middle is a good option.

The Output sliders control the wet and dry levels for the entire reverb. You will need to listen carefully to how it sounds while adjusting these sliders, because the results are very subjective. The best advice I can give is that it is common to set the reverb wet signal too high in comparison with the dry signal. If you are unsure, find a level that sounds good and then turn the wet signal down a little.

Space Designer demo.

Space Designer

This next reverb tool is the real star of the collection. Space Designer is a very powerful convolution reverb. Its strength is in creating very realistic sound spaces, but unfortunately it is a very complex tool to use. I will explain a lot of the basic features, but some explanations are reserved for a more visual explanation on the DVD. Luckily, some of the features have already been covered in the equalization section (see Chapter 7) and so I will not repeat that material here.

Interface

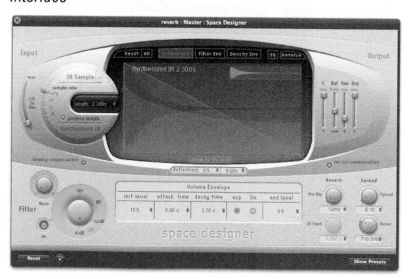

Figure 8-8 Space Designer.

The interface is deceptively simple. The primary area is a graphical representation of the impulse originally created either in a physical space or as a result of the Space Designer Synthesis tool. At the end of this chapter, I will explain about the Impulse Response Utility, which can be used to create presets, so see that section for more information on impulses. The center section of Space Designer is very useful because you can see what the different settings are doing to the sound of the reverb. This section has several different views: Volume Env, Filter Env, Density Env, and EQ. By clicking on each of these buttons, the overlay which is semi-transparent over the actual waveform of the impulse switches to represent the different sections. The Volume Env(elope) controls the volume level over time; the Filter Env controls the cutoff frequency of the filter section; the density represents the level and amount of synthesized reflections; and finally the EQ is a standard equalizer. Let's cover the most important features first and then we'll get to some of the fun stuff.

Level Adjustments

You can easily pick a preset from the list and use Space Designer without ever tweaking any settings. However, you will need to adjust its output level to make it fit in your mix. The interface is different in stereo/mono mode versus surround mode, so we'll need to look at both. In stereo/mono mode, you will find two sliders on the upper right side: Dry and Rev. The Dry slider adjusts the level of the original signal being fed into Space Designer. The Rev slider adjusts the level of the reverb effect being generated by Space Designer (see Figure 8-9).

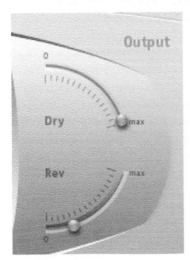

Figure 8-9 Output sliders.

Dave's Video Editor Perspective

Using Tracks, Sends, and Busses

One of the biggest differences between Final Cut and Soundtrack is the mixer functionality. Everything in Final Cut is oriented around clips. If you want to put a filter on a clip, then that is all you have to do. In many situations your hardware will allow the filters to be processed in real time (no rendering necessary), but sometimes the filters will have to be rendered. While Soundtrack Pro has a powerful clip-based architecture, it also has a large amount of track-based functionality. I have spent time explaining this to video editors but with mixed results because it is a foreign concept that seems counterintuitive. Why, they ask, would you want a whole track in your sequence to be processed using the same effect? And if you do want to do it that way, why not just apply the same effect to each of the clips? That way, if you have a clip in the sequence that you want to be kept separate from the filter, you wouldn't have to move it to a new track.

The main issue is that Soundtrack represents the merging of two worlds: music and post-production. In music, a track in a sequence typically holds a single musical instrument which is the same through a whole song, and might not even be split into smaller clips. Instead of applying effects to individual clips, the effects are placed on the tracks in which the clips reside and all clips that are on the track are processed. This is partially because in the pre-digital music production days audio was processed by separate effects units that processed all audio that passed through. Audio tracks in Soundtrack are like funnels. The clips on the tracks are fed through the track funnel and then out to the master. Each clip can be assigned effects, each track can be assigned filters, and so forth. This can be tricky because you have to remember to look in a lot of different places to see what effects are in place.

Sends and busses are where things get a little harder to understand. A send is like a patch cable on a patch bay. It connects an audio track with a bus. A bus is similar to an audio track but it can never hold audio clips; it simply acts as an effects channel that can process audio. The way to use a send and bus is to first create a bus and then tell an audio track to send a copy of its audio to the bus. Once that connection is made, the bus will receive a copy of the audio track's audio and both audio track and bus will send that audio on to its assigned submix (see Chapter 13 for more on this).

There are two situations in which I use this functionality in post-production. The first is when I want to create a headphone mix for dialog replacement and voice over sessions. I send a little from each track that I want the artist to hear in their headphones and then I route the destination bus to a submix that is being sent out of separate outputs on the audio interface. This only works when you have an audio interface with multiple outputs. The second reason I use sends and busses arises when I am using reverb while mixing. This might be when I am creating a musical arrangement with Apple Loops, or matching dialog for a section to a specific location and I have multiple tracks using the same reverb preset. This way I can assign a bunch of audio tracks to the same destination bus by inserting sends on each audio track. Keep in mind that you can complete entire mixes without ever using sends and busses. These are just another option for those who understand them and prefer to work in a traditional audio-style workflow. The only weakness of using clip-based reverb filters that I can think of is that sometimes the tail of the reverb might be longer than the end of the clip and so Soundtrack will cut off the tail. Using a send/bus fixes this problem, but it means that everything being sent to that bus has to use the same reverb setting.

You can adjust the reverb level in several ways. If you are feeding the audio to a bus by using a send, simply turn the send level down using the Send Level slider in the Effects tab in the left pane. You will need to select the track that has the send on it and then expand the Send area in the Effects tab by clicking the arrow next to the Send check box (see Figure 8-10).

You can also turn down the Rev slider (see Figure 8-9). Lastly, you can turn down the fader on the track which holds the Space Designer plug-in.

I prefer to send a full signal to the reverb (leaving the send at 0, which is the default), and then adjust the reverb level using the Rev slider or the track fader. If you are using a send then the Dry should be turned all of the way down to prevent having the dry signal on the original audio track and on the bus. If you are inserting Space Designer on the audio track itself, you will need to turn the Dry up so that you can hear the original audio. The other alternative is to have Space Designer plug-ins on every track or clip in your session, which can be complicated because you'll need to create the same settings on each and it might hit you too heavy on the CPU usage.

On the left side of the interface you should see a slider that adjusts the stereo image of the reverb input. If you leave it up, all stereo information will be retained. Moving it to the middle combines the input into a mono file. Sliding it to the bottom will switch the left and right channels. I typically leave this in the default position.

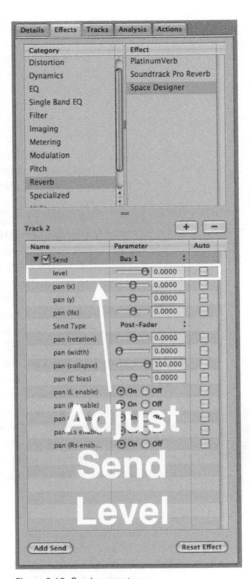

Figure 8-10 Send parameters.

Figure 8-11 Space Designer track fader.

Figure 8-12 Input section.

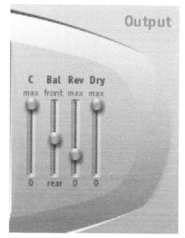

Figure 8-13 Sliders in surround mode.

Figure 8-14
Surround Input
slider.

Figure 8-15 Impulse response
length parameter.

In surround mode you will see a number of different sliders. The way to use Space Designer in surround mode is to insert it on a track or clip that is either a surround item or that is being sent to a surround submix. These sliders affect which channels the reverb will be heard in (see Figure 8-13). The first slider adjusts the level of reverb in the center channel. If you are placing reverb on a dialog track then you will want to leave this fairly high, but you have some flexibility with it.

The Bal slider adjusts the front to rear balance. Pushing this up places the reverb entirely in the front left and right speakers. The Rev slider sets the overall level of the reverb. Typically, you will set this quite low. If you set it high, it will overpower the dry signal and sound wrong. The Dry slider does the same here as in stereo/mono mode: it turns the unprocessed audio signal up and down. When Sound Designer is inserted on an audio track this should be set to the top, but if it is an insert on a bus track it will be set to the bottom. When Space Designer is in surround mode, the slider on the left side switches to an LFE slider (see Figure 8-14).

The LFE slider adjusts the level of the LFE in relation to the input of Space Designer. By default this is set to 0, which means the LFE passes through without actively creating additional reverb. I recommend leaving it this way to prevent the low frequencies of the source material from creating a lot of low frequency reverb. Instead of adding power, it would make things sound extra-muddy.

Length

The next thing to adjust is the length of the impulse. If the reverb tail is too long then it will create a muddy mess. I tend to pick a preset that is slightly longer than I need and then shorten it to the perfect length. To shorten the impulse you can use the Length setting. When using an IR sample you can never make the length longer than the actual impulse file. When using a synthesized impulse (which is covered below), you can make it as long or as short as you like. The trick is in knowing how long or short to make it. Unfortunately there is no magic bullet for this issue.

Equalization (EQ)

The EQ panel is the next area of Sound Designer that it is important to understand. A preset may be good for what you are trying to do, but with a little EQ you can make it great. The

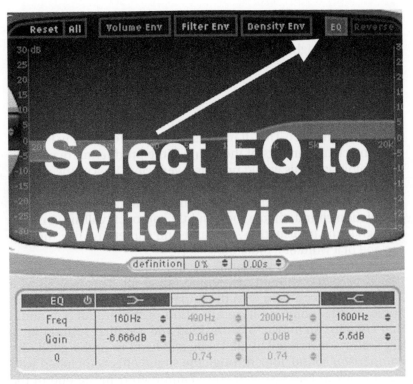

Figure 8-16 EQ view.

approach to take is simple: if the reverb is sticking out too much, then turn down the high frequencies; if the reverb is not sticking out enough, then turn up the high frequencies. If there is too much bass sound coming through the reverb, then turn down the low frequencies. That is just about the extent of typical reverb equalization. Of course, you can always do more as the need arises. For more on equalization, see Chapter 7.

The remainder of the features of Space Designer are better understood with examples. So, instead of further outlines, I am going to push you to the DVD where the rest of the features for normal use are explained and demonstrated.

Additional Space Designer demo.

Synthesized Impulse Responses (IRs)

What I am going to do now is explain how to create a synthesized IR for use in creating custom reverb presets. Instead of loading an IR created in a physical space, Space Designer is able to create an IR based on settings input on the interface. It uses the Volume Env, Filter Env, Density Env, EQ, and Length settings to create an IR that matches those settings. When you make changes to these parameters and then press the Synthesized IR button, a new IR is created to match. This is an extremely powerful tool to have access to. To help you understand why this feature is powerful and how you might use it, let me describe an example situation.

Example

When trying to match the sound of a room used in a particular scene, the IR synthesizer can be used to replicate the room's characteristics. First, you'll need to find a part of the audio track that has a sharp impact. This, if in an isolated moment, really lets you hear the characteristics of the room. If the production team used a clapping slate this would provide a very clear idea of the natural reverb in the room. The clap is heard first followed by the natural decay of the sound in the space. If there is no clear impact in the production sound, then a more subtle approach will still provide enough sonic information – try and find something like the T at the end of a word or a footstep.

Next, find a sound similar to the one in the production sound that is very dry, without any sound tail at all. This is used as a sample for comparison with the impact sound in the production audio. At this point we have a portion of the production audio that contains an impact of some kind and a similar sound that is dry with no reverb tail at all. If you still need to find a good, dry comparison sound, look through the sound effects included with Soundtrack to find a similar sound and then trim the end of the file off until the sound has no tail. It doesn't have to sound good, just similar and dry. Next insert Space Designer on the track with the dry sound. Finally, and this is not a perfect science, tweak the parameters of Sound Designer until the reverb matches the production location reverb. The method for doing this is as follows:

1. Start with the Length parameter to match the length of the reverb. Listen to the production sound and make note of how long it takes for the tail to die out. Match the tail using the Length parameter.

2. You can adjust the Volume Env to match the decay rate. If the reverb dies down quickly at first and then slowly ebbs into nothing, you can set the Volume Env to match this pattern using the graphic section. The shape will need to match the volume decay.

3. After the decay matches, set the Filter Env. This is a little harder because you have to listen carefully to how the decay changes over time. Does it get darker or brighter as it decays? The higher the line in this envelope, the brighter it will typically be. Remember that the Filter Env controls the frequency of the filter located at the bottom of the interface. You can choose between high pass filters, low pass filters, and band pass filters. You can create a reverb tail that starts quite bright and then over time becomes much less so.

4. Once you set the Filter Env, the resulting reverb is often very close. You may, however, want to tweak the Density Env, which is akin to changing the material the walls of the room are made of. The lower the line on this envelope, the more distinct the reflections. You may lower it when emulating a metal, brick, or glass room. Settings that are too low, especially towards the end, may cause quality issues because Sound Designer tries to break the reverb tail into individual reflections when in fact reverb is, in the advanced stages of its tail, naturally made up of completely indistinct reflections. Trying to go against this gives unpredictable results. A part of this density is the Reflection Shape slider, which also changes the smoothness of the reflective surfaces.

5. Next you can adjust the EQ, which will change the overall frequency spectrum. You can make the reverb a little brighter or darker overall, or accentuate specific frequencies throughout the entire frequency range.

6. One of the last things to consider is the stereo image. Sound Designer excels at creating big and beautiful reverbs. If you are trying a match dialog recorded with a single microphone then you probably don't want a big and wide stereo reverb emulation. You can adjust this using the Spread knob. Using a pair of headphones will help when matching the stereo/mono imaging. Headphones act like a magnifying glass for imaging issues. If you listen to the production sound followed by the Sound Designer reverb and the latter sounds a lot wider, adjust the spread until they match better by turning it down.

7. In the end, you may have to do some creative tweaking. I have randomly moved envelopes around to great, but accidental, success. You never know.

Dave's Video Editor Perspective

The Impulse Response Process

As a filmmaker, the impulse response process is very promising and exciting. Many new filmmakers are quick to simply re-record audio and try to replace the audio in a scene. The problem is that, if you are recording in a large room, the audio sounds very different than audio recorded in a small dead room, like a sound booth. If you try to simply replace the audio untreated, the viewer will notice that the audio does not sound like it matches the space that it is in. Often the new filmmaker will also use a different microphone than the one they used on set, producing multiple reasons why the audio sounds 'wrong.' The impulse response process provides you with a tool that will help you to create a similar sound space to that of the original location. This could make ADR a less painful and less expensive experience.

Reverb Usage

I prefer to use reverb as little as possible. I think it has a tendency to muddy things up and it is very easy to overdo. The possible uses of reverb that are typical include:

1. Matching ADR, Foley, and other sound effects to visually determined locations;
2. As an effect for scary/ominous/intense/flashback scenes;
3. When creating a music bed from individual Apple Loops.

When using reverb, err on the side of just enough or too little. Whatever you do, don't think that putting reverb on replaced dialog will make it fit all by itself. Automated dialog replacement fits when there is a combination of dialog, Foley, other sound effects, and then reverb. Combine that with some surgical equalization and then the reverb will do its job.

Surround Reverb

Placing a surround reverb onto a dialog track is generally a bad idea. Dialog is typically panned to the center channel in a surround mix, and hearing dialog tails coming from the rear is often confusing for the ear unless done with a high level of subtlety. However, placing an exploding car into a surround field with an appropriate surround reverb might be just the ticket. Just don't overuse the 'surround' reverb option.

Delay Effects

This is another set of plug-ins in Soundtrack that is aimed primarily at music production and is not as useful in post-production. A delay takes the input signal, saves it in memory for a period of time, and then releases it. This pushes the sound back in time from where it originally would have played. You can do a number of things with the delayed signal, such as mixing it in with the original sound, making it repeat more than once, change the panning of the repeats, making the repeats slowly fade out, and a lot of other really creative effects. Instead of explaining every feature of the three delay plug-ins that Soundtrack has, I've picked several post-production tasks that you might want to use them for and explained how to do enough to accomplish them. There is also extra material on the DVD showcasing additional music related tasks.

Delay plug-in demo.

Echo Effect

Creating an echo effect has several uses as a sound design tool. If you are working on a scene in which dialog takes place in a canyon or an alleyway, you might want to create an echo. For each of the following scenarios, we are going to use the Delay Designer. This has a very similar interface to the Space Designer, and is in many ways just as powerful.

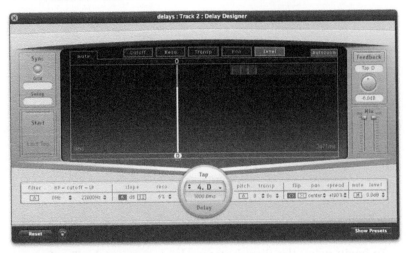

Figure 8-17 The Delay Designer.

Dave's Video Editor Perspective

Echo

Coming from a filmmaker who has shot in an echoey environment, you are better off adding echo in post-production than recording it on set. I once shot a scene in a stairwell for a film I was working on and that space was a bouncy, echoey location, so much so that some lines were hard to understand and the natural decay of the audio would bleed over the lines spoken by the other actors. What any sound designer will tell you is that there is no magic button to remove this sort of echo problem. Generally, if this is the location you shot in, you have two options: one, re-record the audio or two, live with the sound quality as you recorded it. In hindsight I would have chosen a better location, or perhaps I could have brought sound blankets to minimize some of the echo, but that may or may not have helped.

There have been times when I've wanted to create an echo effect and what I did, right in Final Cut, was to duplicate the audio track a few times and offset those audio clips with a bit of a reverb effect applied. Also, Final Cut has a pretty simple echo effect that can do this fairly well.

The center section of the Delay Designer is easy to use once you understand how it works. Each line is a delay of the original signal. You can click on each and then adjust the parameters at the bottom and on the line itself. Let's start by creating a set of delays that sound like an echo. You can add delays by clicking in the lane below the graphic center or by using the Start/Last Tap feature on the left side of the interface.

Figure 8-18 Start tapping.

To begin using the Start button, also known as the Tap feature, click it once to activate. Then click the Start button again at the intervals at which you want to add delays. This is a real-time process, which means that from the moment you start the tap it will run like a clock, creating time-accurate delay markers when you click. To create an echo, think of the sound you wish to achieve and imagine the echo repeating in your head. Click Start, using the initial start click as the sound that creates the echoes, and then click again at the points in time when you imagine the echoes.

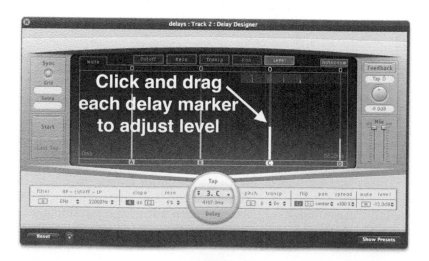

Figure 8-19 Adjusting the level of the delay.

Once you have done this, you may want to morph the delays to sound more realistic. As the echoes repeat, they will become softer and duller. Use the Level control to make each delay progressively lower. You might also want to adjust the Cutoff frequency by switching the view to Cutoff and pulling these sliders down as well.

The last settings you should adjust are the Dry/Wet sliders. The dry signal is the original non-delayed signal, which should be mixed in with the delayed wet signal. Set these based on the resulting sound.

Figure 8-20 The Dry and Wet sliders.

Special Warped Sound Effect

Whether the character is waking from a nightmare, in a chemically induced trance, or in a heightened state of frenzy because they are lost, the Delay Designer plug-in can add plenty of psychedelic sound to the scene. The best way to find the desired result is to explore the presets to find one that is similar in concept to what you are looking for. Especially useful for this type of effect are the Warped delays, available as presets in Delay Designer.

The preset I loaded in Figure 8-21 is a prime example of a Warped delay. Each delay point is transposed to the extreme using a trade-off pattern of one high and then one low. To accomplish this, all you would need to do is to set the pattern as described above, then switch the view to transpose mode, and finally drag each line in opposite directions. As you can see in Figure 8-22, there are many more drastic possibilities available.

Figure 8-21 Transposition view in Gears preset.

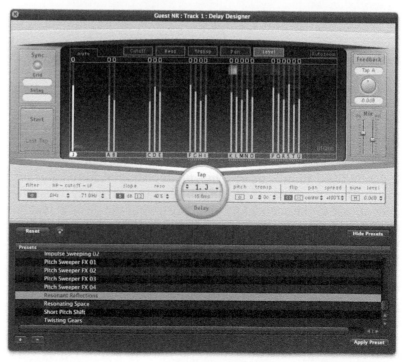

Figure 8-22 Extreme delay setting.

Doubling

The last fairly standard use for delays is doubling. This effect requires that the sound be on a stereo or surround track, meaning that it won't work in mono. If you have a file of general walla (unidentifiable background conversation), you could use Delay Designer to thicken it up. The same is true for traffic noise, avalanche sounds, water effects, and so on. Any time you want to subtly double sounds, a delay is an option. You could also copy and paste files onto different tracks with a similar result, but the Delay Designer allows you to change the repeated portions so that they sound different from the original.

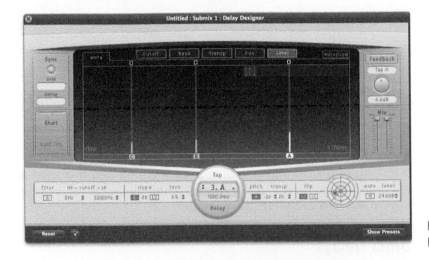

Figure 8-23 Doubling sounds with various levels.

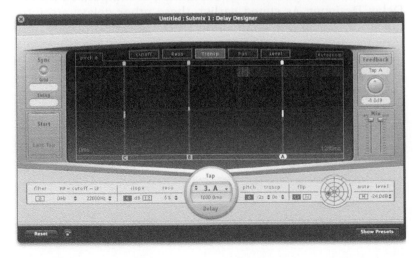

Figure 8-24 Doubling sounds with various pitch transpositions.

Figure 8-25 Doubling sounds with various pan settings in surround.

In Figures 8-23 through 8-25 you can see a doubling scenario that repeats the original sound three times. Each of these repeats has a different level (see Figure 8-23), each of these repeats has a different pitch setting (see Figure 8-24), and each of these repeats has a different pan location in the surround image (see Figure 8-25). All of the settings combine to create a unified texture that is hard to identify as a group of individual elements, and rather appears to be a complete wall of sound.

Other Delays

The other delays are useful but limited in comparison with the Delay Designer. As stated earlier, these other delays are introduced further on the companion DVD. You will probably never use them but you never know what will come up. If you are working on a lot of music tracks, you may find yourself using them all of the time. As we move into the next chapter we leave the discussion of effects behind and begin to look at the mixing process.

9

MIXING

In the type of projects you'll probably be working on in Soundtrack, there are two normal experiences. The first is that you will edit and mix as you go along, ending up with a finished project. The second is split into more defined sections, starting with editing, passing through mixing, and ending with the final deliverables. You may have even done a lot of the work while still in Final Cut, only passing the audio into Soundtrack for finishing. No matter which process you follow, the mixing capabilities of Soundtrack are a huge asset towards creating a high quality final audio track in an efficient manner. What this chapter is not going to cover is the process of mixing full-length feature films in the 'Hollywood' tradition. Soundtrack is not the right tool for those types of projects, although it is getting closer with every version. The problem is that its set of functions is limited in two key areas: automation and surround sound implementation. While Soundtrack does have automation and surround sound capabilities, they are still less developed than the tools that a professional mix engineer requires. What this means is that, if you are a video editor working on audio, you will probably have plenty of power to complete the tasks you have in front of you. But, if you are an audio editor working on tight deadlines day in and day out, some of the features that would help you to perform your job efficiently are not available in Soundtrack. For instance, the automation in Nuendo is a highly complex system that has a great many features that take recording and editing automation to a whole new level. There is an entire control panel with options such as recording current automation level retroactively to the previous starting point. This means you can work on automation for a section and find the right level, and then have it added onto earlier portions of the track using a shortcut. In Soundtrack, you would have to either re-record the earlier section or use the mouse to change the part. The difference is one click versus an additional pass or manual changes. This is one example of how Soundtrack

169

is still on its way to becoming a true competitor of the big post-audio tools. However, it can still accomplish the same tasks and it has a lot of other features that are unique.

Tools for Mixing

The two primary areas of Soundtrack that are used for mixing are the Mixer tab and the envelope lanes on the timeline. The mixer interface is based on hardware mixers that use a vertical track layout and vertical level faders (see Figure 9-1). Each track on the timeline is attached to a track on the mixer. You may already be used to this because Final Cut also has an audio mixer; however, there are some differences. The main divergence is that Soundtrack allows you to use both clip-based and track-based effects, while Final Cut only allows clip-based effects. Further, in Final Cut you can only add filters when a clip is selected and you cannot add effects to the sequence track itself. There are a few reasons why it is important to have these features in an audio mixer.

Figure 9-1 Audio mixer. Reproduced with permission of 42 Productions - Boulder, CO.

The first reason deals with the time-based effects covered in Chapter 8. When you place a reverb on a clip in Final Cut, the reverb ends when the clip ends. When the effect is track-based, in Soundtrack, it continues after the clip ends because the track continues. There are three places in Soundtrack in which to open track-based effects: the Mixer tab in the Insert area (see Figure 9-2),

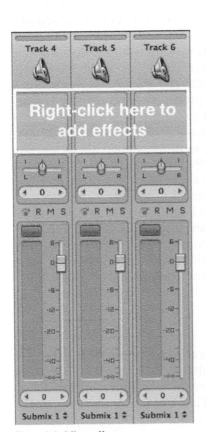

Figure 9-2 Mixer effects.

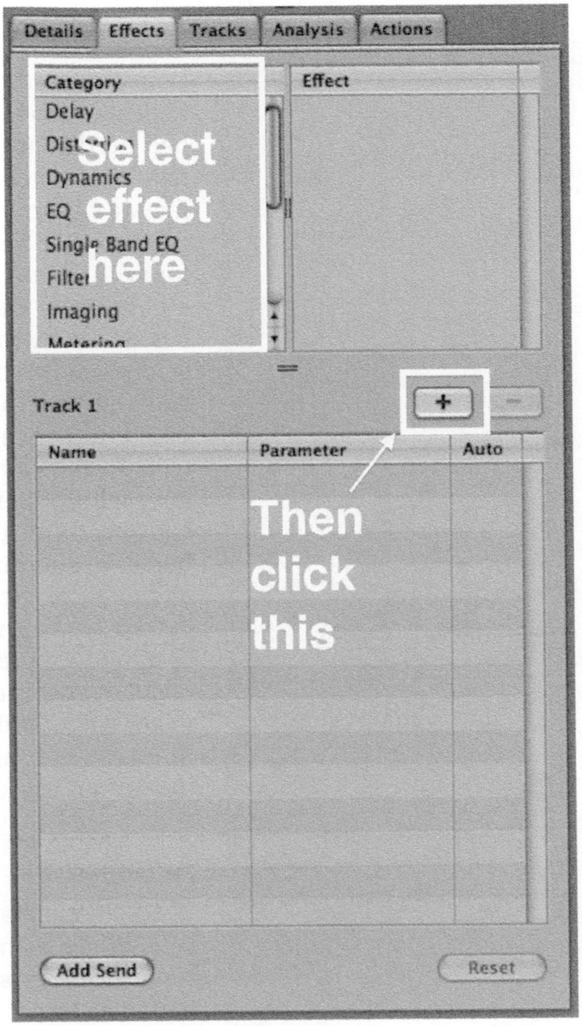

Figure 9-3 Effects tab.

the Effects tab in the left pane (see Figure 9-3) and the Tracks tab in the left pane (see Figure 9-4).

The effects that you insert in these locations will affect everything that is on that track. Every clip on a track that has a reverb plug-in will be processed through the reverb. In a lot of ways this seems limiting to video editors who are moving to audio for the first time. 'What happens if you want to put a single clip through a reverb – do you have to waste an entire track to do it?' Since the beginning of moving pictures everything has been defined in frames of still

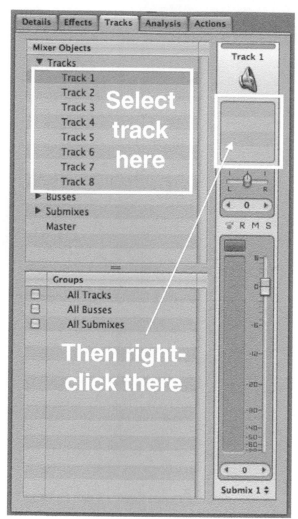

Figure 9-4 Tracks tab.

images that have a distinct and tangible existence. Conversely, audio started as grooves on cylinders and later moved to magnetic tape. These formats had no distinct 'frames' and were continuous in nature. Until computers matured, audio processing was primarily implemented using real-time effects, while film has always been processed one frame at a time. This history is expressed in modern software design, although the dividing line has definitely grayed over the years. Soundtrack is capable of both clip-based (frame-by-frame and clip-by-clip) processing and real-time track-based processing (continuous, like a groove on a record). You can put a reverb on a track that contains a lot of files to process them all, or you can add reverb to individual clips. In fact, using the busses or submixes, you can add a single reverb to any or all of the tracks at the same time. In various places in this book I explain this system. In Chapter 13 there are a few 'recipes' that help demonstrate how the various tracks, busses, and submixes work. Additionally, we'll be spending some time in this chapter explaining how you will use the various tracks during the final mix.

Automation

Automation is a critical part of the mixing process. While Soundtrack does not have the most sophisticated system of automation, it has enough to do most work. Final Cut has similar automation nodes, which are commonly called keyframes. In Soundtrack the automation lives in envelope lanes on the timeline. This is one area that could use some further development by Apple because there should really be track-based automation and clip-based automation. In Soundtrack there is only track-based automation and in Final Cut there is only clip-based keyframing. When you adjust the level of a clip in Final Cut, it is attached to the clip. When sequences are sent to Soundtrack, the keyframes are converted to track-based automation and it becomes too easy to lose the link between clips and levels.

Automation Modes

Aside from drawing automation in manually using the Arrow tool, you can also record automation in real time using the

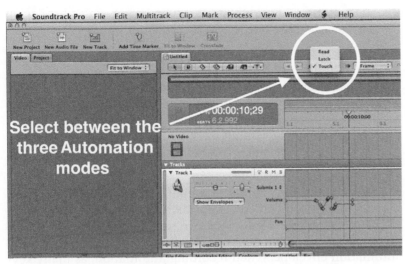

Figure 9-5 Automation mode selection.

controls on the mixer or on the plug-in interfaces. You can also attach a control surface which provides tactile control over the different effects and track levels. The modes are as follows:

- Read – allows the automation to be read by the tracks and plug-ins.
- Latch – sets the tracks into read mode until a parameter is touched and then the mode is switched to write mode.
- Touch – reads the automation unless a parameter is currently being held, in which case the mode switches to write until the parameter is let go.

Each of these can be broken down even more by category.

Read Mode

Read mode is the default automation position. Unless you are actively recording automation, this should be set as the automation mode. The reason is that if you are in one of the other modes, you can easily mess up the automation by touching any parameter.

Latch Mode

Latch mode starts off in read mode until an automatable parameter is adjusted, which instantly switches the mode to write. Write mode is not a mode in and of itself, but is half of what latch mode does. It takes the current setting and writes automation at that level. If you move the automatable parameter, the change is recorded into the envelope lane. Even when the parameter is released the automation will continue to be recorded until playback stops. The write mode is the most dangerous of all modes because it will erase all of the previous data.

Touch Mode

Touch mode is the most used automation mode because it reads the current data and switches into write mode only when a parameter is in use. Once the parameter is released, everything switches back into read mode. Further, you can alter small portions of the envelope without having to worry about accidentally overwriting previous data.

Thinning

You can adjust the amount of thinning that takes place by moving the Automation Recording Sensitivity slider under the General tab in the Soundtrack Preferences. Thinning is the process of automatically reducing the number of keyframes used to represent the automation envelope. When recording automation, as many keyframes as needed are used to represent the automation envelope and the thinning takes place upon completion of the automation recording. The further to the right (Low) that you slide the parameter in the Preferences, the more of the data is removed during the thinning process (see Figure 9-6). When the slider is set all of the way to the left (High), no data is removed at all (see Figure 9-7).

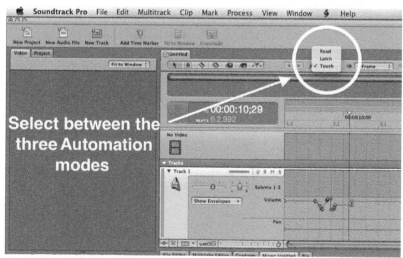

Figure 9-6 More thinning.

The primary reason for thinning automation is processing power. The more automation nodes that are present in a project, the higher the processing hit. A long film with many tracks will

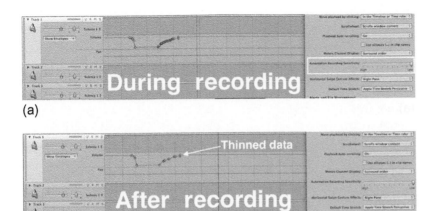

(a)

(b)

Figure 9-7 No thinning.

require a lot of computer power to complete. Thinning also helps with editing automation nodes; the fewer you have, the easier it is to manipulate them. It is possible to thin too much and create a sound different from what you originally recorded and so the default is the recommended setting. If you are constantly having CPU problems, consider this as one way to reduce the load.

Control Surfaces

Control surfaces are a great way to efficiently mix projects. A control surface allows you to take control of multiple tracks, with fader controls to set the levels for each of the tracks. While control surfaces often look like audio mixers, they are rarely more than an extension of your computer's mouse. This means that you can almost always do the same work with your mouse and it is only for efficiency purposes that you would use a control surface. Soundtrack works with several of the prominent control surface protocols, including Mackie Control, Logic Control, and Euphonix EuCon. These three cover most of the standard control surfaces you might typically use.

To set up a control surface, navigate to **Soundtrack Pro > Pref erences > Control Surfaces**. In order to install a device, you have to have it currently attached with all required software installed. In fact, you'll need to carefully read the documentation that comes with the control surface. Once it is installed and attached, you'll be able to choose the type of controller from the dialog in the Preferences (see Figure 9-8). You can also click the Control Surface Buttons button in the Preferences to open a window in

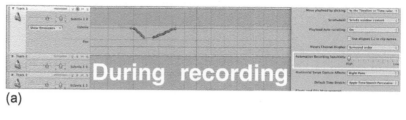
(a)

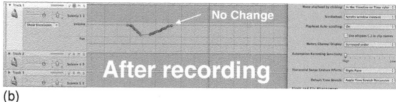
(b)

Figure 9-8 Euphonix controller not installed message.

Figure 9-9 Euphonix controller.

which you can choose, in a limited way, what some of the buttons can control in Soundtrack (see Figure 9-9). Select an item from the list of commands and drag it onto the available list of controls.

You have to be really good with the control surface to mix using the faders. It is very tricky to set audio levels in 'real time' because you have to remember how the levels sounded originally, have a clear concept of what you want them to sound like, and have

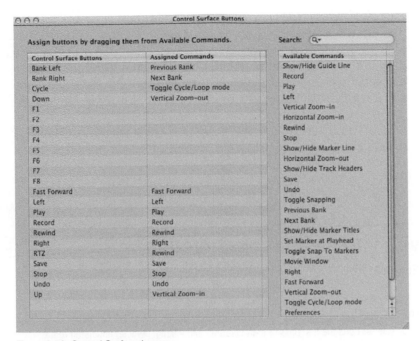

Figure 9-10 Control Surface buttons.

the coordination to implement it on the   y. This takes practice! Most of the time control surfaces are used for their other key commands, which means you might as well avoid them and stick with your computer keyboard. One really nice thing about a control surface is that it lends credibility to your mixing environment with clients. A good-looking control surface can become the centerpiece of a room, even if you end up using your mouse most of the time; just don't use that justification when proposing it to your accounting department!

Mixing

The process of mixing involves a number of different components. These include setting volume levels, panning items, applying effects, and creating the final audio files. By the time the project arrives at the final mix in a traditional setting, all of the sound effects, Foley, replaced dialog, music, and ambient tracks will have been put into a single session file. This allows you to have access to all of the parts of the project so that they can be balanced together. Of course, the other option is to put all the pieces together as you progress through the mix process.

This only works for very simple projects that don't have complex sound design and thousands of audio clips. If you are dealing with a complex project, it is recommended that you pass the project on to a post-audio facility because they can handle large projects in an efficient manner. If you have a decent sized budget, it will probably save you money to have the 'professionals' do it because if someone without the right experience works on the project it will take longer and most likely cost even more. Let's go through each of the typical parts of a mix.

Dave's video editor perspective

Interactions with the Audio Engineer

If you are able to hire a professional audio engineer, you are more likely to save a great deal of time and headaches. Once I've given the OMF files to that audio person, I will basically leave him or her to do what they do best. That is, clean and improve the existing audio. When that person has done the first pass of their cleaning and mixing, I will sit and listen to the film while they are present. As the director, I will make comments and suggestions and he or she will make notes and discuss what can and cannot be accomplished. After I leave they will make the adjustments and continue sweetening. Basically, I find it counterproductive to sit in the room with the sound designer. Most people do not work best when someone is watching (or listening) over their shoulder. So, let them be, and let them use their ears and training without worrying about what the director is thinking from moment to moment. When they are done with that pass I will get the call that the mix is ready for another listen. We'll go through the film again, making notes, and hopefully will then be close to completion.

Levels

The process of setting levels does not necessarily have a 'set in stone' procedure. I have experienced many different workflows for accomplishing this task. The primary considerations regarding how to do this begin with a discussion about what your project needs. The dialog is almost always the most important element and so I typically put that in place first. I mute all of the other tracks and then slowly un-mute them as I progress through the mix. My entire group of dialog is typically sent to a dedicated dialog submix. This means I can automate individual dialog tracks or automate the dialog submix. All of the ambient matching on the dialog should have already been completed, so you should be able to focus on the big picture of making sure that the dialog can be understood and that the music and sound effects don't bury it. In light of this, you will set the overall levels using automation throughout each scene. I have seen a number of 'audio engineers' use compressors/limiters on all of the tracks to control the dynamic range so that they don't have to create automation. Sometimes this works, but it often creates less desirable results because the audio has no room to breathe and is constantly squashed.

Instead, you can use automation to level each line of dialog as you match it to the other elements. You can accomplish this task by either using a control surface/mouse controlling the faders, or manually drawing in the automation on each track. Obviously, using a controller can save time, but only if you can master its use. If you are starting the mix with a clean slate (no previous leveling), then use the latch automation mode. This lets you record the automation as any previous automation points are deleted. You can set a level and then let go of the fader and it will continue as long as the project is playing. On the next pass (unless you messed up the first pass), you should use the touch mode and make changes as needed. The touch mode will only record new automation when the fader is held; when you are finished updating a section, let go of the fader and it will return to the previously recorded level. As you set the levels for each of the elements you will also set the panning and use processing to achieve a balanced mix.

Panning

Panning is the process of choosing which speakers the sound will be sent to. In a stereo setup, you only have two speakers and so you can pan between them. An interesting phenomenon that happens when you pan between two speakers is called a 'phantom image.' Any sound that is equal in two speakers will sound like it is coming from between

Figure 9-11 The panner.

them. This phantom image is what allows a stereo image to sound very realistic. The problem is that the image does not have a solid anchor and depends on the listener being exactly between the speakers. If the listener is closer to one speaker, the image will shift towards that speaker. So, if you are sitting near a speaker, the sound will come from the side instead of the center. If a movie in a theater is played in stereo, you should avoid sitting on an edge row near the front because all of the dialog will sound like it is coming from the side of the screen instead of the center. In surround, dialog is almost always set to come from the center speaker to avoid imaging problems. With the center channel, dialog will always be anchored in the center.

As you move through the different elements in a mix, you may have to try a few different things to help the balance work. If you are working in surround, you can sometimes place sounds around the surround image to help prevent sounds from stepping on each other. However, sounds placed around the surround image have no place to hide if they are sub-par. If you are working in stereo, even more care will need to be taken to prevent sounds from stepping on each other sonically. One of the tools you will use to do this is the panner. The anchor of both the stereo and surround mixes is the dialog. Since the dialog is so important, you will often need to avoid placing anything else in the same location, opting instead to pan other sounds outside of the center location.

Think of panning in terms of sync items. The most important sync item is dialog, and it is panned in the center. Next are hard sound effects associated with the people or elements on screen and these will need to be panned either near the center or to match the location of the action they are associated with. If someone is walking across the screen, you can pan the footsteps to match the movement. Any dialog that is taking place will no longer be stepped on by the footstep sound effects. A red flag may have just popped up for some of you because there are two levels of project that typically exist. If you have to use mostly production dialog for all of your sound, then panning sound effects is often out of the question unless your audio person recorded stereo/surround sound on location. The reason for not being able to pan effects is that production audio typically uses a boom mic with various wireless lavs. If you are using the boom for the dialog, the footsteps may already be a part of that dialog track. Hollywood blockbusters use mostly replaced dialog and the effects are recreated by Foley artists and sound effects libraries. This means that they can be panned wherever you like, completely separately from the dialog track. Lower budget films often don't have the luxury of replacing all of the production sounds, leaving them to coexist with the dialog.

Next in the order of sync items would be sounds that don't have any hard sync with related visuals. Examples of this are ambient tracks of birds and nature sounds, city traffic, and walla (unintelligible dialog tracks representing crowds). These can be panned wide in the stereo image, leaving room in the middle for higher priority items. Most of these types of sounds come in stereo/surround formats and might work without panning, but some them will need to be panned away from the center.

Dave's video editor perspective

Wild Sounds

It is always necessary to augment the soundscape of your film by adding sounds that may not have been present when you shot the film. As a filmmaker, you should be thinking about your sound before the shoot and imagining all the sounds that you'll need to gather in order to better tell your story. Sometimes this happens in the editing phase, when you see what would improve the impact of the edit. Basically, you will make a list of the audio that needs to be gathered that is non-synchronous to the picture, for example car sounds, hitting sounds, footsteps, keys jingling, and so on. These are called 'wild sounds' because they are independent of the picture prior to you placing them in your edit. Often the sound designer will suggest and even gather this media for you, but it is really up to the director to decide what goes in. Remember, a good film is at least 51% audio. People will forgive a bad image, but not bad audio.

Last is the music, which is an important part of the process but often not directly related to the visuals in terms of sync. It is often a large amount of what is placed in the surround channels and furthest out in the stereo image.

One last thing about panning is that you will also want to check for consistency between the panning of various clips. This is kind of like having a continuity check on set. You need to make sure that the panning remains consistent from clip to clip. The best way to do this is to use headphones because they act as an audio microscope for imaging issues, allowing you to hear the slightest shift left or right of the audio files in the stereo field. Of course, this doesn't work with surround because there are still very few surround headphone sets. Just make sure you listen very closely. You can also automate the panning settings to adjust various sounds in the mix. This works in exactly the same way as automating the volume levels.

Panning demonstration.

Dave's video editor perspective

Panning

Since I tend to work on small projects for video and television and use only mono microphones, I generally choose not to mess with the pan settings. My thinking is that I really cannot anticipate where the film will be screened and what sort of listening environment might be available. So, I will generally try to have my audio set to left and right mono, with both channels equal in strength. This way, if the film is played in a theater, or on a television where one of the speakers might be inoperative, I know at least that all of the sound will be available to the listener. If the music I am using is in stereo, I may leave it as stereo, since as the filmmaker I am more concerned with the spoken word. For me, it's about communication. If you are trying to make people sound like they are in separate parts of the room through speaker selection, you could be burned in a lesser venue. Case in point: I screened a film at a festival in Upstate New York. The venue had a problem and only one speaker was working, so many filmmakers were upset when they could not hear a portion of the sound. I would have preferred to hear from both left and right, but at least the viewers heard everything, even if it was just on one side of the theater. So, to summarize, if you don't know where it will be played and you cannot make multiple versions of the audio, play it safe. Two-channel mono is a safe bet.

Processing

Once your levels are set and the panning completed, you may find that some of the items are still not sitting correctly in the mix, which might have one or more of the following symptoms:
- Some sounds are covered up by other sounds.
- Too much dynamic range – a sound may be soft one moment and then too loud the next; automation can help with this but not in every case.
- Some sounds might not sound natural and so stick out.

If you have a scene where there is dialog, music, and sound effects, then you might have to use a variety of processing tools to balance the elements. This is the hardest part to fully explain in text format because of the nature of audio mixing. The reason for a sound not fitting in the mix could be any one of a hundred different things. Instead of going in too deep, I am going to suggest a pragmatic approach. One, listen to all of the different elements together and figure out which is causing the problem. This usually involves deciding which of the elements is the most important and blaming the others for getting in the way. Two, figure out what the problem is with the element that is to blame. Is it a sound effect that is covering up the dialog? Is the music getting in the way because it is too rhythmic? Three, once you can put a label on the problem, you'll need to find a tool that can help. Equalizers can help sculpt the sound. To make the music fit around the dialog you could reduce certain frequencies of the music. If a sound effect is really loud but it has a lot of soft portions as well, consider a compressor/limiter to control its dynamic range. If the sound effect sounds too close to you while the dialog sounds further away, placing reverb on the sound might help it fit better. Specialized effects like phasers or vocoders are not going to help in most cases. Four, process the problem clip(s) and/or the track on which the clip(s) reside(s).

If the problem is small and on a single clip, process the individual clip. If the problem covers a much longer section, consider using a track-based effect.

Dave's video editor perspective

Sergio Leone

Some of the great films of Sergio Leone (*Once Upon a Time in the West, Hang 'em High, Fistful of Dollars*) are memorable for the characters created and their engaging stories of gunslingers, set in beautiful desert vistas. However, in the 1960s, the industry standard of post-production audio was basically one or two tracks of analog audio tape. Leone was known for recreating all of his audio in post and, on location, shot almost entirely MOS (without sound). Watching these films today, you'll notice that the audio does not appear to be coming from the location seen on the screen. A noticeable example is the sound of the harmonica that Charles Bronson plays in *Once Upon a Time in the West*. There is reverb, yet he is playing in the open desert where reverb could not exist. There are no walls for the sound to bounce off. Further, the dialog in the film sounds like it was recorded indoors, when again the image is of people talking in the open landscape.

It is this sort of thing that makes the viewer notice a discrepancy, and it takes us out of the viewing experience. Many new filmmakers don't take these issues into account and try to re-record audio in locations other than where the film was shot. More times than not, this is distracting to the viewer. Soundtrack can help to recreate the presence for audio that is not recorded on location, which is a great benefit to filmmakers who choose to work, as Leone did, MOS. I am sure if Leone had these tools 45 years ago he would have used them. Perhaps one day someone out there will re-edit the audio to fix the issues of the spaghetti western genre. Some will argue that doing so would take away from the feel of the film but, personally, I would love to see such improvements to these great films.

Master Levels – Submixes

Once you have all the elements for each category leveled in their own areas, you can mix using the submixes. For documentary-style projects, this might only include a music submix and a production audio track. Either way, at least you can focus on mixing two faders instead of four or five, depending on the project. Once you have automation in place for the submixes, you can always adjust the original tracks to make fine-tuned adjustments.

Surround Sound Options

If you are mixing for surround, I recommend a book by Tom Holman called *5.1 Surround Sound*. This book covers more about surround sound than just about any other. I wish there was room here to really get under the hood with surround, but all we can do

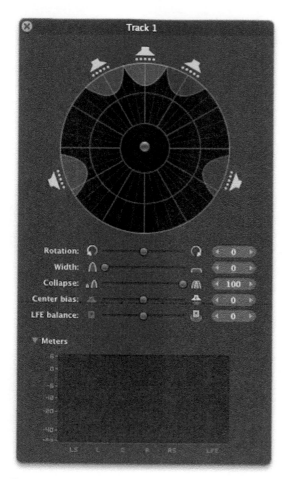

Figure 9-12 The surround panner.

Surround demonstration.

is to cover the basics, such as the surround panner (see Chapter 13, topic 16 for additional surround panner information). The most convenient thing is that the panner interface shows you where the sounds will end up in the surround image. It does this in two ways: through the blue, green, and red bubbles on the interface and through the little white dots outside the circle next to the speakers. The gray puck on the interface can be moved around to anywhere in the surround field. If you are mixing in surround, it might be temping to go crazy with surround panning, but subtlety is most often the best course of action.

Surround Panner Parameters

The first parameter is Rotation. This takes the current surround output and spins the entire thing around. The relationships between sounds remain the same because all items are shifted equally.

The Width parameter spreads the sounds wider across the channels. This is useful for diffusing a sound's location so that it is harder to identify the direction it is coming from. For example, a sound being sent to the left and right channels would be expanded so that it is also in the surrounds and the center channel.

The Collapse parameter is slightly more complex because it changes the fundamental way in which the panner works. When the puck is moved around the panner, the sound is sent to all outputs at varying levels depending on where the puck is located (Collapse at 0), or the sound actually moves between the outputs and the levels only appear to change (Collapse at 100). I recommend leaving this at the default because the implications rarely affect your mixes.

On the other hand, the Center Bias slider is very useful. It is a way to either make the front speakers create a phantom image or to use the center speaker as an independent channel. At a setting of 0%, the center channel won't be used, but you'll still hear sound from the center because anything panned in the center will be sent to the left/right channels, which create a phantom image. If you use a surround sound effect, this could be one way to minimize the potential overlap with the dialog because you can turn off the use of the center channel by setting the Central Bias to 0%. You will see this change re ected in the white dots around the edge of the circle.

Use the LFE Balance to send portions of the audio into the subwoofer channel. At −100, nothing gets through; at 0, everything passes straight through; and at +100, a portion of all channels is combined and sent to the LFE channel. This is one way to take an effects track and add some super subwoofer power to it. I recommend using a dedicated LFE channel instead of sending things via the panner into the subwoofer.

You can also click on any of the white Speak icons to toggle the active/inactive states of the surround channels passing through the panner. Just as with any other parameters in Soundtrack, the panners can be automated. All you need to do is to put the project in latch or touch mode and then, while playing is active, you can move the panners around to record the movements. Once automation is recorded, the panner will move at the exact same time and place from then on.

Mixing Advice

Mixing is a funny thing because on some levels it is very subjective. Two people can listen to the same mix and hear completely different things. One of the major problems lies in how the ears work. They are comparative and adaptive. Not unlike a frog being placed in cold water as it slowly boils, ears get used to things slowly as well. Taking breaks and resetting your hearing experience is almost as important as enlisting the help of third parties who haven't yet heard the mix a hundred times. Changing listening environments can help as well. In fact, you should be listening to most of your mixes on a variety of sound systems anyway. As discussed in Chapter 6, there are a variety of different level standards and so it is important to mix what is expected of the deliverables. If you are working on a theatrical mix, you will need to have a room specially calibrated to −85 dB. If you are mixing for broadcast then the room matters less, but your metering tools matter more because you have to hit specific audio levels. If you are mixing for DVD, then you have a little more exibility. If you are mixing for the web, then you will probably make it as loud as possible! With the exception of the theatrical mix, you should be listening on a variety of sound systems. For broadcast, I always have a television hooked up to make sure the mix translates well. For DVD, I will burn a disc and watch it on my home theater system – which I admit is a fairly poor comparison with the average setup because, as an audio geek, I have kind of a high-end system; so, I will also play the DVD on a smaller television in my family room. I know how the average television program sounds on the set and so I can gauge how close I am to the mix I am looking for. During this process I take copious notes and then return to the project and implement any changes to fix problems that really stuck out.

Summary

In most independent/small-scale/short format/low budget projects, I almost always have to get through a lot of work in a short amount of time. The bulk of the work in those situations takes place in the 'audio editing' phase. I try to make sure the dialog is level and consistent long before I enter the 'mixing' phase. I make sure things are panned consistently and that the overall levels are in the right pocket. The mixing process provides an opportunity to make sure all of the elements are working together. On big budget projects, the elements are often combined for the first time at the mix and so it really is a critical phase in the process. Assuming that you will not be using Soundtrack for that type of project, I encourage you to work on the 'mix' throughout your entire project. Use Final Cut to get things ready. If you need to process a clip with an equalizer, use the Send to Soundtrack feature to make sure all work will translate to Soundtrack in the later stages.

10

EXPORTING FEATURES OF SOUNDTRACK PRO 3

Exporting audio, sometimes referred to as 'mixdown' or 'bouncing,' is the process by which the audio and/or video in your session are consolidated into a single file, or batch of files, that is easily transferred or delivered. Many users gloss over the importance of understanding exporting features. There have been countless times when I have heard someone say, 'It's just exporting – it can't be that difficult.' That statement couldn't be further from the truth. As a matter of fact, as today's DAWs (digital audio workstation) become more and more integrated, and as audio and video formats and technologies become more sophisticated, the need to understand exporting functionality is greater than ever. In addition, efficiency is a crucial ingredient in today's job marketplace. Understanding the different facets of exporting will help the user to get the job done right the first time, preventing embarrassment and undue added stress in the studio.

Overview

Typical DAWs, such as Digidesign's Pro Tools, are somewhat deficient in the area of exporting when it comes to time management. DAWs like Pro Tools require that the user bounce the session in real time (for example, to export a seven-minute film you need seven minutes). This becomes extremely laborious when dealing with feature-length films at the independent level. Issues like hardware buffer size and memory are likely to cause a crash in the middle of bouncing. Apple has helped to bypass those issues by incorporating non-real-time processing into Soundtrack for many of the options in the exporting process.

Soundtrack Pro 3 performs exports of all types in a fraction of the actual runtime of the session. This, combined with the flexibility and number of options available at the exporting stage, means that Soundtrack Pro is becoming more useful in the world of post-production audio for film, especially for independent filmmakers and production houses.

Even those who are sound designers or mixers rarely deal solely with audio anymore. Video is nearly always part of the process. Being able to handle both audio and video formats/codecs (data compression algorithms) will make you invaluable in a post-production house. In order to put yourself in this position you should have a thorough understanding of how DAWs handle audio/video exporting. The sections below will help to put you on the right path to understanding both in Soundtrack Pro.

Soundtrack Pro sessions, with accompanying metadata, can be exported for continuation of work on another application or machine. The program is also capable of exporting master stereo and surround mixes, and selected tracks including submixes and busses, video only, and audio/video interleaved masters. There are also several additional options for the exportation of surround sound mixes. Each of these exporting features contains several options for modification (some more than others), which are detailed further in the sections that follow. When installed as part of the Final Cut Studio package, the program also has expanded data compression and authoring exporting options. Step by step examples are included in the final sections of this chapter.

Interleaved Audio

The term 'interleaved' refers to files that have multiple parts of audio/video tracks. Instead of being stored as separate files, they are all combined into a single file. In video this is sometimes called a 'self-contained movie.' A stereo audio file is interleaved, but an interleaved file may have many more than two audio tracks.

Exporting Multitrack Session Data

Dave's Video Editor Perspective

Exporting OMF from Final Cut

You've been staying up late to edit, tweaking the video and audio, and finally you think the project is ready to be labeled 'picture lock.' You can now send the video and audio files on to your audio post person to do the final mix and sweetening. If you have done some audio work in Final Cut and you want the audio person to see that work, you have to export it in a format that they can use. The one that I use consistently is the OMF format. In your Browser window, Control + click or right-click the icon for your final sequence and select Export Audio to OMF. You then get a dialog box in which you can select the handle length. It is important to give at least one second so that the sound designer has enough media on either side of the edit to work with for various reasons. There are also check boxes for Include Crossfade Transitions, Include Levels, and include Pan.

It is always unclear whether these check boxes actually translate to the audio software you are using, but if you are exporting for a Pro Tools system these are the selections you'll need to think about. Further, that Pro Tools system will also need a piece of software called 'DigiTranslator' in order to use the OMF files. Once you have finished, you can take the files to your audio engineer on a DVD or send them via FTP. I use a service called 'Filemail.com,' which allows transfer of large files. It's free unless your files are larger than 2 gB.

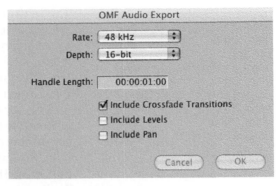

Figure 10-1 Export OMF dialog.

There are two types of audio export: audio-packed files and data packages. Audio-packed files are playable with just about any standard audio playback software, for example QuickTime, and can easily be burned to a compact disc or DVD. An audio-packed file results in a file with extension AIFF, WAV, or MP3 and others. In contrast, data packages include both session file exports and project data files. The session export files are based on an object model, allowing for session data to be read by various media editors. A session file export repackages all content and data information and some audio settings of a multitrack session into a single file that can be transferred to another program for editing (i.e. OMF or AAF).

It is very important to note that session file exports do not retain all settings and are not the same as Soundtrack Pro project files. Most session file exports will maintain volume and pan information when imported into another program. For example, sessions exported from Soundtrack Pro and imported into Pro Tools will retain volume and pan levels. However, real-time processing effects, or inserts, are not retained in the session file exports. Therefore, if you are looking to maintain an exact copy of all session data, including plug-ins, you should save as a Soundtrack project file.

Soundtrack Pro project data files have an STMP extension. However, session exports have a file extension of OMF or AAF. OMF stands for 'open media framework' and was created to standardize audio content for sharing between programs and between picture and sound editors. AAF stands for 'advanced authoring format' and is an updated standardization supported by more programs and built on a more efficient object-packing model. The AAF model also allows for the transfer of metadata, which provides information on the original files in the session including location, length, etc.

There is a major difference between the two formats. An OMF export is a single file with all settings and content packed together.

The individual files are limited to 2 gB in size. However, programs are capable of dividing OMF files automatically if the project extends beyond the 2 gB limit. AAF, on the other hand, contains a data file with the metadata and content information as well as individual audio files. This makes exchanging projects back and forth much more difficult as all audio files must remain with the AAF file for the opening of the session file. Typically, audio editors will receive OMF files from picture editors. AAF packages are more commonly exchanged among sound editors.

In Soundtrack Pro both OMF and AAF data files can be imported. However, only an AAF session file can be exported. Pro Tools can import these AAF files. (Pro Tools requires the addition of DigiTranslator to import any OMF or AAF file). However, other programs often only handle the importing of OMF files and not AAF. For more exporting control of sessions, Apple's Logic Studio has the ability to export and import both AAF and OMF. So, this is one area that Soundtrack Pro must work on in order to become more compatible with other audio and video editing programs.

So why are session file exports important? Well, these files allow for easy transfer via high-speed data lines to other post-production houses. Often projects will be farmed out to other houses for completion of specific portions. An OMF session export gives the other editing house a way to import the data without the need for folders full of original audio and video files. Everything necessary is contained in a single file. The same logic works in reverse. It is more efficient to receive a single file back than to wait for a DVD of files through snail mail. This is why it is important for audio programs to both import and export OMF files. If sharing a Soundtrack Pro session export, the recipient is going to have to battle with an AAF file and the associated plethora of audio files. While OMF is more limited in the metadata arena than AAF, the trade-off is that all necessary files are packed into a single OMF file so nothing will get lost in the transfer.

To export a multitrack session, go to **File** > **Export AAF ...** There are no options other than the save destination. I recommend creating a new folder as the Export AAF function will create one AAF file and numerous audio files, one for each mono track and two for each stereo track in your session. Note: In OMF and AAF exports, session stereo tracks will reopen as two mono tracks and pans will be placed in the center.

Exporting Single Audio Files

Unlike many DAWs, Soundtrack Pro can function as a single-file editor. If trimming or processing is necessary on a single audio file, Soundtrack Pro will allow you to open the file in a new window. The good thing about this function is that it takes away from the confusion of a multitrack session. You only have to look at one piece of audio.

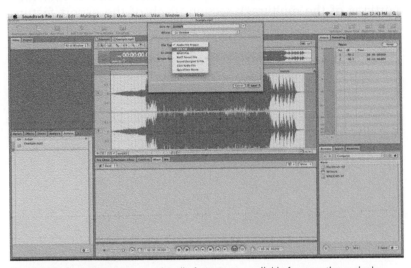

Figure 10-2 Several uncompressed audio formats are available for exporting a single audio file. The single audio file can also be exported as a QuickTime movie by selecting the option in the File Type dropdown.

When viewing a single audio file the Export option is not available. Instead, it is as simple as going to **File > Save As ...** Below the window area in which you choose the save destination, there is a section allowing you to choose which format to save the audio as. The file can be saved as any of the five sound formats supported by Soundtrack Pro, which are AIFF, WAV, NeXT, SDII, and Core Audio; each shall be discussed in more detail in the next section. Another possibility is to save as an audio project file for continuing work on the single audio file at a later time without making all changes permanent (all items in the Actions List are preserved). Lastly, the single audio file can be exported as a QuickTime Movie with the extension .MOV (no video will be attached to the audio file in this situation).

Selecting any option other than audio project file will also give you the option to choose a sample rate and bit depth. Dither can also be applied by selecting the check box underneath the Sample Rate pulldown.

Dither

Dither is used to help with the conversion of audio files from one bit depth to another. A small amount of random noise (sometimes sculpted noise) is added to an audio file that is about to be converted to a lower bit resolution. The random noise helps prevent certain types of errors in the process and results in a better conversion. If you compare this with changing the resolution of a photograph, you would take a high resolution print and add some blur to the pixels before converting it to a lower resolution. While the results are not exactly the same, the process is similar.

Exporting Multitrack Session Mixes (Stereo)

This section demonstrates some of the different methods and uses for the main Export function in Soundtrack Pro. The main export feature of the program is much more exible than other DAWs. It allows the user to export master mixes or individual portions of the multitrack section. Each of the export features contains various modifying options, which depend on the type of export selected.

The main export screen is accessed via the File menu or by using the shortcut Command + E. Note: The export function will be grayed out if you are currently using the single-file editor window.

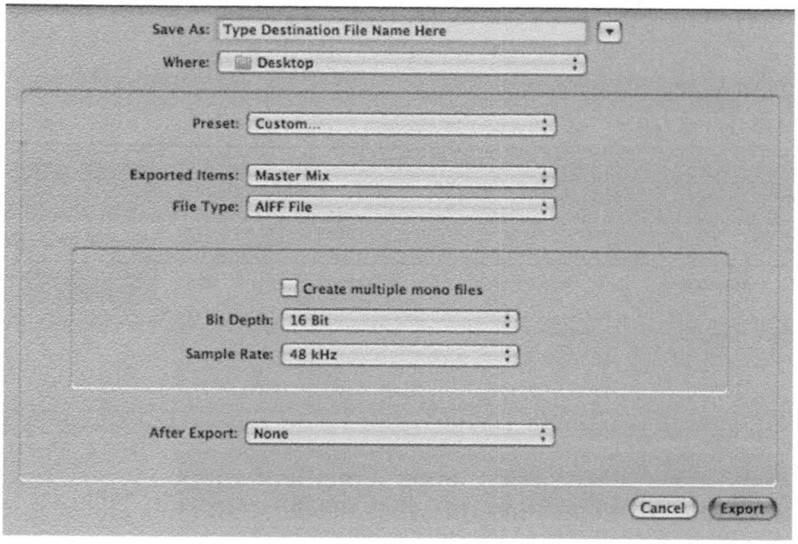

Figure 10-3 The main window for the exporting of multitrack session mixes is available via the Command + E keystroke.

When viewing the export window there are several default parameters: Save Destination, Preset, Exported Items, File Type, Multiple Mono, Bit Depth, Sample Rate and After Export. The availability of all these items is dependent upon the selection made in the File Type and Exported Items pulldown menus.

The Exported Items Menu

The Exported Items pulldown menu allows the user to specify what content is to be exported from the multitrack session. By default the Master Mix option is selected. This option will export the entirety of the session, excluding those tracks that are muted or inactive. The Master Mix export is the overall output as defined by the Master Fader in the session. The Master Mix option is typically used when the final project is completed and ready for mastering. However, a Master Mix is also useful if the picture editor, director, etc. need audio that is a work-in-progress.

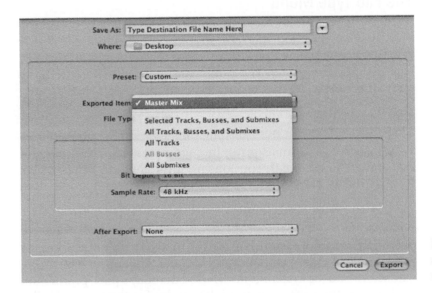

Figure 10-4 The Exported Items dropdown allows for the exportation of various mixes other than the Master Mix.

The next choice in the Exported Items pulldown menu is Selected Tracks, Busses, and Submixes. Selecting this option will export each of the selected tracks, busses, and submixes as separate files. Tracks are selected using the Command or Shift key while clicking individual tracks in the session prior to going to the export window. If no tracks are selected, this option will export all unmuted or inactive tracks, busses, and submixes as individual files. With most DAW systems the user must export each track, bus, or submix separately.

The third option in the pulldown menu is to export All Tracks, Busses, and Submixes. This option is virtually the same as the one above. It will export all unmuted sections of the multitrack session as individual files. Exporting everything as individual files is a good way to consolidate the project into an easier-to-manage session. This feature is useful for preparing a session for mixing as it makes it easier to group aspects such as sound effects and Foley.

The final three options in the Exported Items pulldown menu are All Tracks, All Busses, and All Submixes. Each of these options will export all tracks of the designated type to individual files. This is simply a variation on the above grouping of tracks, busses, and submixes. Depending on the needs of the audio editor and other members of the post-production team, these options could prove to be useful.

The File Type Menu

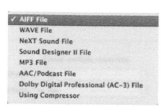

Figure 10-5 The File Type dropdown presents various options for compressed and uncompressed mixes.

The File Type pulldown menu allows the user to choose the encoding scheme that the files should be outputted as. This is also the section where output can be set to video only, audio only, or video/audio masters. The pulldown menu contains the basic audio file formats for audio-only applications.

AIFF and WAVE

The first options in the File Type pulldown menu are AIFF and WAVE. These two formats result in uncompressed data audio files and should be among the options used for creating a master file. By far, AIFF and WAVE are the two most common uncompressed audio file formats.

NeXT and Sound Designer II

Soundtrack Pro provides the user with two other uncompressed formats, NeXT and Sound Designer II. NeXT files appear with an .au extension. The file system is rarely used in today's post-production facilities. In the early days of digital audio for the web, .AU files had the ability to be encoded in one of 27 formats, each based on a particular bit depth. Some of the formats were lossy, while others were the same as uncompressed PCM (pulse code modulation) encoded files. In the case of Soundtrack Pro, the NeXT files contain the same data rate as the more common uncompressed file formats. The reason why the format is included in Soundtrack Pro seems to be that the founder of the NeXT system (back in 1985), Steve Jobs, later returned to Apple and so, when Apple subsequently purchased NeXT, they were able to integrate the company's DSP creations into their software such as Soundtrack Pro.

The other uncompressed audio file format is Sound Designer II. This format was extremely popular for a time, when Pro Tools was nearly exclusive to Apple computers. When Digidesign began building Pro Tools systems for PCs, the Sound Designer II file system was thrown out in favor of WAVE. Due to the manner in which WAVE files are written, they are compatible with both MAC and PC systems. Sound Designer II files, however, are not cross-platform compatible.

The AIFF, WAVE, NeXT and SDII options each contain three modifiers: Bit Depth, Sample Rate, and Multiple Mono. By default, 16-bit is the selected Bit Depth. The only other option is 24-bit. I highly recommend using the Bit Depth that corresponds with the multitrack session. Soundtrack Pro does not contain a Dither option, and thus it is not optimal to down-convert the Bit Depth of your session if using 24-bit.

The user may also change the Sample Rate to 32, 44.1, 48, 88.2, 96, 176.4, and 192 kHz. Once again, I would advise matching the exporting sample rate to that of the current multitrack session to avoid variations in the runtime of the audio file.

Dave's Video Editor Perspective

Shooting at 32K

Many consumer cameras default the audio setting to shoot at 32K. This is usually acceptable for home video and even sometimes for professional use. However, you need to know what the setting is on your camera, so check. If you are shooting at 32K and your timeline in FCP is set at 48K, your audio will surely fall out of sync. So, try to be aware of what you are doing and be consistent.

The final modifier is the ability to choose whether or not to create multiple mono files. This option is only available during the selection of these four uncompressed audio formats. Checking the box for multiple mono will create two separate audio files for each stereo pair. So, if the user exports a stereo master mix with the box checked, the resulting export would contain one audio file for the right channel and one file for the left channel. This feature is mainly for when another program is used to create a specific or proprietary audio file for authoring to disc. For example, using multiple mono files is a good idea if creating a DTS-HD Master Audio package.

MP3

The next option in the File Type pulldown menu is MP3. Soundtrack Pro comes with the ability to create an MP3 directly from a multitrack session. When this option is selected, further modifiers appear below the File Type pulldown: Stereo Bit Rate, VBR (Variable Bit Rate), Channels, Joint Stereo, Smart Encoding Adjustments, and Filter Frequencies Below 10 Hz. As with the uncompressed exporting options, the user may also select the desired Sample Rate. By default Soundtrack Pro selects 160 kbps as the Stereo Bit Rate. This means that each of the channels in the stereo pair is allocated 80 kbps. Soundtrack Pro allows the user to select any of the popular bit rates from 32 to 320 kbps – the minimum and maximum MP3 encoding bit rates. Below the Bit Rates

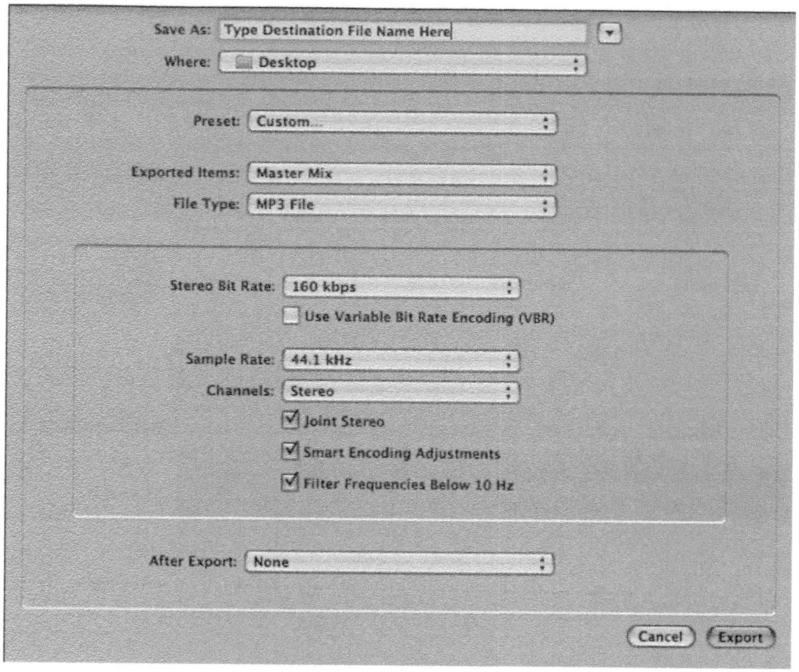

Figure 10-6 Selecting the MP3 file type option expands the window with more modifiers including Variable Bit Rate, Joint Stereo, and Stereo Bit Rate.

option is a check box that allows you to select whether or not to use VBR. By default it is unchecked. Due to the data loss incurred, use of the MP3 option should be limited to mixes that need to be sent via email, or for other uses that do not require a high quality version of the multitrack session.

Dave's Video Editor Perspective

Problems with Using MP3 Audio in Final Cut

Because so many people walk around with all their music on their iPod or iPhone, they often think that the music they have can simply be included in their video edits. Copyright issues are beside the point and will not be talked about here; what we are talking about is a compatibility issue. Many people will try to include MP3 files in their 48K timelines with less than satisfactory results. You may hear pops and clicks and digital distortion if you import into Final Cut in that format. However, if you are ripping the music from a 'legal' CD source, you can use iTunes or QuickTime Pro to convert the audio file into a 48K AIFF file instead of an MP3. If you are using iTunes v.9, go to **Preferences** > **General Settings** > **Import Using** and select AIFF Encoder. Then select Custom under Settings and in the sample menu select 48K. This will make all the files that you import from that point on huge and in a useable format. However, be sure to change this back because you'll see that not doing so will quickly fill up your iPod with your music. These files are significantly bigger, but they will now work fine in Final Cut.

The MP3 selection also contains other modifiers. The Channels pulldown menu allows the user to define whether the mix should be stereo or mono. Stereo is selected by default. There are three check boxes that follow underneath. By default all three are checked. The first is Joint Stereo. This tells the encoder to place all information that is common to both the left and right channels onto one track and put all the unique information onto another track. Based on the MP3 encoding algorithm, Joint Stereo should likely be reserved for lower bit rates, such as those below 224 kbps; above that bit rate it is best to use Normal Stereo. Normal Stereo keeps the left and right channel information on their own tracks. Smart Encoding Adjustments allows Soundtrack Pro to analyze the decisions you have made and alter them as the program sees fit. It is recommend that if you know what you are doing then this box should be unchecked. If you are questioning the settings you have chosen then you may want to leave it checked. Lastly, Filter Frequencies Below 10 Hz does exactly what it says. While human hearing extends at most down to 20 Hz, high-end equipment and properly acoustic-treated rooms will be able to recreate 10 Hz, which can be felt. However, since you are dealing with lossy MP3 data, it is likely that you are not concerned about recreating the 10 Hz range. Therefore, I would suggest leaving this box checked as it will slightly reduce file size and allow the bits to be used by more audible frequencies.

AAC/Podcast

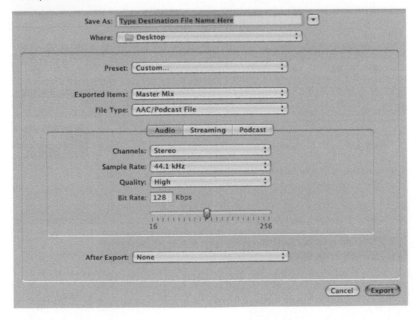

Figure 10-7 The Audio pane of the AAC/Podcast File option allows for the modification of quality settings.

This option in the File Type pulldown menu allows the user to create a podcast for the Internet, an iPod, or iTunes. When this option is selected a window with three option panes – Audio, Streaming, and Podcast – appears below the File Type pulldown. The settings present in this section determine the type, quality, and compatibility of the podcast. In the Audio pane the user can select whether the podcast should be stereo or mono and the sample rate. The Quality pulldown contains three options – Low, Medium, and High. There is no scientific guideline as to which of these settings to use. The Low setting is the quickest to transcode but also results in the lowest audio quality, while the High setting takes longer and results in higher audio quality. The difference in speed of the transcode is not gigantic and so I would recommend using either the Medium or High quality setting. The last option in the Audio pane is the Bit Rate. The Bit Rate can be set anywhere from 16 to 256 kbps either by using the slider or manually typing in a number.

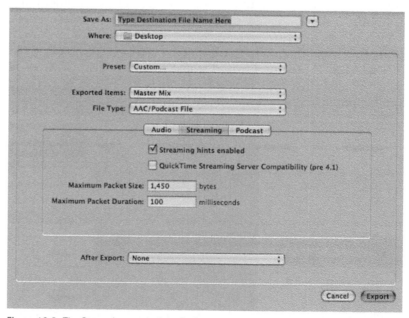

Figure 10-8 The Streaming pane of the Podcast section provides advanced options that work fine in the default mode, but advanced users will want to modify these settings to work more efficiently with the remote hosting server.

The next pane is Streaming. It allows the user to modify the manner in which servers will handle the podcast. The settings are not straightforward, and unless you have an advanced knowledge of server communications I would recommend using the defaults. The box for QuickTime Streaming Server Compatibility should be checked if the user will be using a version of QuickTime that is earlier than 4.1. However, since most media applications require at least version 7, this setting is of little use. The options for Maximum Packet Size and Maximum Packet Duration determine the amount of data that can be transferred between a server and user in a given time interval and the amount of audio data that can be contained in that packet. These settings will work in their default modes but sometimes tweaking settings is half the fun, or perhaps half the frustration.

The last pane is Podcast. This area allows the user to define what type of podcast is to be created. There are three options: No Video, Enhanced, and Video Track. The first option will simply create an AAC-compliant audio file with a .M4A extension. The Enhanced option should be used if the podcast contains still images and/or web links. This option will create a .M4V file with an interleaved AAC-compliant audio track. The last option, Video Track, should be selected if the video track of the multitrack session should be used in the podcast. Once again, this will create a .M4V file with an AAC audio track.

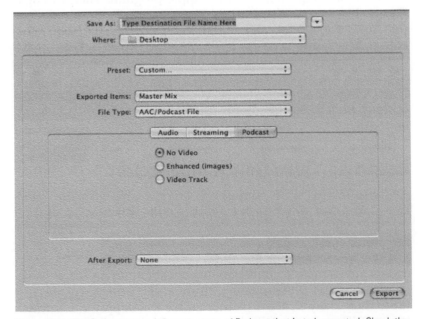

Figure 10-9 The Podcast pane defines the type of Podcast that is to be created. Check the appropriate bubble depending on the use of video in the project.

The settings used by selecting the AAC/Podcast export option are pulled directly from the Compressor program. Compressor will be discussed in the following section on video exporting.

Dolby Digital and Compressor

The two final options in the File Type pulldown are Dolby Digital Professional and Compressor, which will be discussed further in the surround sound exporting sections.

Toward the top of the export window there is a pulldown menu labeled Preset. This allows the user to save any changed settings in the export window. If a lot of exporting is performed in the same way, this Preset utility is rather useful, especially when changing the default settings for the more advanced export options. Once all the changes have been made in the export window, choose Save Preset from the pulldown menu and give the preset a name that is easy to recall.

The export window also contains a pulldown menu called After Export. In this pulldown menu it is possible to choose actions to be completed once the exporting process has finished. This allows the user to perform an export that might take some time without having to wait around just to complete the next step. The After Export options include sending the files to a Final Cut sequence, importing them back into the Soundtrack Pro session as new tracks, or sending them to other Apple programs such as Logic, iTunes, Motion, or WaveBurner. These are really simple options that only remove a tiny step in the overall process; however, many editors have grown accustomed to the After Export options.

An important note in this section is that selecting only Master Mix allows the user to choose from any of the File Type settings. If anything other than Master Mix is selected, the only export options are the four uncompressed file types: AIFF, WAVE, NeXT, and SDII.

Exporting Video Only (Compressor)

Unlike many DAWs, Soundtrack Pro gives the user the ability to export just a video track from the multitrack session or from the single-file editor. So, in a way, on a basic level Soundtrack Pro functions like its sister program, Final Cut Pro. Exporting just the video file from the audio editing program is rare, but it has its advantages. Primarily, it allows the audio house to create a video file that is compliant with their authoring software. It is more than likely that the picture editor will supply video which is not DVD-compliant. In this case, it is not possible to create a temporary screening mix on a DVD for the client. Soundtrack Pro,

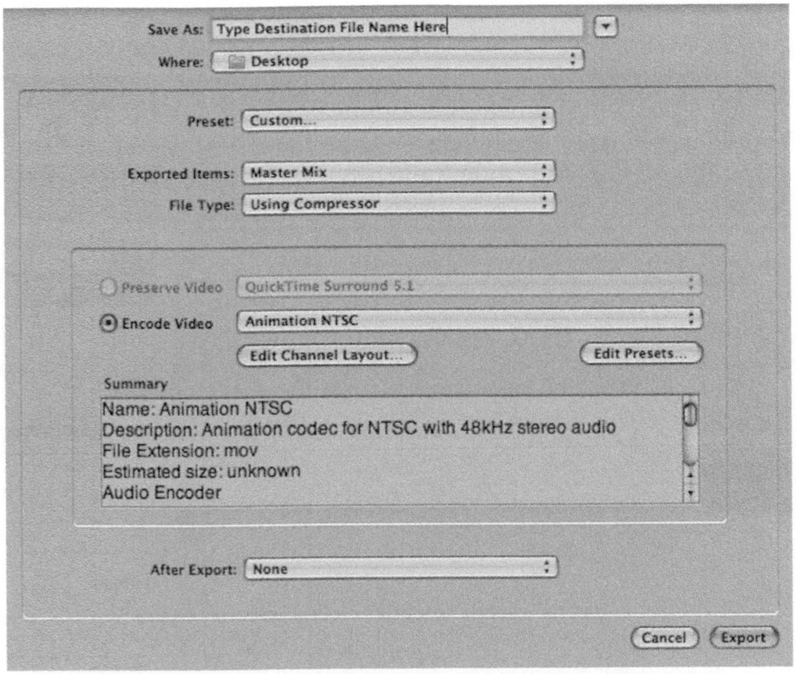

Figure 10-10 Selecting Using Compressor in the File Type dropdown expands the export window to provide a consolidated view of the actual Compressor program. Using Compressor is an efficient way of compressing audio and video without resorting to a stand-alone program.

however, lets the user export the video file independently from the audio track using Compressor. Compressor is a stand-alone program that is included in the Final Cut Studio package. When installed, it embeds itself into the Soundtrack Pro program, giving the user the ability to create numerous files of different audio and video encodings.

Compressor has increased the number of its encoding presets over the years. It now comes complete with different quality encode settings for MPEG-4 files, DVD MPEG-2 files, Web-Ready files, High Definition HDV, and XDCAM files, among many others. The addition of high definition exporting comes with this latest version of Compressor (3.5). Several of the presets contain export options for both audio and video. In this section, however, we will concentrate on the video presets. The DVD and HD DVD (MPEG-2) presets, as well as the high definition (HDV and XDCAM) presets are the primary video-only encoding presets.

When Using Compressor is selected in the File Type pulldown menu of the export window, the window extends down, displaying options pulled from the Compressor software package. The first modifier is Preserve Video. Marking this bubble will keep the video track the same as the original video file. The pulldown menu that is located next to it provides options as to what format the audio should be rendered as. There is not much use for this function and it should only be used when there is a specific need for it.

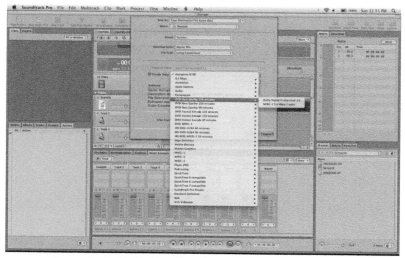

Figure 10-11   When exporting video only that is destined for a standard DVD, begin by using the DVD Quality presets in the Encode Video dropdown. This is a good way to export video to be burned to a standard DVD for client use.

Below this option is the primary pulldown menu, Encode Video. This menu displays all of the Compressor presets for both audio and video. In the middle of the list are the options for DVD, HD DVD, and high definition. When mousing over these options, the list extends to the right, revealing the available presets in each category. The DVD options are divided into two groups of three. The first group of options are named DVD Best Quality, followed by a length of time (120 minutes, 90 minutes, and 60 minutes). These presets indicate roughly how much video at the preset setting, along with uncompressed PCM stereo audio, can fit onto a standard single-layer DVD-5 disc. What changes between these three settings is the video bit rate. The more data the program says can be fitted onto a disc, the lower the video bit rate and thus the worse the video quality.

The second group options are named DVD Fastest Encode, followed by the same lengths of time as listed above. The difference between these two groups lies in the number of passes. The Best

Quality group does two passes over the video for more accurate encoding and better image quality. However, this takes twice as long as one pass. The second group uses the one-pass function, making only one pass through the video during the encoding process. This generally yields less desirable image quality results; however, for a test disc it would be perfectly suitable. I would not use the one-pass setting if the export were going to be used as a master copy.

Compressor still provides the option to export video files compatible with the now defunct high definition format, HD DVD. The presets for HD DVD result in either an MPEG-2 encoded file with a video bit rate that is beyond the bit rate limit of a standard definition DVD, or a file encoded with the H.264 codec. Also, with this version of Compressor, high definition video at 720p, 1080i, and 1080p resolutions can be exported using the presets set forth. These settings should only be used when the situation calls for them as the encoding process of such large video bit rates takes quite some time.

While the presets are generally suitable for DVD authoring, some advanced editing of the presets can be done. Below the Encode Video pulldown menu there is a button, Edit Presets. Engaging this button will open the stand-alone version of Compressor. In the new window the user can choose to make changes to any of the existing video presets and save them as a new setting.

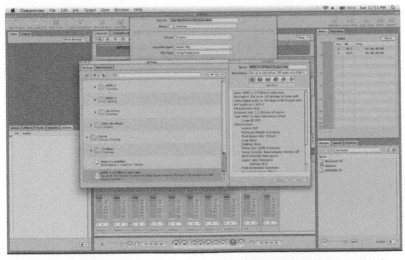

Figure 10-12 To edit the chosen preset simply highlight the initial template preset and click the third button from the left at the top of the Settings window. Make sure to give the new preset a unique name at the top of the Inspector window.

When Compressor opens there are multiple windows. To edit settings you only need to be concerned with the Settings and Inspector windows. The other three windows can be closed if they are distracting. In order to start editing settings a copy needs to be made of the existing preset that you have chosen to use as the template. To do this, click the preset in the Settings window and click the Duplicate Selected Setting button (third from the left at the top of the Settings window). This will create a copy under the Custom folder at the bottom of the Settings window. Click the duplicated setting and move it to the Inspector window. The first thing you should do is change the Name at the top of the Inspector window. This will be the name under which you will find the preset in the Soundtrack Pro pulldown. The modified preset can be found in the Encode Video pulldown under the Compressor tab. In the Inspector window there are six buttons underneath the Description that allow you to toggle through the different panes of video encoding. The first button is a summary of the settings, the second is the video encoder settings section, the third is the frame control section, the fourth and fifth are the video processing sections, and the sixth is an advanced tab for scripting. There are numerous options to modify in the Inspector window, much beyond the scope of this book. However, these are some of the more important ones to take a look at.

Video Format

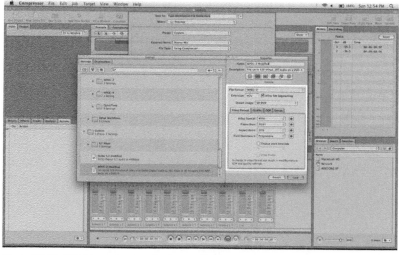

Figure 10-13 Editable options for the format of the outputted video can be found under the Video Format tab of the Encoder pane on the Inspector window. Make sure to match these settings with the original video file to avoid a distorted video image.

This pane allows the user to control: the region encoding of the video, either NTSC or PAL; the frame rate, which defaults to 29.97 fps but other standard frame rates are available; the aspect ratio, which can be either 4:3 or 16:9; and field dominance, which allows the user to select whether the video material is progressive or interlaced. It is advised that these settings be left to match the original specifications of the video file to avoid distorted images and changes in the runtime of the video file. Note: There are buttons to the right of each of the pulldown menus that by default are pushed in, indicating that automatic settings are being used. To edit these fields, those buttons must be deselected.

Quality

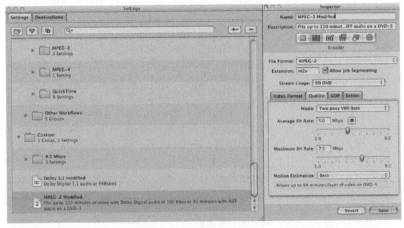

Figure 10-14 The Quality tab allows for different data rate settings. Using a two-pass setting will scan the entire video twice, causing it to take twice as long as a one-pass scan. Use the Bit Rate sliders to select the average and maximum bit rates of the video file. *Remember: A standard DVD has a maximum bit rate of 9800 kbps for the audio and video combined so plan accordingly.*

This pane allows the user to manually configure the video bit rate. The Mode pulldown menu allows the selection of various one-pass and two-pass modes. Remember, two-pass takes twice as long as one-pass, so make sure two-pass is absolutely necessary before it is selected. When a VBR (variable bit rate) is chosen, there are two sliders available for setting the video bit rate. The first is the Average Bit Rate and the second is the Maximum Bit Rate. The Maximum Bit Rate becomes extremely important when authoring video to a standard DVD. The overall bit rate (the addition of both the video and audio bit rates) of a standard DVD must never spike above 9800 kbps. Therefore, it is important to make sure enough room is left after the Maximum Bit Rate setting to accommodate for the audio track. If, for example, an uncompressed stereo PCM audio file is used for the audio track and its audio bit rate is 1411.2 kbps, the Maximum Bit Rate should not be higher than about 8.3 mbps, or 8300 kbps. When using the CBR (constant bit rate) mode, the Average Bit Rate slider functions as the Maximum Bit Rate. Following the previous example, the Average Bit Rate slider would be set to no higher than 8300 kbps.

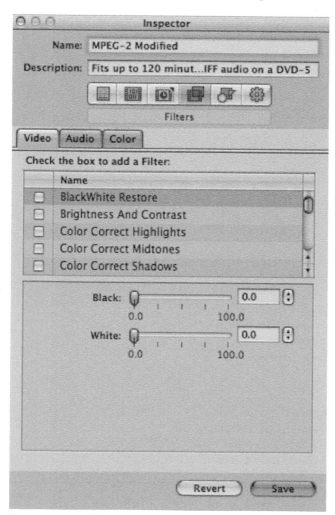

Figure 10-15 The Filter pane of the Inspector window allows for the editing of the video on a basic level. Changes in the brightness, gamma, color, etc. can be made here.

Filters

In the Filters section it is possible to change some of the video attributes. There are options for changing the color balance, applying a de-noise filter, changing the video to a letterbox format, de-interlacing, gamma correction, watermarking, edge enhancement and fade-ins and -outs. These filters should not be applied without the approval of the picture editor or director. For personal use, this section offers an easy way to fix a video problem without resorting back to rendering the original video edit session.

Geometry

The Geometry section of the Inspector window is handy for trimming any edges of the video that contain distracting noise. Once again, this should not be applied without approval from the picture editor or director. Cropping can be done to any or all of the four sides of the video and happens in increments of one pixel. It does not change the dimensions of the video. Instead, cropping will simply overlay a black line of one pixel in width on the chosen side of the video, hence removing a portion of the picture. This function can also be used to change full frame 4:3 video content into letterboxed widescreen content, assuming that losing image content on the top and bottom of the video is not a concern.

Upon the completion of editing a preset, make sure to click the Save button at the bottom of the Inspector window. Back in Soundtrack Pro, find the edited preset in the Encode Video pulldown and check the settings in the summary box. As this is the main export window, the facility to save a preset of the entire export window, and the After Export options, is also available. Lastly, type in a name for the file to be saved as and click Export.

Exporting Audio with Video (Compressor and Soundtrack Pro)

Perhaps more useful to an audio editor is the ability to export the current video and audio together as a completed mix. As with exporting the video only, Soundtrack Pro provides a great many options for audio/video exporting. Like most audio editing programs that support video import, Soundtrack Pro imports the attached audio with the video. While there is no way to edit the picture, there is a way to edit the audio attached to a video file, in either the multitrack session window or the single-file editor. This can prove to be useful to an audio editor who needs to apply a filter, volume level change, and so on to the entire audio track of the video file. Deletions and insertions can also be done to the audio track. After the changes have been applied the file is easily saved as a new movie file.

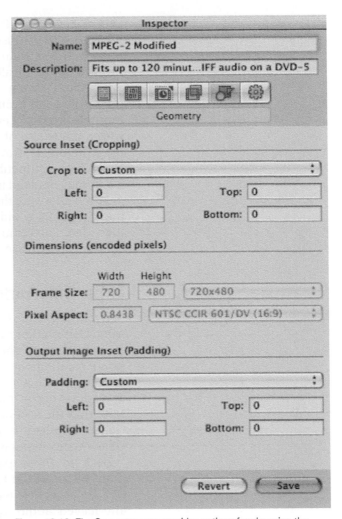

Figure 10-16 The Geometry pane provides options for changing the dimensions of the video file. Both padding and cropping can be done via the dropdown menus or by using the numerical boxes. Each numerical value corresponds to one pixel in cropping or padding.

Exporting Audio/Video from the Single-file Editor

When working with an audio track attached to a video file in the single-file mode, the only way to export the video and audio is to choose Save As ... from the File menu. In the File Type pulldown menu the user must select QuickTime Movie. There are no settings for this selection in terms of modifying the video. Soundtrack Pro will automatically choose the output format, which will be a .MOV file. Typically, the program will retain the video settings of the current file if already using a QuickTime movie format. For example, an H.264 encoded video file loaded into Soundtrack Pro with a frame size of 512×268 pixels will be saved with the same file structure. However, if the video settings are not recognized as QuickTime-compatible, the file may appear differently upon saving or may not load into the program in the first place.

When choosing the Save As ... function, it is possible to change the Sample Rate and Bit Depth of the audio track associated with the video. The option to apply dither is also available if the user chooses to decrease the Bit Depth.

Exporting Audio/Video Using Compressor

Exporting audio/video projects using Compressor is much like using Compressor to export just the video file. This time, however, we will focus on the settings that interleave the audio with the video, creating one seamless multimedia file. One of the primary uses for creating an interleaved audio/video file is to be able to upload a work-in-progress file to a server for the client to view. Note that the section on Podcasts focuses on low quality audio/video compilations. Using Compressor affords higher audio and video quality along with more advanced options.

Back in the export window we once again choose Using Compressor in the File Type pulldown menu. The DVD and HD DVD settings discussed in the previous section do not allow for interleaved audio and video. This is because, with the audio attached to the video, the file would no longer be compliant for a DVD authoring program. Therefore, those options are out for this section. We will focus on the bottom half of the pulldown screen, primarily the QuickTime compatible, Standard Definition, and Apple Devices tabs.

The QuickTime Compatible Tab

The QuickTime Compatible and Apple Devices tabs provide presets for audio/video files for use on mobile devices, such as the iPod, and Internet streaming. The QuickTime Compatible tabs are divided among version 6 and 7. I recommend using the QuickTime 7 compatible tab to enable the Internet streaming capabilities which allows media to be streamed online. QuickTime 7 uses H.264 encoding, which is more efficient than previous QuickTime versions, which were based on MPEG-4 encoding. Under this QuickTime tab there are various presets, each with a different bit rate (i.e., 300 kbps, 400 kbps, 800 kbps, etc.). For each there is also a preset labeled 'Streaming,' indicating that the settings have been tweaked to be more web-efficient. The difference between the Streaming and Non-Streaming presets is the video frame size and the QuickTime hint. The Non-Streaming QuickTime 7 presets contain a frame size of 480 × 360 pixels. They are also marked for a fast start, meaning that the entire audio/video file should be played from a local hard drive. The Streaming presets have a video frame size of 320 × 240 pixels and are hinted for QuickTime streaming, meaning that there is metadata included in the resulting file that indicates it is optimized for Internet streaming. Streaming is useful because the content is seen over the Internet without actually having it download first. The presence of both of these preset options makes exporting audio/video files for clients who are local, and clients who are away, simple and efficient. Note: Make sure your export settings for the video size match the original settings or the export may be stretched incorrectly.

While the video is encoded using H.264 technology, the audio that accompanies the video is encoded as AAC. This format was discussed in the section on Podcasts. AAC is more efficient than MP3 and provides intelligible quality at low bit rates. As AAC is a lossy compression scheme, the use of it is only recommended when creating a presentation for Internet streaming.

As discussed in the previous section, these presets can also be modified and saved using the Edit Preset button and following the path laid out above. In addition to being able to edit the video controls, you will now be able to edit the audio controls. It is in this section that you can modify the encoding scheme that should be used for the audio track. While the default may be AAC, it can readily be changed to AIFF for higher quality audio. However, AIFF is not advised if the media file is destined for the web.

The Apple Devices Tab

The Apple Devices tab contains presets that create video for Apple devices such as the AppleTV and iPod. It is important when choosing these presets that the fundamental aspects of the video and audio are not changed. These devices have specific requirements as to the video frame size, video codec, and bit rate, as well as for the audio codec. It is best to leave the presets alone for this tab. While experimentation is always welcome, do not be surprised to find the resulting audio/video file is no longer compliant with the selected mobile device.

The Standard Definition Tab

The final main Compressor preset for exporting audio/video files is the Standard Definition tab. Here there are several presets that correspond directly with those used by Final Cut Pro. DV NTSC is perhaps the most commonly used video codec on the MAC platform, along with the other presets in the tab: DV NTSC Anamorphic, DVCPRO50 NTSC, and DVCPRO50 NTSC Anamorphic. The primary difference between DV NTSC and DVCPRO50 NTSC is that the latter has twice the video bit rate. However, both codecs use higher than typical video compression codecs. DV NTSC uses a bit rate of 12.22 gbph while DVCPRO50 NTSC uses 24.28 gbph. Both are substantially more than the average standard MPEG-2 compressed files running at a max of 9.8 mbps for standard DVDs. Notice the latter is only megabits per second as compared with the former's gigabits per hour, which translates into about 203 mbps for the DV NTSC codec. This gives you an idea of how much data compression is done to fit content onto a standard definition DVD.

The anamorphic preset should be used when the video file being exported is encoded at 720 × 480 pixels but is meant for 16:9 displays. A pixel aspect ratio correction ag is included in this preset that tells the playback engine to stretch the video's image pixels horizontally to recover the true aspect ratio of the video. In order to know which preset to use, it is best to refer to the production notes given by the picture editor, which should have indicated the encoding of the file being used.

The audio track settings for these presets default to AIFF, 16-bit, 48 kHz, and stereo. Make sure the preset settings match those of the Soundtrack Pro multitrack session. These settings, along with the video control settings, can be edited by selecting the Edit Preset button in the Soundtrack Pro export window and following the guidelines set forth in the previous section. When using the main export window in Soundtrack Pro, all the settings may be saved as a preset using the Preset menu pulldown option above Exported Items.

Using Compressor to export audio/video files provides a great deal of exibility. However, it does take time to encode the video to the specifications of the chosen preset. So, if you are unsure about the settings that you have chosen, it is best to try the export settings on a small piece of audio and video to make sure they are going to turn out properly. There is hardly anything worse than exporting an entire project only to find that the wrong sample rate was chosen so the audio is out of sync with the video, or that the video frame size was not proportionate with the original video and so the video is now distorted. Professional-quality work will take you a long way in the industry. While some issues will go unnoticed if they are done properly, almost all issues will be noticed if done improperly. So, make sure to check your work before sending it to clients.

Exporting Surround Sound Using Soundtrack Pro and Compressor

It is becoming more of the standard for DAWs to incorporate the ability to mix and export in multichannel formats, typically 5.1 or lower. However, some platforms allow for the mixing and exporting of 6.1 audio and greater. Pro Tools recently integrated 7.1 surround mixing into the LE version of their software, with the purchase of the Music Production Toolkit.

Soundtrack Pro is one of the DAWs that has full integrated multichannel audio exporting. This is a terrific feature for independent movie houses that need surround sound capabilities without the huge expense. As Soundtrack Pro is paired with the Compressor program, there are numerous options for exporting the 5.1 content from the multitrack session. Typically, programs will export six uncompressed audio tracks to a 5.1 audio file or six individual audio files. Separate software is then needed to create a Dolby Digital or other file that is compatible with standard DVDs. Soundtrack Pro goes one step further. The program incorporates the ability to go directly from the multitrack session to a compressed Dolby or AAC file.

In addition, due to the program's ability to export different groups of tracks, it is easy to create stems of your work. Stems refer to the individual components of a film's soundtrack. Typically there are stems for sound effects, music, and dialog. In order to set up these various stems in the multitrack, the outputs of the corresponding tracks can be assigned to different submixes. Then, by selecting these submix tracks, the stems can be exported in one easy step. Refer to the step-by-step example at the end of the chapter for more information.

Exporting Dolby Digital Multichannel Audio

In Soundtrack Pro there are two ways in which to export Dolby files from the program. Apple has simplified the process by making

Dolby Digital Professional one of the built-in options in the export window. The other way is to select Compressor in the File Type pulldown menu.

By selecting Master Mix and Dolby Digital Professional, the export window expands to display the options for Dolby exporting. There are three panes: Audio, Bitstream, and Preprocessing. All three panes contain important settings to ensure correctly exported Dolby Digital files.

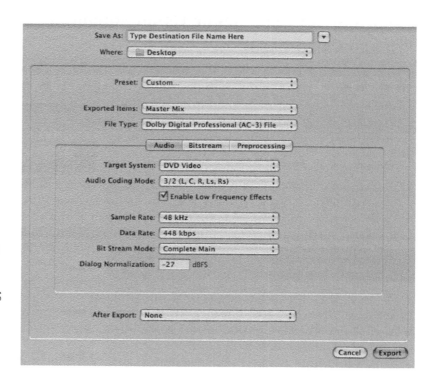

Figure 10-17 The Audio pane of the Dolby Digital Professional export option contains some of the most important metadata for Dolby encoded files. Choose the channel layout that corresponds with the Soundtrack Pro session. The dialog normalization setting should be −31 dBFS for a zero gain reduction in the output Dolby file. For more information on Dolby metadata refer to the Dolby Metadata guide on Dolby's official website.

In the Audio pane, the first pulldown is Target System. By default, DVD Video is chosen and this is likely the setting that should be used for all standard DVD authoring. You may also choose DVD Audio for when you are authoring music to the DVD-A format. The Audio Coding Mode is one of the most important fields. It is here that the selection of the number of channels in the multichannel audio stream is made. The default is 5.0. This includes Left, Center, Right, Left Surround, and Right Surround. In order to enable the .1 (LFE channel), the box below the field (Enable Low Frequency Effects) must be checked. There are other Dolby encoding modes, including simply Dolby 2.0 for stereo mixes. Make sure to choose the setting that correctly matches the number of channels used in the multitrack session.

Next in the Audio pane is the Sample Rate. The only choice here is 48 kHz when DVD Video or DVD Audio is selected in the Target System field. This is to ensure compatibility with standard DVD authoring and playback. The Data Rate is the amount of data per second that is allocated to all the channels combined, at any given time. The highest setting is 448 kbps while the lowest setting allowable is 224 kbps. Typically in high definition television broadcasts there will be a data rate of 224 to 384 kbps. If using Dolby Digital compression I recommend using the highest data rate possible. The next field is Bit Stream Mode. This setting allows you to select what this particular track will be used as, i.e. a commentary track, a track for the hearing impaired, and so on. Complete Main is what should be chosen for audio tracks that will be the main audio content. The last setting in the Audio pane is Dialog Normalization. This is perhaps the most crucial setting in the Dolby Digital metadata. At the risk of over simplifying, Dialog Normalization determines how much the overall volume of the Dolby file will be lowered. This setting is used in broadcast to try and balance the level between commercials and programming, and other functions. A −31 dBFS value represents a change of zero in the volume level between the original mix in the session and the output level of the Dolby file. The default setting in this field is −27 dBFS. This means that the output volume of the Dolby volume will be 4 dB lower than the original volume. The value of −31 dBFS should be viewed as a zero level change and not as the reference volume level of −18 dBFS. In short, the closer to zero that the value in the Dialog Normalization box reaches, the more gain reduction will be applied to the outputted Dolby file. For more detailed information on this topic, the Dolby Metadata Guide can be found on Dolby's website.

The Bitstream pane contains settings regarding how the Dolby surround mix should be downmixed for playback on stereo systems. It is important to assign values to the center and surround downmix fields. By default, each field is set to downmix by 3 dB. Depending on the mix, these settings may need to be changed. If the surrounds should be left out of the stereo downmix, that can also be specified in this section. The last pane is Preprocessing. The Compression Preset is perhaps another important field to pay attention to. It defaults to Film Standard Compression; however, there are various other settings depending on the content of the audio track. Detailed information as to how to handle these presets can also be found in the Dolby Metadata Guide. However, in order to avoid any alteration to the original mix, the selection of No Compression is best. This pane also contains information on modifying individual channels in the Dolby stream including low pass filters, DC filtering, phase shifts, and digital de-emphasis.

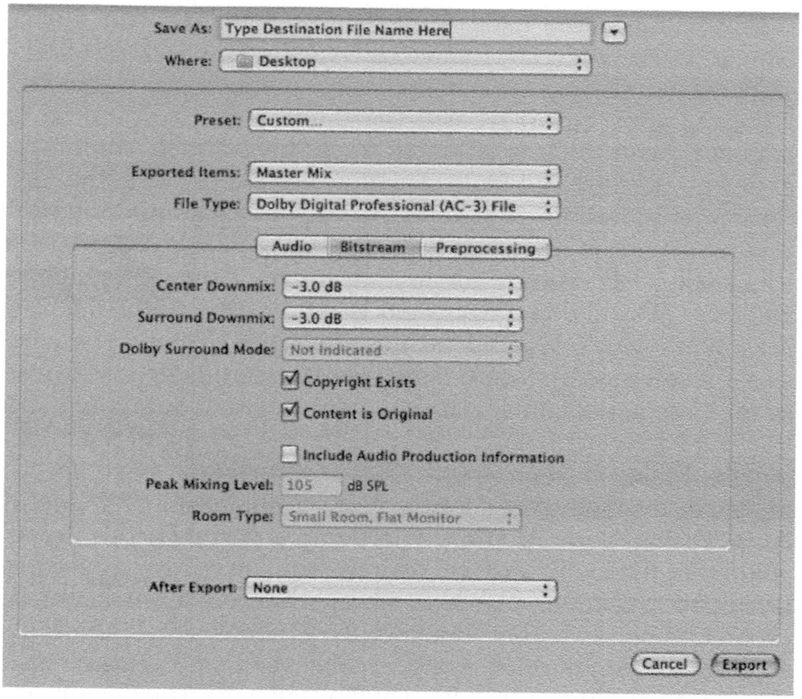

Figure 10-18 The Bitstream pane defines how the multichannel surround sound Dolby file will be downmixed for stereo systems.

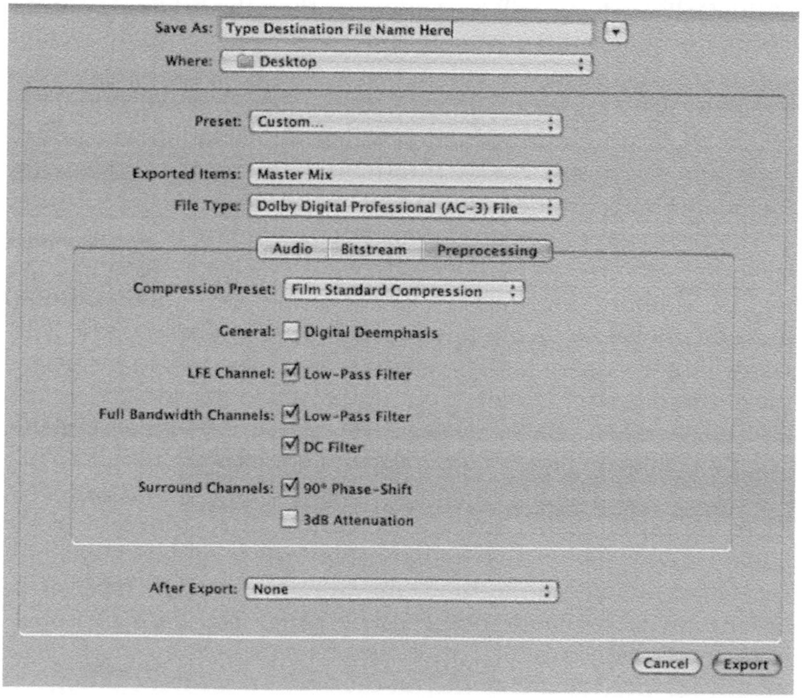

Figure 10-19 Audio filters and compression settings can be defined in the Preprocessing pane. Make sure to select the appropriate Compression Preset to avoid major alterations to the original mix in the resulting Dolby file.

The other way in which to export Dolby files is to select Using Compressor in the File Type field. Presets for Dolby Digital 5.1 and 2.0 can readily be found on the Audio tab under Encode Video. However, these are presets and only allow editing via the Compressor program. This is accomplished in the same manner as described in the section on editing video presets and contains the same metadata options as described above.

Exporting Uncompressed Multichannel Audio

While sometimes it is useful to export mixes directly to a Dolby compressed file, generally mixes should be exported as uncompressed audio files. This can be accomplished in a couple of ways. While it can be done through Compressor, in doing so it is much easier to make a mistake in assigning the channel order. By default, Soundtrack Pro uses the SMPTE/ITU standard for the channel order of the surround audio. This means that the order of the channels progresses as follows: left, right, center, LFE, left surround, and right surround. If you are trying to modify the presets to conform to a different standard, such as DTS (L, R, Ls, Rs, C, LFE) it is almost a guarantee that the channel order will be different than that desired. Therefore, I recommend simply using the export window for surround mixes.

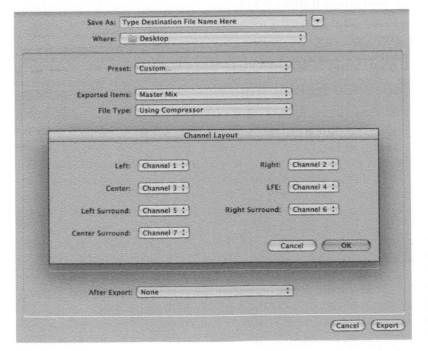

Figure 10-20 When using Compressor to export surround sound in a different channel order than that defined by SMPTE/ITU (L, R, C, LFE, Ls, Rs), make sure to change the channel order by selecting the Edit Channel Layout button in the main export window.

Once the multitrack session has been set for using surround sound, exporting the final surround mix, individual surround tracks, or submixes for use as stems is quite easy. The export feature of Soundtrack Pro automatically knows when a surround session is being exported; therefore, getting uncompressed surround mixes out of Soundtrack Pro is as simple as exporting the master mix as an AIFF file. If the other settings in the export window are left at their default positions, the program will create one AIFF audio file with a channel order of L, R, C, LFE, Ls, Rs. However, authoring programs typically need mono audio files, with one file for each of the channels. Therefore, I recommend checking the box to create multiple mono files. This option creates a folder with the chosen target name and places six mono files inside it. The naming convention is as follows: Untitled. L.aiff, Untitled.R.aiff, and so on and so forth, where Untitled represented the name given in the Save As field. These mono files can now be dropped into an authoring program such as DTS-HD Master Audio Suite or combined in a custom channel order by using QuickTime.

The process of uncompressed exporting is less time-consuming than exporting directly to Dolby Digital. In addition, uncompressed audio files are the desired format for a master mix. While exporting directly to Dolby is a nice feature, it is perhaps less useful than it may initially seem.

Exporting Interleaved Video and Surround Sound Audio

Occasionally, clients and other recipients may request a QuickTime file with surround sound. While it is not common practice today, with the growing rise of ISDN connections in studios and FTP transfers, it is nice to see that Soundtrack Pro has included the ability to accomplish this interleaved task for the future. In order to perform this export, you will need to use Compressor; thus, it will only be possible to export the master mix along with the video.

As has already been seen, there are numerous presets under the Encode Video pulldown menu. The first that can be ruled out are all the presets dealing with DVD compliancy. This is because DVD compliancy mandates that the video be in the form of .M2V, which does not support the addition of audio. Instead, we want to export a QuickTime file with encoded audio. There is no available interleaved preset that will allow for video and surround audio.

Therefore, we are going to have to create one. The best preset to start with is under the QuickTime tab. It is called H.264. When selected, the Summary window will show that the audio encoder is set for Linear PCM stereo. This needs to change. Using the steps outlined in the video section on editing presets, enter the Compressor program and make a duplicate copy of the preset. In the Inspector window click the Audio Settings button under the Encoder pane (second button from the left). This will bring up a new window that looks exactly like QuickTime's encoding option window.

In this new window you will want to decide whether you want the audio to be compressed or uncompressed. For uncompressed audio, leave the format as Linear PCM. In the Channels pulldown you will find many options, both in terms of the number of channels and channel order. Make sure to select the channel configuration that matches your session. When selecting 5.1 channels, remember that Soundtrack Pro defaults to an SMPTE channel order. It is recommended that you use that setting in the pulldown (5.1 L, R, C, LFE, Ls, Rs). Note: The channel order is editable back in the main export window; however, it is recommended to avoid trying to change the channel order within Soundtrack Pro due to ease of error. Approving these new settings will make your session ready for export. The video is also editable by selecting the Video Settings button in the Inspector window.

Uncompressed Linear PCM audio does not have to be interleaved with the video. If you decide to use a compressed format, AAC is the best option. In the popup Sound Settings window, change the format from Linear PCM to AAC. This will limit the options present in the Channels pulldown menu. The AAC format uses a custom channel order, one not used by Dolby (Film), DTS, or SMPTE. AAC uses a C, L, R, Ls, Rs, LFE channel order. Once you save the preset and return to the export window you must click the Edit Channel Layout button. In the popup window you must assign the same channel order that AAC uses. So, the left should become channel 2, right channel 3, center channel 1, etc. However, please note that sometimes the channel still reverts back to the SMPTE standard. Make sure to check your channel order using QuickTime or by importing your saved file back into Soundtrack Pro.

Exporting uncompressed surround mixes is by far the easiest and most surefire way to export your multichannel project. However, if you must use Dolby or Compressor, make sure that you double-check all your settings and also that the export turns out correctly before handing the project over to the client.

Exporting Examples

Exporting a Compressed Stereo Mix Master From Soundtrack Pro

1. Save the Soundtrack Pro project via **File** > **Save** or Command + S.
2. Go to the export window via **File** > **Export** or Command + E.
3. Choose Mix Master in Exported Items.
4. Select 320 kbps as the Stereo Bit Rate and change the Sample Rate to 48 kHz.
5. Un-check the Joint Stereo and Smart Encoding Adjustments boxes.
6. Type a name in the Save As box and choose an export destination.
7. Click the Export button.

Exporting Uncompressed Surround Sound Stems From Soundtrack Pro

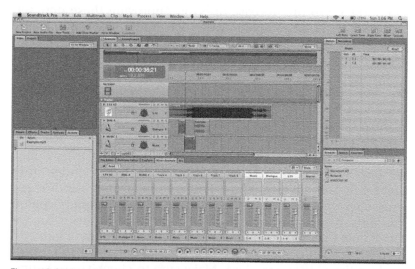

Figure 10-21 In order to export surround sound stems (mixes that are a subset of the master mix), select the various submixes in the Mixer window of the multitrack session.

1. Save the Soundtrack Pro project via **File** > **Save** or Command + S.
2. In the Mixer pane at the bottom of the Soundtrack Pro window click once on the green bar above the first

surround submix (either Submix 1 or the custom name used, such as SFX Stem).

3. Hold the Command key down while clicking once on the green bar of each of the other stem submixes in the session (Music Stem, Dialogue Stem, etc.).
4. Go to the export window via **File** > **Export** or Command + E.
5. Choose Selected Tracks, Busses, and Submixes in Exported Items.
6. Choose AIFF from the File Type menu.
7. Check the box for Create Multiple Mono Files.
8. Conform the Bit Depth and Sample Rate to that of the session (i.e. 16-bit, 48 kHz).
9. Type a name in the Save As field and choose a destination.
10. Click the Export button.
11. Find the finished files in a folder with the same name as that entered in the Save As field at the corresponding destination.

Exporting a QuickTime Audio/Video Interleaved File with Surround Sound

1. Save the Soundtrack Pro project via **File** > **Save** or Command + S.
2. Go to the export window via **File** > **Export** or Command + E.
3. Select Master Mix in Exported Items.
4. Choose Using Compressor in File Type.
5. Click the Edit Presets button.
6. In the Compressor program's Settings window find the H.264 preset (**Apple** > **Formats** > **QuickTime**).
7. Select the H.264 preset and click the Duplicate Selected Setting button.
8. In the Inspector window change the name from H.264 copy to a unique name.
9. Switch to the Encoder pane of the Inspector window and click the Settings button next to Video.
10. Make changes to the Quality settings if necessary (in this case: Medium; Faster Encode [Single-pass]) and click OK.
11. Click the Settings button next to Audio.
12. Change the Channels setting to 5.1 (L, R, C, LFE, Ls, Rs).
13. Match the Sample Rate and Size with that of the Soundtrack Pro Session.

14. Select OK.
15. Make other changes as necessary in the Inspector window.
16. Click the Save button at the bottom of the Inspector window and return to Soundtrack Pro.
17. In the Encode Video pulldown navigate to **Apple** > **[name of the edited preset]**.
18. Review the Summary window.
19. Type a name in the Save As field and select a destination.
20. Click the Export button.

Things to Remember When Exporting

- You should utilize Soundtrack's options for efficiency. Plan ahead and use the most sensible setting for exporting.
- The Master Mix setting is the only item that is capable of using all of the exporting options, so organize your mix session accordingly.
- While uncompressed formats export in quicker than real time, compressed audio such as MP3 takes longer.
- If routinely exporting items from a mix session, make use of the Custom Preset option in the export window.
- In most cases make sure to match the Sample Rate and Bit Depth of the export window with those of the mix session.
- Soundtrack Pro's default multichannel export channel order is the SMPTE/ITU standard (L, R, C, LFE, Ls, RS). If you need a different channel order make sure to change the channel order of Soundtrack Pro using the Edit Channel Layout button.
- Finally and most importantly, *be professional*. Always double-check your exports to ensure proper playback and quality.

Special Thanks

Scott Selter, graduate student at the University of Colorado, Denver, is currently working on a thesis on the topic of audio and video codecs as part of a Master of Science in Recording Arts degree. Thanks to Scott for preparing the majority of the material in this chapter.

ACOUSTICAL DESIGN AND CONFIGURATION

In order to help you to be as successful as possible in working with audio, it is important to at least touch on the subject of acoustics and studio design. While this section is not a comprehensive exploration of acoustics, it will help you to understand the complexity of the situation and provides some practical advice on what you can do to make your audio environment better.

Configuring the ultimate acoustic setup for a specific space is not an easy task to jump in to. There are many factors that play a part in creating a space that works best for the engineer and equipment utilized. This section will present a basic understanding of how sound reacts with certain materials and discuss problems and solutions for many misunderstood creations, and the placement of your sound equipment.

Sound Development

First, to understand how to properly fix troublesome frequency peaks and dips, the development of sound must be addressed. Sound is caused by variations in air pressure, and is most commonly described as the vibration of air particles. The particles in the air move by way of compression and rarefaction.

During compression, the air particles are forced together, creating higher atmospheric pressure, whereas rarefaction is when the particles begin to move inward and create lower atmospheric pressure. This same concept holds true for sound travel within other mediums besides air, such as wood or metal. Instead of air particles vibrating to create sound, the other material becomes the vibrating object that produces the perceived sound.

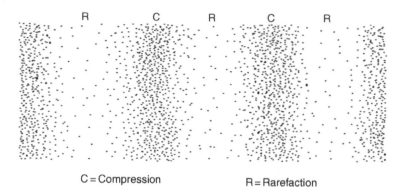

Figure 11-1 Compression and Rarefaction.   C = Compression   R = Rarefaction

The Waveform

Sound development is universally represented graphically as a waveform (see Figure 11-2). A waveform visually describes the characteristics of what we perceive to be sound, such as frequency, amplitude, length, and, in some cases, phase.

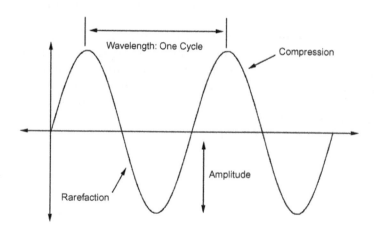

Figure 11-2 The waveform.

The frequency of a waveform is the number of these waveforms or cycles produced per second, also known as hertz (Hz). The length of a waveform can be determined through a simple equation:

$$\text{Wavelength} = \frac{\text{Speed of Sound (1130 ft/sec)}}{\text{Frequency (Hertz)}}$$

The amplitude is how much pressure there is in the waveform; the higher the pressure, the greater the displacement from the uninterrupted position. Amplitude is mostly perceived as being the loudness or signal level of a particular sound. For example, when recording an audio file into Soundtrack, the higher the signal level, the higher the amplitude. There is a limit, depending on the recording equipment, as to how much amplitude a signal can handle before it begins to peak and distort. Phase is an occurrence that happens when the time relationship is displaced between two of the same frequencies. Figure 11-3 demonstrates how a simple waveform of the same frequency is increasingly put out of phase, beginning with 90 degrees. Once the waveform reaches 180 degrees out of phase, the compression and rarefaction sync up in time. The resulting output of this particular phase shift has an amplitude of zero. Often, the ill effects of out-of-phase audio are not noticed when dealing with more complex waveforms.

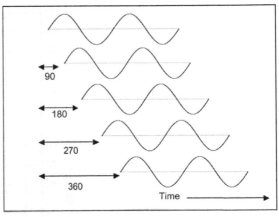

Figure 11-3 Phase.

Sound Levels

Not all frequencies can be heard by human ears, nor do they have the same perceived loudness. The typical range of hearing by human ears is approximately 20 to 20 000 Hz. This range does not apply to all people and is subject to change as we age, as the frequency range of the human ear becomes smaller as we get older. Ears are more sensitive to certain frequency ranges than others. To help put this sensitivity into perspective, see Figure 11-4, which represents information taken from a case study originally performed by Fletcher and Munson, then later revised by Robinson and Dadson in 1956. This graph displays how human beings perceive loudness at different frequency levels.

There is also a limit to the loudness sensitivity of our ears. The threshold of hearing and the threshold of pain levels are represented as decibel values. The loudness of sound is accurately measured in pascals (Pa), which is a unit measurement of pressure. The range over which human beings can hear is vast; therefore, to help represent loudness in a more manageable range, the decibel was created. The decibel is a logarithmic ratio which helps to describe the wide span of human sensitivity to loudness. The ratio is typically between a measurement of power or intensity and a specified reference level. Instead of viewing our range of hearing as 0.00002 Pa to 200 Pa, the decibel makes it possible to reference loudness between 0 and 140 dB. Table 11-1 gives a sense of reference between decibels and pascals.

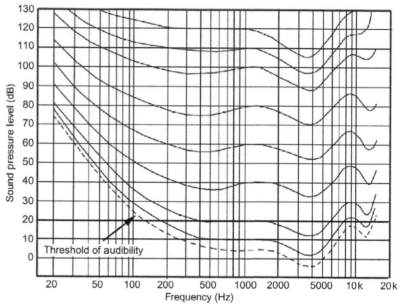

Figure 11-4 Loudness curves.

Table 11-1 Sound pressure levels.

Sound source	Decibel level	Sound pressure (pascals)
Sonic boom	194	100 000
Jet engine	160	
Threshold of pain	140	200
Gun muzzle blast	140	
Thunder	120	
Chainsaw	110	
Heavy traffic	100	2
Telephone dial tone	80	0.2
Conversational speech	60	
Residence, private office	40	0.0002
Recording studio	30	
Whisper, ticking watch	20	
Threshold of hearing	10	0.00002

Table 11-2 Speed of sound in various materials.

Medium	Speed of sound (ft/sec)	Speed of sound (m/sec)
Air	1130	344
Sea water	4900	1493
Wood	12500	3810
Stainless steel	18800	5730
Brick	13700	4175
Concrete	10500–11800	3200–3596
Glass	13000	3962

Sound Reacting to the Room

Sound typically travels 1130 feet per second in air that is 70 degrees Fahrenheit, but this varies according to temperature and the travel medium. The higher the temperature, the faster sound will travel. Sound also travels at a different speed in water and through solids such as wood.

Because the speed of sound is known, the calculations to determine wavelength and frequency are easily obtained through the equation given earlier in the chapter. Resonating frequencies are common in many different rooms for many different reasons. When a specific frequency resonates in a particular cavity, that sound is perceived as being more intense than all of the other frequencies being produced. A space, such as a small control room or the body of an acoustic guitar, will resonate at a certain frequency dependent on the size of the area. How does that frequency end being up so much louder than the rest? Many different frequencies can resonate in a particular space. For example, if the listener is in a rectangular room, a wavelength the size of the room can bounce back and forth off two parallel walls. Because the sound wave bounces off the surfaces, it is multiplied and its loudness increases. When two waveforms are added together and they are in phase with each other, the amplitude will increase. This leads to the frequency becoming louder and lasting slightly longer than the other frequencies. By understanding the equation above, we can determine at least one frequency at which a specific space will resonate. If the resonant frequency of a space falls within the human range of hearing, adjustments such as low frequency absorption and diffusion can be made to help reduce the excited tones. Using this same method of simple algebra, peaks, dips, and potential phasing can be calculated within

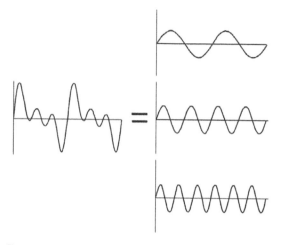

Figure 11-5 Wave interaction.

the known dimensions of a given space. Other than resonating frequencies, boosts and cuts in particular frequencies will occur as well. Often, when a waveform reflects off a hard surface, it will interact with other oncoming waveforms. This process results in other phasing problems and peaks or dips in the frequency spectrum (see Figure 11-5).

Other problematic issues may arise, such as comb filtering and flutter echo. Comb filtering occurs when two signals of the same frequency arrive at a hard surface at two different times and, when reflected, are added together in a way that creates both varying peaks and dips in the resulting signal. A graphic analysis of the output typically looks like a comb with extreme peaks and dips in the amplitude. Flutter echo is aurally perceived as being a fast echo between two parallel hard walls. Higher frequencies are easier to hear as flutter echo, and contain a ringing characteristic. The listener may not notice any problems to begin with, but, as time passes and as the signal continues and grows in volume, these waveforms will continue to add to and subtract from each other. This in turn can produce several different effects. As discussed before, resonance, peaks, dips, and echoes may occur from all of the interacting waveforms. Sound localization becomes unclear because phasing is introduced. In some cases, bouncing waveforms can be delayed long enough to create an echo or reverb. If the delayed signal is as loud as the fundamental sound, then aurally locating the original source becomes inaccurate. Many of these situations only occur in large concert halls or large rooms made up of hard surfaces. In a near-field monitoring system (small speakers close to the listening position) or smaller recording spaces, the room is not big enough to produce such a phenomenon.

Sound and Materials

Sound reacts to various surfaces in many different ways. For the purposes of this chapter, three primary reactions will be discussed. When a sound approaches a surface, it will either be reflected, absorbed, or diffused. Reflected waveforms are typically produced by hard surfaces, such as a wooden floor or a concrete wall. Reflection of sound is simply expressed in Figure 11-6.

Other materials, such as insulation and fabric, exhibit absorptive properties. The frequency range absorbed depends on the surface's thickness and density. For example, four inches of rigid fiberglass

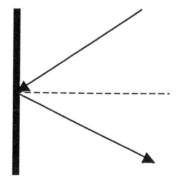

Figure 11-6 Reflection.

will absorb lower frequency content than one-inch thick foam. Each piece of material will absorb down to a certain frequency limit and have a specific absorption coefficient. Determining the specific absorption coefficients of certain materials is beyond the scope of this book. Although certain materials can absorb down to very low frequencies, there will still be a specific frequency range that cannot be absorbed (see Figure 11-7).

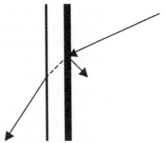

Figure 11-7 Absorption.

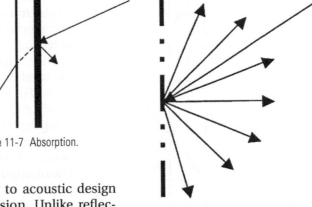

Figure 11-8 Diffusion.

Another occurrence that is still fairly new to acoustic design and is continually being re-invented is diffusion. Unlike reflection, diffusion disperses the waveform evenly into the room (see Figure 11-8).

Many diffusion structures utilize mathematical sequences to determine the reaction of the waveform to the surface. There are many different ways to effectively incorporate diffusion into a space. Naturally, old churches and concert halls have built-in diffusers to help distribute sound evenly throughout the audience. Most of these structures include curved panels and oddly shaped architectural walls. Diffusion helps to bring life back into the workspace. In the past, audio engineers would completely cover the control room and recording space with acoustic foam and other materials to deaden the sound. There is nothing wrong with this concept; however, working in a completely dead space tends to drain a person's hearing stamina. Today, studio owners tend to take a more sound-friendly approach to meeting the needs of a particular editing and mixing space.

Optimizing a Room

Before a space is examined and tested to determine its specific acoustical needs, speaker placement must be addressed and optimized. The positioning of the monitoring system can help to reduce the unnecessary use of certain acoustic constructions. Rooms that are easy to calculate, such as those that are square or rectangular, can be ideal in some situations. The even shape of the room means that the engineer can easily determine the resonant frequency and some possible

Figure 11-9 A treated audio edit room. Reproduced with permission of 42 Productions – Boulder, CO.

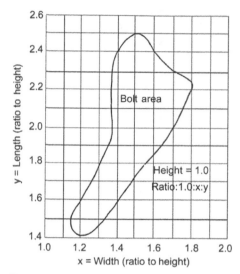

Figure 11-10 Ideal proportions for a small space. Based on research by Bolt.

peaks and nulls in the room. More complex rooms are much harder to calculate, but will inherently reduce the effects of flutter echo and comb filtering. Figure 11-10 displays a range of rectangular room proportions that yield a smooth low frequency response for a small space. The inside of the area is the ideal dimensions for a room used for mixing or editing audio. For example, for a room with a height of 10 feet and a width of 12 feet, it would be ideal to have a length of 13 feet, using the ratio 1.0 : 1.2 : 1.3.

Lower frequencies have a tendency to build up in corners and small partitions in a given space. Keeping this information on hand helps to determine an optimal position for the playback system. Centering the speaker monitors in a corner is not ideal; however, certain acoustical constructs can help reduce the low frequency build-up produced in the chosen corner. The more centered a playback system is in a room, the more symmetrical the reacting sound will be. If the speakers are in the center of a rectangular room, the distribution of sound can be easily determined and further decisions for acoustical structures can be optimized.

In the ideal space, the speaker monitors should be as far from the back wall as possible. If the back wall is untreated, then sound will reflect right off that surface back to the listener. This can lead to phasing problems with waveforms adding to and canceling each other. The same theory is applied to the front wall. If the monitors are mounted right in front of the wall, the sound may have a tendency to bounce off that wall directly after the initial sound and construe the listener's opinion of the frequency spectrum. There are many different ways to place setup monitors in a control room and minimize the amount of error from sound bouncing off certain objects. Placing the speaker monitors on top of a mixing console can be harmful to the mixing experience. The engineer will usually sit in front of the console and listen to the speaker monitors; however, if they are placed on top, there will be a misinterpretation of the signal as it reaches the engineer's ears as well as the top of the mixer, which then reflects the signal back to the engineer shortly after the direct signal. As discussed before, this can lead to phasing, peaks, and dips in the signal. To help fix these phenomena, the speakers can be mounted on speaker stands directly behind the mixing console, or the monitors can be mounted into the front wall if space permits. Placing the speakers into the structure of the front wall will not produce the same effects as simply placing the units directly in front of the wall. While in the wall, the drivers inside the speaker cabinets are at the same level as the wall and leave very little room to reflect the same signal at different times.

Room Size

The size of the room will help determine what speaker setup will best suit the engineer's needs. The right size of speaker for the right size of room will make a large difference to the acoustics used. It is not advised to place very large speaker monitors in a very small room. This would be like wearing very big headphones. A lot of sound can be created with larger speakers, therefore leading to louder waveforms that have more energy. The more energy these waveforms contain, the longer they will stick around in the studio, ultimately making way for phasing problems, peaks, and nulls. Lower frequencies tend to take longer to lose energy, especially in a smaller room where they become trapped. With this simple knowledge, a large subwoofer would not be ideal for a small room. Rooms smaller than 8×10 feet function well without a subwoofer or large speaker monitors. Bigger rooms benefit from slightly bigger speaker monitors and an added subwoofer, or just a pair of larger speakers to reach that lower frequency range.

Construction

With this knowledge of how sound works in a given space with certain materials, the studio can be optimized for the specific needs of the engineer/owner. Before the construction process begins, the room should be analyzed. During this time, the designer will pick out any parallel hard surfaces, such as the walls or floor and ceiling, and determine speaker placement. Depending on the financial budget of the studio owner, a full building reconstruction may not be preferred. This is when nonpermanent or portable acoustical solutions are ideal. As earlier suggested, different materials and structures will react differently to sound. Egg crates and foam can absorb some of the higher frequencies and are cheap; however, these two materials are not ideal for more broadband absorption. Materials such as rigid fiberglass, rockwool, and cotton/jean fiber are very dense and have high absorption coefficients. Other materials that you can find in a typical home are strongly suggested for use for diffusion. Without having to get overly technical and mathematical, a multi-pattern structure such as a bookshelf will help tremendously in the back of a control room. In cases where engineers are using homemade acoustical formations, a little diffusion is still better than a flat, hard surface.

Checklist for Audio Setup Issues

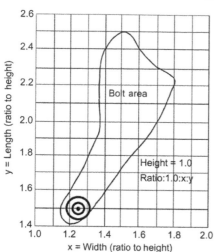

Figure 11-11 An acceptable room dimension.

1. Pick the right room, using Figure 11-11. This chart uses the height at the common denominator, but you should use the shortest distance. Divide each dimension of the room by the shortest dimension. Once you do this you will have three numbers that vary between one and three. Use Figure 11-11 to find the point your room is on. Divide each number by the height; for example, if your room is 8 feet tall, 10 feet wide, and 12 feet long, you will get 1 (8 ÷ 8), 1.25 (10 ÷ 8), and 1.5 (12 ÷ 8). If you plot this on the chart, you will see that it falls inside the Bolt area, which means the dimensions of the room are acceptable for audio monitoring.

2. Use a mirror to find potential problem spots in your audio mix area. This will require two people: one to move the mirror and one to sit at the mix location. As the mirror is moved along the edge of all surfaces in the room, the person sitting in the mix location should look at the mirror and keep track of any time they see the speakers. These instances indicate the specific places in the room where the audio will leave the speakers and bounce off a surface aimed directly at the listening position. These locations are where you can place acoustic treatment material to help prevent/reduce the negative effects of reflections. Don't forget to check the ceiling and floors.

3. Use speaker stands instead of placing the speakers on the desk surface. This will also help to prevent harmful reflections.

4. Arrange the speakers and listening position in an equilateral triangle when using stereo speakers. This ensures that you will hear a balanced image. Also make sure you have a clear line of sight to the speakers.

5. You should be using full range speakers (full range means able to reproduce at least 20–20 000 Hz). If not, then at least use a subwoofer as a means to hear the entire range of sound. You should also be using high quality cables to connect devices. Typically this means that you will be using balanced cables, which refers to cables that have three connection parts: hot, cold, and ground. This could be an XLR or a quarter-inch TRS (tip ring sleeve). These are the best options for ensuring that your signal is free from unwanted noise interference.

6. Calibrate the level of the speakers. There is more information about this in Chapter 6. You should make sure

you know exactly where the level should be for the room when mixing for different types of projects. Most audio interfaces will have a monitoring knob, and I recommend using a marker to mark the standard levels.

7. Use comprehensive metering. Not only should you be taking care to make sure your room is accurate, but you should also use software meters to make sure you are meeting the expected level standards.

8. Have reference files available at all time. This is important when mixing because it is so easy to lose track of what your mix sounds like. Use a 'known' project as a method of comparing your mix. This will keep your efforts more accurate.

9. Set up a typical consumer television to hear what your project will sound like in a standard setting. This can be useful when trying to make sure your mix works in as many spaces as possible.

10. Keep a pair of headphones handy so you can listen critically to various portions of your audio. If your room sounds very bad, you might consider moving to headphones for more of the time, but be aware that you really can't trust them for final mixes.

Special Thanks

Tira Neal, graduate student and instructor at the University of Colorado, Denver, is currently working on a thesis on the topic of acoustics as part of a Master of Science in Recording Arts degree. Thanks to Tira for preparing the majority of the material in this chapter.

12

SHORTCUTS AND ADDITIONAL MATERIALS

While this chapter is primarily devoted to the key commands of Soundtrack, I am also including two sections of additional information. The first details the Apple Loops content and the second is a comparison chart with the other audio software packages to provide you with an idea of where Soundtrack fits in.

Figure 12-1 Keyboard shortcuts (photograph by David Liban).

Keyboard Shortcuts

Originally I had thought the help file document included with Soundtrack was enough to provide information about the key commands, but after a closer scrutiny of the document I realized that many of the commands were not clearly explained, others were not explained in enough detail, and some were just plain wrong. Instead of simply putting the entire list of commands here, I have taken the majority and rewritten their entries. Some I have made even simpler (shorter), while others have a much longer explanation. When appropriate, I have explained how a command might help your workflow. I have removed some of the more obvious commands, such as Command + S (save) to help keep this section as simple as possible without completely reinventing the wheel.

General/File

Command + N	New multimedia project.
Command + Shift + N	New audio file project.
Command + B	Takes an audio file in any media tab and places it in the Bin of the open project. This is useful because it allows you to place a file into the current project's Bin without having to place it on the timeline. I do this sometimes to keep a file with a project for organizational purposes, even if I am not currently using the file.
Command + ,	Open Preferences.
Command + Shift + ?	Open Help.

Layouts, Tabs, and Heads Up Displays (HUDs)

F1	Opens default layout.
F2	Additional default layout with separate video/mixer tabs.
Control + A, S, or D	Toggles the view status of the left, lower, and right panes respectively.
Command + 1	Video tab.
Command + 2	Mixer tab.
Command + 3	Project pane.
Command + 4	Browser tab.
Command + /	Details tab.
Command + 5	Effects tab.

(Continued)

(Continued)

Command + Shift + C	Sound Palette. I never use this because the Sound Palette is automatically opened when you switch to the Lift/Stamp tools.
Command + Shift + {	Switches to tab to the left of actively selected tab.
Command + Shift + }	Switches to tab to the right of actively selected tab.
V	Multipoint video. If you click-and-hold a clip before pressing V, the HUD will remain open for the duration of the edit and then disappear when the mouse is released.
Control + V	Toggles the video output device. I have had to use this to turn off video when screen resolution changes or when the Cinema Desktop is activated and I want to turn it off.

Navigating the Timeline and Project Playback

Return or Home	An efficient way to return the playhead to locations that are to the left of your current location. When pressed, the playhead moves to the following items in this order: 1. last starting place, 2. start of cycle region, 3. start of project. If you move back to 1, press it again to go back to 2, etc.
End	The same as Return or Home above, but to the right instead of to the left.
Option + M	If you use markers a lot, you will be using this command and the one below quite a bit to help navigate. Moves the playhead to the immediately preceding marker. This is great for setting locations of ADR you want to record or sound effects that need editing.

(Continued)

(Continued)

Shift + M	The same as Option + M above, but to the immediately following marker.
Option + ← or →	Move forward or backward by a frame. Audio editors rarely seem to navigate using frame controls, but as a video editor this will probably be the first key command you look up. One very important use is to constantly check sync. You should see visual cues that match the audio waveforms as you go through your project. Look for hard sound effects such as footsteps or anything that makes a sharp sound. Frame through to make sure the waveform matches the visuals.
Space	Play/Stop.
Shift + Return	Returns to the previous start time and then plays. This is useful when checking edits because you can play across the edit point numerous times to make sure it sounds good without having to manually adjust the playhead.
J	Play backwards. Press multiple times to speed up reverse. I use this a lot when editing because it allows me to quickly go back through a section and then press the L key (below) to start playback again.
K	Stop.
L	Plays normal unless pressed multiple times, which speeds it up. I use J, K, and L a lot while editing because it makes moving through material so much more efficient.
K + L	Slow motion. This is another great tool while editing because you can hold K and then push L once to move a single frame forward. If you want to move forward in slow motion, then hold down L and you will advance slowly with the sound playing at a slower rate.

(Continued)

(*Continued*)

J + K	Slow motion in reverse. This is used hand in hand with K + L. Basically, hold the K key down and you can push the J key once to move a frame in reverse and hold it down for slow motion reverse playback. I hold K and can go backward or forward using the J and L keys as modifiers.
Option + Space	Allows you to start and stop playback of files previewed in the Bin or other media tabs.

Cycle Region

C	Toggles the cycle region. If you have the cycle region activated, it affects the starting points and looping. You may want to turn off the cycle quickly, which is what this does.
X	Use this to set the cycle region to match the length of a specific clip, or whichever clip is in the upper most track and is touching the playhead. Useful for setting loop points for recording ADR: If you have lines needing replacement separated into their own clips, you can place the playhead on the clip and press X to create the loop boundaries. This works during playback as well, which means you can press X to create a cycle region for instant looping of a file. When you want to move on, press C to deactivate the cycle and then press X over the next clip to set the new boundaries. Re-press C to re-activate the cycle, and the new region will be looped.
Option + X	Removes cycle.
Shift + A	Similar to X but works with selected clips regardless of where the playhead is.
I	Cycle In point.
O	Cycle Out point.

(*Continued*)

(Continued)

Option + I	Moves the In point of the cycle to the start of the project.
Option + O	Moves the Out point of the cycle to the end of the project.
Shift + I	Moves the playhead to the beginning of the cycle.
Shift + O	Moves the playhead to the end of the cycle.

Editing

Command + Z	Undo.
Command + Shift + Z	Redo.
Command + X	Cut.
Command + Shift + X	Ripple cut. This is useful for editing voiceover because you may want to take out a section to put it somewhere else. This removes the portion, slides the rest over, and then you can paste it where you want it.
Command + C	Copy.
Command + V	Paste.
Shift + Delete	Ripple deletes.
Command + D	Duplicate.
Command + A	Selects all.
Command + Shift + A	Deselects all. Because Soundtrack works in a selection-based system (processing applies to selected items) you should get in the habit of clicking this command to make sure you aren't processing more that you think you are.
Command + Shift + Option + X	Ripple cuts to the following clip edge.
Shift + Option + Delete	Ripple deletes to the following clip edge.
Command + Option + V	Allows you to paste the clipboard file multiple times. Often useful for laying down long sections of ambient noise.

(Continued)

(Continued)

N	Toggles snap.
S	You can use the Blade tool to split clips or you can split them (selected clips or clips on selected tracks) by pressing S with the playhead in the desired location. You can do this in real time if you are roughing out clip definitions. You can also select a portion of a file to cut in two places, resulting in three files.
Option + S	Rejoins clips that have been separated.
D	Uses the playhead to set the left clip edge on a selected clip. Useful for trimming clips.
G	Uses the playhead to set the right clip edge on a selected clip. Useful for trimming clips.
Command + F	If you use the Timeslice tool to select across the edges of two clips that are side-by-side, this will create a cross-fade. Once you have a cross-fade, you can double-click it with the Arrow tool to edit the fades.
Option + D	Uses the playhead to set the right edge of a clip fade-in on a selected clip.
Option + G	Uses the playhead to set the left edge of a clip fade-out on a selected clip.
Command + Option + Z	Uses the Timeslice tool's selection to trim the edges off the clip.
Command + Option + Drag	Slips the audio inside of a clip. It only works when there are available handles under the edges of a clip, but is useful for moving sound effects around while maintaining their ambient noise for the audible clip.

(Continued)

(Continued)

Command + \	Uses the playhead to determine where a selected clip or portion of a file selected using the Timeslice tool moves to. In both cases, the clip is moved to the playhead time on the currently selected track.
Command + Shift + \	Similar to Command + \, but uses a dialog to set the time code position for the new position.
E	Toggles envelope display for selected tracks.
Option + E	Toggles between envelope selection modes. One leaves keyframes at their track position even when moving clips and the other mode moves them with selected clips.

Moving Audio Clips and Envelope Points

Command + Option + ←	Envelope points (keyframes) are moved a ruler gridline to the left.
Command + Option + →	Envelope points (keyframes) are moved a ruler gridline to the right.
Command + ←	Envelope points (keyframes) are moved a nudge value to the left.
Command + →	Envelope points (keyframes) are moved a nudge value to the right.
Option + Control + B	Toggles locking on clips. I typically lock clips after I am done editing them to prevent accidental repositioning.
Control + B	Toggles the active state of clips. You can deactivate clips, effectively turning them off. This is useful because you can keep clips on the timeline in case you need them later without having to hear them.
Command + ↑	Two functions: • Selected clips are moved left to earlier edit points. • Adjusts the level of selected envelope points (keyframes) by a coarse value.

(Continued)

(Continued)

Command + ↓	Two functions: • Selected clips are moved right to later edit points. • Adjusts the level of selected envelope points (keyframes) by a coarse value.
Command + Option + ↑	Two functions: • Selected clips are moved up to a higher track. • Adjusts the level of selected envelope points (keyframes) by a fine value.
Command + Option + ↓	Two functions: • Selected clips are moved down to a lower track. • Adjusts the level of selected envelope points (keyframes) by a fine value.
Command + Shift + E	Envelope points are added based on the edges of clips that are currently selected. This is so much easier than adding them manually.

Viewing the Timeline

Command + =	Horizontal zoom in.
Command + −	Horizontal zoom out.
Control + Command + =	Track height zoom in.
Control + Command + −	Track height zoom out.
Option + Z	Current selection zoom.
Command + 0	Default zoom.
Control + Z	Toggles sample level zoom. This means you will be zoomed in as close as possible. Only works in audio file projects and the File Editor.
Shift + Option + Z	Cycle region zoom.
Shift + Z	Horizontal zoom to fit entire project.

(Continued)

(Continued)

Command + Shift + =	Waveform zoom in. This makes your audio look louder without actually making it louder.
Command + Shift + −	Waveform zoom out. This makes your audio look softer without actually making it softer.
Command + Shift + 0	Waveform default zoom.
Command + 6	Mini track view.
Command + 7	Small track view.
Command + 8	Medium track view.
Command + 9	Large track view.

Timeline Tools

A	Arrow tool.
B	Blade tool.
B + B	Blade All tool.
W	Timeslice tool.
U + U	Lift tool.
U	Stamp tool.
H	Scrub tool.

File Editor Project View Tools and Commands

W	Frequency Selection tool.
P	Sample Edit tool. This is also called the Pencil tool because you use it to draw the waveform.
T	Audio Stretching tool.
Z	Zoom tool.
H	Scrub tool.
Control + Z	Toggles sample level zoom. This means you will be zoomed in as close as possible. This only works in audio file projects and the File Editor.
Option + Z	Current selection zoom.
Shift + Z	Horizontal zoom to fit entire project.

(Continued)

(Continued)

Command + Control + Y	Copies a selection of audio to a special clipboard for use as an ambient noise print.
Command + Y	Takes the current audio and adds the ambient noise print to it.
Command + Shift + Y	Deletes the current audio and replaces it with the ambient noise print.
Command + Shift + I	Moves both edges of a selection in to the nearest zero crossing points.
Command + Shift + O	Moves both edges of a selection out to the nearest zero crossing points.
[	Moves the left edge of a selection to the nearest zero crossing point towards the left.
]	Moves the left edge of a selection to the nearest zero crossing point towards the right.
Shift + [	Moves the right edge of a selection to the nearest zero crossing point towards the left.
Shift+]	Moves the right edge of a selection to the nearest zero crossing point towards the right.

Processing and Editing Audio Files

Command + Control + N	Takes the current selection and creates a new audio file project. When you use this on a clip in a multitrack file project, it replaces the audio on the timeline with the new clip automatically, retaining effects and sync.
Command + Shift + Control + N	Takes the current clipboard and uses it to create a new audio file project.
Command + L	Normalize. Use this to adjust audio levels to a specific amount.
Command + Shift + L	Adjust Amplitude. Use this to change a file's level by a specific amount.

(Continued)

(Continued)

Command + Shift + V	Paste mix. In the File Editor or an audio file project, you can use this to paste mix two files together. It adds the copied file into the selected file using a dialog which lets you adjust the mix ratio.
Command + Delete	Turns a selection into silence.
Control + F	Flattens audible actions. The purple marker on the side of the Actions List can be moved above or below effects. Any effects that are below the purple bar will not be flattened.
Shift + Control + F	Flatten all actions.
Command + F1	A/B last actions.
Command + Control + Y	Set ambient noise print.
Command + Y	Add ambient noise.
Command + Shift + Y	Replace with ambient noise.

Tracks, Busses, and Submixes

Command + T	New track.
Command + Control + T	New bus.
Command + Option + T	New submix.
Command + Shift + T	Delete selected track.
T	Mute track.
Y	Solo track.
Control + ↑	Moves track selection up.
Control + ↓	Moves track selection down.
Shift + Control + ↑ or ↓	Toggles selection of tracks above and below currently selected track.
F5	Locks track. This is useful to protect the contents of the track from being altered. Final Cut has the same feature.

(Continued)

(Continued)

E	Toggles automation (keyframes) view for a track.
Command + G	Groups tracks that are selected.
Control + G	Toggles groups' active/inactive state.

Markers

M	Insert time marker. The marker is added at the current playhead position and can be added during playback for efficient organization.
Control + M	Adds region marker. Region markers are the same as time markers, but cover a range of time instead of just a specific time code position. This command adds a region marker based on a selection on the timeline.
Option + Control + M	Instead of adding a region marker, this command places time markers at the start and end of a selection.
Option + B	Insert beat marker.
Command + Option + M	This command opens the Details tab for the selected marker and is useful for quickly seeing details about the maker.

Selecting Audio Clips in the Timeline

Shift + End	Selects every clip from the playhead until the project end marker, including clips that are under the playhead even if they start before it. If you have a track selected, it will only affect clips on it, but if there is no selection it will work on all clips to the end.
Shift + Option + End	Same as Shift + End except it always works on all clips from the playhead on.

(Continued)

(Continued)

Shift + Home	Selects every clip from the playhead until the project start, including clips that are under the playhead even if they continue after it. If you have a track selected, it will only affect clips on it, but if there is no selection it will work on all clips to the beginning.
Shift + Option + Home	Same as Shift + Home except it always works on all clips from the start to the playhead.
Shift + T	Clip selector for selected track, unless no tracks are selected, and then it works in the same way as Shift + Option + T.
Shift + Option + T	Same as Command + A, but for tracks. On the timeline they work the same.
Shift + A	Sets cycle region to the edges of a selected clip.
Shift + ↑	Playhead is shifted to previous edit and the selection state is toggled for clips starting at that point. I have never found a good use for this or the following few commands.
Shift + ↓	Playhead is shifted to following edit and the selection state is toggled for clips starting at that point.
Shift + Option + ↑	Same as Shift + ↑ but only for selected tracks.
Shift + Option + ↓	Same as Shift + ↓ but only for selected tracks.
Video Out	
Control + V	Toggles video output. This is useful when you need to turn off an external output quickly.
Recording	
R	Prepares selected tracks for recording by 'arming' them.

(Continued)

(*Continued*)

Command + R	Begins recording. You can only record on existing tracks by 'arming' them. Think of this as log and capture straight onto a sequence track in Final Cut.
Control + 1 through 9	When loop recording, the various passes of recorded audio are stored in a single file with each pass, called a 'take.' Use Control + 1 through Control + 9 to move the corresponding take from 1–9 to the top level, which makes it the audible take. This allows you to easily pull the best take to the top of the clip. Also the default OS X Spaces Switch command.

Using Arrow Keys to Move the Playhead

↑	Move to previous edit.
↓	Move to next edit.
Option + ↑	Previous edit/selected track.
Option + ↓	Next edit/selected track.
Option + ←	One gridline earlier.
Option + →	One gridline later.
←	Earlier by nudge amount.
→	Later by nudge amount.

Working with Timeslices

Shift + Option + ←	Lengthens the timeslice by a gridline to the left.
Shift + Option + →	Lengthens the timeslice by a gridline to the right.
Shift + ↑	Lengthens the timeslice to the immediately preceding edit point. Once you click ↑ you can click ↓ to move the left edge back to the right as long as you keep the Shift key pressed. You will need to let go of the Shift key to begin adjusting the right edge.

(*Continued*)

(Continued)

Shift + ↓	Lengthens the timeslice to the immediately following edit point. Once you click the ↓ you can click the ↑ to move the right edge back to the left as long as you keep the Shift key pressed. You will need to let go of the Shift key to begin adjusting the left edge.
Command + ←	Keeps the current timeslice length, but shifts it earlier by the nudge amount.
Command + →	Keeps the current timeslice length, but shifts it later by the nudge amount.
Command + Option + ↑	Keeps the current timeslice length, but shifts it up a track.
Command + Option + ↓	Keeps the current timeslice length, but shifts it down a track.
Command + Option + ←	Keeps the current timeslice length, but shifts to an earlier gridline.
Command + Option + →	Keeps the current timeslice length, but shifts to a later gridline.
Command + Shift + ↑ or ↓	Keeps the current timeslice length, but extends the selection to the track above or below. If you start the selection with a clip in the middle of the timeline, you can select in either direction, but you will need to release Command and Shift before crossing over the other direction.

Apple Loops

Below is a list of the categories of Apple Loops that are bundled with Soundtrack in the Final Cut Studio package. To help clarify things I am only including the items that are concrete in nature (yes to Acoustic Bass but no to Acoustic). This is because some of the categories are very general and would overlap with the more specific areas (Acoustic Bass is in the Acoustic category). For each category I am listing how many loops are found there.

This is designed as a quick reference to help you find the files you are looking for.

Category	Number of Files
Acoustic bass	106
Acoustic guitar	159
Ambience	358
Animals	76
Bagpipe	1
Banjo	48
Bass	419
Beats	575
Bell	1
Bongo	40
Cello	5
Chime	2
Clave	8
Clavinet	30
Conga	53
Cowbell	17
Cymbal	14
Drum kit	306
Drums	964
Electric bass	193
Electric guitar	261
Electric piano	133
Explosions	16
Flute	8
Foley	123
French horn	1
Guitars	514
Harmonica	24
Hi-hat	51
Impacts and crashes	168
Keyboards	652

(Continued)

(*Continued*)

Category	Number of Files
Kick	6
Mallets	120
Mandolin	23
Marimba	2
Motions and transitions	511
Orchestral	135
Organ	12
People	208
Percussion	505
Piano	190
Rattler	3
Sci-fi	128
Shaker	38
Sitar	13
Slide guitar	23
Snare	6
Sports and leisure	84
Synth bass	120
Synths	287
Tambourine	21
Textures	116
Tom	6
Transportation	183
Trombone	9
Vibes	78
Vinyl	50
Viola	3
Violin	9
Vocals	21
Weapons	43
Work/home	256
World	733

Selected Feature Comparison with Pro Tools and Nuendo

The question always comes up of whether Soundtrack is really able to keep up with the other audio software packages. I have created a chart comparing the features of these applications to help answer that question. This is only a selected feature comparison and I have focused both on features that Soundtrack has which are unique and the features which are its weaknesses. Putting aside the fact that, obviously, this is a book about Soundtrack, I believe that it has a place in the post-audio workflow, even if it isn't going to replace either of the other apps.

I have listed the names of the features as they are called in each system and then ranked them using the numbers 1–3 (1 being the best implementation of the feature according to my personal opinion).

Soundtrack	Nuendo	Pro Tools
Multitake Editor – 1	Lanes – 2	Playlists – 3
Actions List – 1	Offline Process History – 2	–
File Editor – 2	File Editor – 2	Each Track – 1
Multipoint Video	–	–
Restoration tools	Partial set	Partial set
Final Cut Conform	–	–
Audio Engine uses the OS X Core Audio System – 3	Core Audio and others – 2	Proprietary (Pro Tools hardware required, which ensures compatibility) – 1
Control surface functionality – 3	Control surface functionality (most flexible) – 1	Control surface functionality – 2
Export to AC-3 (bundled with Compressor) – 1	AC-3 requires third party plug-in – 2	AC-3 requires third party plug-in – 2
Convolution Reverb (Space Designer) – 1	Non-real-time version – 3	Often bundled – 2
Mac compatible only – 3	Mac and Windows (better on Windows) – 2	Mac and Windows – 1
Ambient Fill tool	–	–
Spectrum edit	–	–
Audio Stretch functionality – 1	Audio Stretch functionality – 3	Audio Stretch functionality – 2
Single window interface – 1	Multiple windows – 3	Two primary windows – 2

(Continued)

(Continued)

Soundtrack	Nuendo	Pro Tools
Designed for audio post – 2	Designed for audio post – 1	Designed for music production and post – 3
–	MIDI functionality – 2	MIDI functionality – 1
–	Music notation feature costs extra – 3	Includes music notation editor – 1
Automation – 3	Automation – 1	Automation – 2
Default plug-in quality – 1	Default plug-in quality – 2	Default plug-in quality – 3
–	–	Hardware DSP
Rank of software availability in studios – 3	Rank of software availability in studios – 2	Rank of software availability in studios – 1

Some of the data require further explanation. The problem with making a comparison like this is that Soundtrack has a lot of specialized tools which make editing audio very efficient. If you look at these features all by themselves, then Soundtrack appears to be the best tool. However, there are several other features which count for a lot more, and probably hundreds of features that Pro Tools and Nuendo have that Soundtrack doesn't. In comparison, Soundtrack is a small program. The features that count for a lot more are availability in studios, automation, and control surface compatibility. However, Final Cut Conform and the specialized tools make a strong case for Soundtrack to be a competitor in the future.

13

SCENARIOS AND PRACTICAL TUTORIALS

This is a reference chapter covering 20 basic features of Soundtrack Pro. In addition to the descriptions, there are detailed illustrations that will help you to use the features in the most efficient way possible. Think of this chapter as a cookbook, with each feature as a recipe. Each illustration is labeled with numbers that correspond to a more detailed textual explanation. These 'recipes' cover everything from recording audio to more complex tasks like using those specialized tools that are useful but not necessarily intuitive. Along with an explanation of each number in the illustration, there is a short paragraph that explains why the function is important and how you would typically use it. Understanding why you might use a feature is probably just as important as understanding how to use it. As with cooking, the best way to understand and integrate the recipes into your workflow is to try them out, so have Soundtrack Pro open while reading this chapter.

The Functions

Below are the 20 topics covered, first in the order in which they appear and then in alphabetical order by function name. They are organized in such a way as to help you move from basic advanced tasks. Having an index of both actual order and alphabetical order will help you to find exactly what you are looking for; however, there are only 20 so I suggest looking through and discovering each recipe individually.

Chapter Order

1. Recording audio.
2. Sharing files between projects.
3. The Actions List.
4. Copy/paste clip effects.

5. Leveling clean dialog.
6. Leveling noisy dialog.
7. Recording automated dialog replacement (ADR).
8. The Multitake Editor.
9. Placing sound effects.
10. The Audio Stretch tool.
11. Adding ambient noise.
12. The Spectrum Selection tool.
13. The restoration tools.
14. Noise Reduction.
15. Stem routing.
16. Using the surround panner.
17. Adding reverb on a bus.
18. Automating effects plug-ins.
19. Project music settings.
20. Exploring music loops.

Alphabetical Order by Function Name

3. Actions List.
11. Add Ambient Noise.
13. Analysis tools.
10. Audio Stretch tool.
18. Automation (plug-ins).
2. Bin.
5. Lift Voice Level.
4. Lift Process Effects.
7. Loop recording.
9. Multipoint video.
8. Multitake Editor.
20. Music Loops.
19. Music Settings (project).
14. Noise Reduction.
6. Normalization.
1. Recording.
17. Reverb.
12. Spectrum Select tool.
15. Submixes.
16. Surround panner.

1. Recording Audio

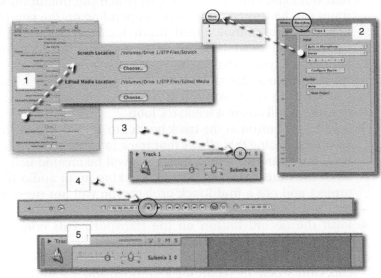

Figure 13-1

Introduction

Recording audio might seem pretty straightforward, but there are a couple of things that it is important to know about. While the basics of getting Soundtrack to record are here, the fundamentals of setting up your audio interface are not. You will need to look in your interface's instruction manual for information detailing how to set up and use the interface. The good news is that Mac OS X is fairly easy to use and I have not run into any problems as long as the interface has driver software that is compatible with the current version of the operating system.

Steps

1. In the Soundtrack Preferences under General, you need to set the Scratch Location to determine where the files will be recorded. Much like Final Cut, this needs to be set on a project-by-project basis. Soundtrack is one of the only audio programs that does not set this by default to the saved project location.
2. In the Recording tab (right pane by default) you need to set the input device and channel information. The channel number should be set to mono when using a single microphone to record voiceover or ADR. If you want to configure the device, then choose the Configure option from the tab

and the Core Audio application from the operating system will load. This is one place in which the microphone input can be turned up or down depending on the source material. You cannot adjust input levels in Soundtrack itself. If you need to hear what is being recorded by Soundtrack, you should select a Monitor output. Be careful not to place the microphone near the speakers when you turn this on or you might damage your speaker/ears because it will create a feedback loop.

3. Select the r button in the track header to 'arm' the track for recording. Doing this allows that track to be recorded into. If no tracks are 'armed,' a new track will be created below all of the other tracks. If you are working in an audio file project and not a multitrack project, you will not need to arm any tracks.

4. Push the Record button on the transport. This engages record and Soundtrack will begin to record.

5. Note: The track will record what looks like an empty red clip. Only when the recording is stopped will the audio clip waveform appear.

2. Sharing Files Between Projects

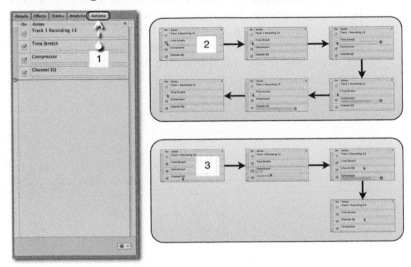

Figure 13-2

Introduction

This is a super-powerful feature that allows you to have multiple projects open at the same time, consequently allowing you to drag files from any open project into another. This is an efficient way to work when editing sound effects because you can open a project that has files you would like to use in a different project and, instead of importing these files, you can drag them from your Bin tab. It's as easy as that. The Bin is organized into projects, which makes it easier to find the files you are looking for. It has a number of different tools to help you find files, but perhaps the easiest way is to find the file on a track in the project and select it. This highlights the track in the Bin and makes it easy to find.

Steps

1. After opening a project, open the Bin, which is located by default in the bottom pane.
2. Open a second project containing a file or files that you would like to bring into the original project.
3. You can also see a variety of details about each file in the Bin, including length, type of file, positional data for current project, and other things. The Bin is a great place to find out more information about the files in your projects.

4. Click and drag the file you want to bring into a different project only after making sure the destination project is currently visible. You may drag it onto any track in the project. Once it is on a track the Bin will show the file as being in both projects and you may close the project that the file came from and not worry about the file losing its connection.

3. The Actions List

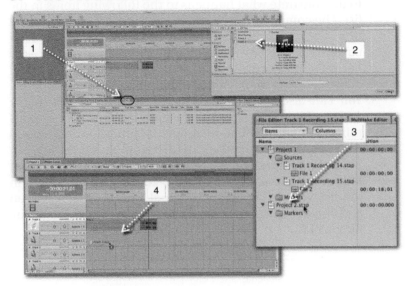

Figure 13-3

Introduction

The Actions List is an important area to master in Soundtrack because it plays a central role in the editing of audio files. Everything you do to each clip is stored in its own Actions List. The Actions List allows you to change these things, re-order them, or completely delete them. In a typical post-production project where there might be thousands of sound effects and many hours of dialog, it is refreshing to have an individualized history for each and every audio clip. Of course, Final Cut has been working this way for years, but only a handful of audio software tools provide this level of functionality. If you look at each item in the list you will see a bar below the name. Sometimes there is a wider section coupled with a skinny line. The wider section indicates how much of the file has been processed and how much has not. This helps to show you when only a portion of a file has been changed.

Steps

1. The Actions List is in the Actions tab in the left pane. The top entry in the list represents the file itself and the items below represent different actions taken on the clip. In this example you can see that the audio clip has been through a time stretch, a compressor, and a channel EQ.

2. In this example I am turning off the time stretch process to demonstrate what happens to the following items in the list. The compressor is automatically recalculated once the time stretch has been removed, and then the EQ is recalculated. This is an efficient way to make a comparison between how a clip sounds with a process turned on and off at any point in the Actions List.

3. You can also change the order of the processes in the Actions List. This is useful to audition how the various things sound in different orders. Maybe it would sound better to time stretch the clip after you pass it through an EQ and a compressor. It is very easy to discover the answer to that question. Also, by double-clicking on each item in the list you can open the original process dialog screen and make adjustments that will then ripple through the Actions List.

4. Copy/Paste Clip Effects

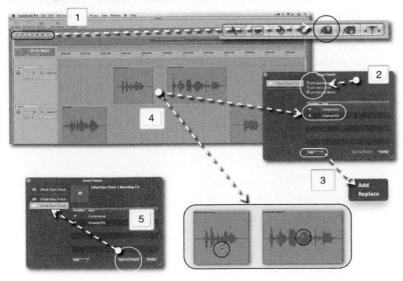

Figure 13-4

Introduction

While the Actions List (Tutorial 3) creates an individual effect history for each clip, the Lift Process Effects option in the Sound Palette provides a tool to copy a set of process effects off one clip and onto another. Not all items that are stored in the Actions List for a clip can be copied, but all effects initiated from the Process menu are available. The primary reason that this is a useful tool is that you can fine-tune a set of effects on one clip knowing that when it is complete you can use this tool to paste it onto a bunch of other clips. You can even customize what gets pasted.

Steps

1. Select the Lift tool from the toolbar. This automatically opens the Sound Palette window.
2. In the Sound Palette choose the lift Process Effects option while disabling the other lift options.
3. Choose Add or Replace to determine what happens to any existing effects on the destination clip. If you want to retain the original effects, choose Add. If you want to delete any previous effects, choose Replace.
4. Use the Lift tool on the clip that has the effects you want to copy. Immediately after the list of effects is copied, the tool

switches to a Stamp tool which is ready for pasting on any other clips. At this point the Sound Palette will show you a list of effects that will be pasted. You can easily uncheck any of these to prevent them from being pasted.

5. You can also save the lifted set of effects as a preset for use at a later time. This is useful for groups of effects that you use frequently.

5. Leveling Clean Dialog

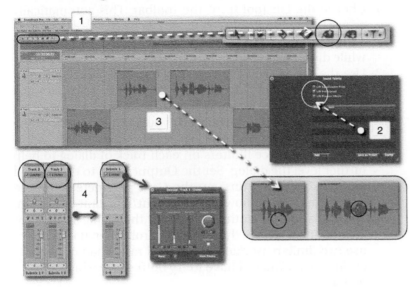

Figure 13-5

Introduction

This is a new feature in Soundtrack Pro that is designed to make dialog leveling easier. It analyzes the average level of the dialog and can then be stamped onto other clips to bring them to the same average level. The primary limitation is that it doesn't do anything with varying levels of ambient noise. This means that if you match the average level of dialog in a clip that has loud dialog and soft ambient noise to a clip that has soft dialog and more ambient noise, it will match the dialog but the ambient noise will jump from clip to clip. This creates an unusable match. You can use the Lift Voice Level tool to match dialog that is similar in level and has similar ambient noise. For leveling dialog with varying levels and ambient noise, see Tutorial 6 and possibly Tutorial 14 (Noise Reduction). In this example, I have also included putting limiters on each track and the submix, which helps in the leveling process by further controlling the dynamic range. Controlling dynamics is like cutting hair. The Lift Voice Level tool is like cutting off the longer portions of the hair with scissors. Once the levels are manageable, you use the electric razor to trim the edges. The limiters represent the electric razor: you use them to fine-tune the levels. The submix track acts like a funnel for any audio tracks that are assigned to it, and the limiter inserted on it will do another pass of fine-tuning as they all pass through.

Steps

1. Choose the Lift tool from the toolbar. This automatically opens the Sound Palette window.
2. In the Sound Palette choose the Lift Voice Level option while disabling the other lift options.
3. Use the Lift tool on the clip that has the dialog you want to match. Immediately after the dialog level is copied, the tool switches to a Stamp tool which is ready for clicking on any other clips whose levels you want to match to the original.
4. You can also place limiters on each track of dialog to help further level the dialog. Set the Output Level to the desired loudness and then turn up the Gain parameter until the Gain Reduction is showing consistent/constant reduction. You can also use another limiter on the dialog submix for an additional level of dynamics control. Often it is better to use two limiters working at reduced rates than one that is limiting a lot. You will have to try both to see which sounds better.

6. Leveling Noisy Dialog

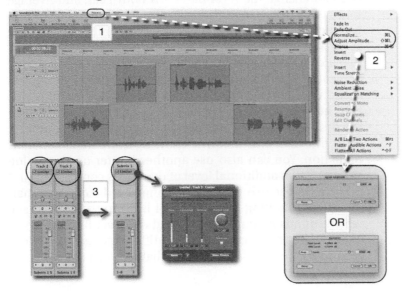

Figure 13-6

Introduction

When there is a lot of ambient noise coupled with dialog, using the Lift Voice Level tool (Tutorial 5) in the Sound Palette becomes unreliable. Instead, you will need to use a couple of other tools which require manual operation and critical listening. The process includes processing the clips, listening to see if you have achieved the right results, and then either re-processing or moving on to the next clip. What you are listening for is a consistent dialog level between clips and an ambient noise level that is not distracting. If you get the dialog perfect and the ambient noise is not working then you may have to either use a Noise Reduction tool or re-record the dialog and add in artificial ambient noise.

Steps

1. Once you have selected a clip on a track, choose the Normalize or Adjust Amplitude options from the Process menu.
2. Both the Normalize and Adjust Amplitude options work towards the same result of making your clip louder. The Normalize option lets you determine the Peak or Average level that you want the clip to end up at and Adjust Amplitude lets you turn the clip up or down by a specific amount. Listen to the clip and then make changes based on whether it needs

to be louder or softer. The Normalize option is nice because you can change the level based on both Peak and Average levels. This is closer to the Lift Voice Level tool and so you can pick an average level you like and set other clips to the same amount. Listen carefully to the ambient noise and try to match that as well as the dialog level.

3. You can also place limiters by right-clicking on the effects section of each track in the mixer. The reason for doing this is to help further level the dialog. Set the Output Level to the desired loudness and then turn up the Gain parameter until the Gain Reduction is showing consistent/constant reduction. You can also use another limiter on the dialog submix for an additional level of dynamics control. Often it is better to use two limiters working at reduced rates than one that is limiting a lot. You will have to try both to see which sounds better. Keep in mind that over limiting noisy clips might accentuate the noise differences and therefore hurt your attempt at leveling the dialog. Don't overdo it.

7. Recording Automated Dialog Replacement (ADR)

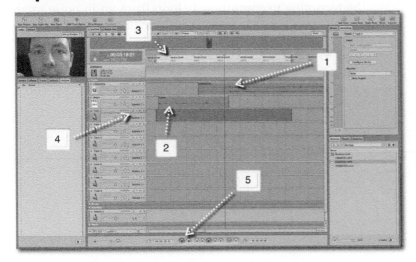

Figure 13-7

Introduction

Recording ADR is a standard process in post-audio. When production dialog isn't useable, it needs to be replaced. Soundtrack Pro, like many audio programs, does not have any specialized ADR tools. However, it is possible to use Soundtrack to record ADR and there are some great tools which can be used for editing. It is recommended that you read Tutorial 1 to help with the recording setup and then you can use Tutorial 8 to help you edit the various recordings. First, you'll need to have the video in Soundtrack and then you can decide which lines need to be replaced. You can easily make markers to keep track of dialog that needs replacing. I use an audio file with three beeps to cue the actor. The three beeps play and then the line starts where a fourth beep would have been. You can download a beep file from www.practicalsampling.com although it is possible to make using Soundtrack. If you are trying to match ADR to production dialog, it is a good idea to use the same microphone that was used on location. If you are replacing everything, then this is less of an issue.

Steps

1. Pick the line you want to replace and take note of where it starts.

2. Import the beep file and line up the right edge of the clip with the beginning of the line you want to replace.

3. Set the loop cycle (which is a Ruler selection that allows the recording to continuously loop from an In point to an Out point) so that it starts at the beginning of the beeps and continues until after the entire line of dialog. You may want to add a little extra time if the actor wants to have a pause between takes. You can set the In/Out points of the cycle using the I key for Ins and the O key for Outs. The C key activates/deactivates the loop cycle.

4. 'Arm' the track for recording (see Tutorial 1).

5. Push Record on the transport.

8. The Multitake Editor

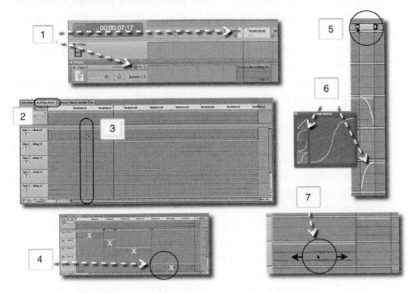

Figure 13-8

Introduction

The Multitake Editor is a very powerful tool that makes editing ADR (see Tutorial 7) very easy. The typical way to use this begins with recording a looped section of audio into Soundtrack. When you loop record, each recording pass in the looped section automatically becomes a part of a multitake clip. Once the recording is complete, it looks like a single clip, but in fact is a collection of all of the clips recorded and can be accessed through the Multitake Editor. You can quickly edit these takes to create a compilation of all of the best parts. The top layer (the one that is heard when you press Play) is treated like an individual clip that can be copied, exported, and so on.

Steps

1. Record using a loop selection to create a multitake clip.
2. Once you have selected a mutitake clip, open the Multitake Editor in the bottom window pane.
3. Use the Blade tool to cut the clip up into smaller chunks. Typically with dialog this will consist of words and/or phrases. Notice that the top layer is not cut using the Blade, only the other sections below the top layer.

4. Once you have cut the clip into sections you can use the Arrow tool to select different portions of the file. The portions you choose are displayed in a different shade to the rest and these are the parts that are compiled into the top layer. The compiling happens automatically and all you need to do is choose portions of the lower layers.

5. At the edge where you cut the files using the Blade tool, you will see a set of arrows. Click and drag these apart to create audio fades. Doing this smoothes out potentially glitchy transitions between sections.

6. Double-click on the individual fade to open the Fade Editor. You can choose between four different fade options. The default works well in most situations and you would only need to try out other types if you aren't achieving smooth results.

7. Since you cannot cut the various files at different locations using the Blade tool, you might need to slip the audio horizontally to move a line of dialog into place. Use the Arrow tool in combination with the Option and Command keys to slip the audio inside the region. This moves the audio but not the clip borders.

9. Placing Sound Effects

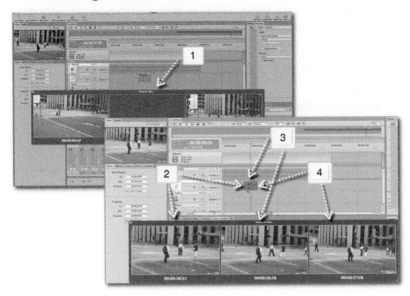

Figure 13-9

Introduction

The key to efficient sound effects placement is an HUD (heads up display) in Soundtrack called the Multipoint Video HUD. This is a unique tool in the world of audio software. It allows three frames of video to be seen simultaneously. The first frame corresponds to the left edge of a selected audio clip; the right frame corresponds to the right frame of a selected audio clip; and the middle frame is blank when a clip is simply selected but shows the frame that corresponds to a click-and-hold selection, representing the frame that lines up with the current mouse location. The implication of this is that you can place a sound effect, such as a footstep, exactly where it should go by clicking the file on its initial transient and then activating the Multipoint Video display without letting go of the clip. The boundaries of the file determine the left and right frames of video displayed and the middle represents the beginning of the footstep. Move the clip until the middle frame of video matches the sound effect. One effective way to use this tool is to have it turned off when you make the initial clip selection. While the clip is held, press V on the keyboard, which opens the HUD. Once you are done positioning the clip and have let it go, the HUD disappears as well. It only remains while the clip is held.

Steps

1. The Multipoint Video HUD is active with no currently held clip selection.
2. The left frame corresponds to the left edge of the audio clip.
3. The right frame corresponds to the right edge of the audio clip.
4. The middle frame corresponds to the currently held mouse placement on the audio clip, in this example a footstep sound effect that is being matched to the man walking away from the camera position.

10. The Audio Stretch Tool

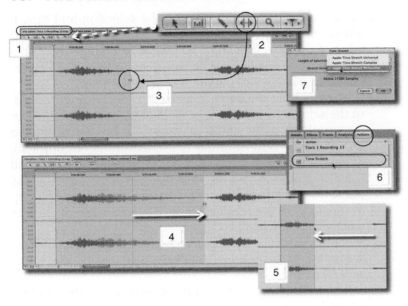

Figure 13-10

Introduction

The Audio Stretch tool is a powerful way to tweak the timing of audio to match picture needs or to simply alter the audio to increase/decrease the rate of speech. It is used to stretch the audio in time without changing the pitch of the file. I use this most often when matching recorded ADR (see Tutorial 7) to the actor's original lip movements. While this is a powerful tool, it is not a golden bullet that can fix any and all problems. The more you have to stretch, the worse it sounds, so it is best used in moderation. There is a key modifier that provides an additional feature. If you hold Option while clicking-and-dragging, the audio immediately following will either be pulled to the left to fill the void created or pushed to the right to make room for the lengthened selection. If you don't use this modifier there will either be a gap of silence created or a portion of the following audio will be deleted.

Steps

1. Once you have a clip selected, open the File Editor tab in the lower pane.
2. Choose the Audio Stretch tool from the File Editor toolbar.

3. Make a selection of the audio you wish to stretch or condense.

4. Click and hold the right edge of the selection and drag it either to the left or the right. You cannot adjust the left edge of the selection so, if you want to change the initial placement, you will have to do this by moving the entire clip or by cutting and pasting the selected area.

5. When you drag the edge to the left to decrease the length of the selection, you are supposed to be able to fill the gap automatically with ambient noise (if you have created any using the Add Ambient Noise feature in Soundtrack). At the time of writing I have not gotten this to work and there is always a void of sound left when stretching the audio to the left. Of course, you can always fill the gap manually with the Add Ambient Noise feature (which does work – see Tutorial 11).

6. If you want to change the stretched audio, double-click on the action in the Actions List and a dialog will appear with several options.

7. The most important option that appears is the Stretch algorithm. You can choose between three different algorithms and when you press OK the stretched area will be updated with the new choice. These three can produce wildly varying results and so it is recommended that you experiment with them to find the best one for your material.

11. Adding Ambient Noise

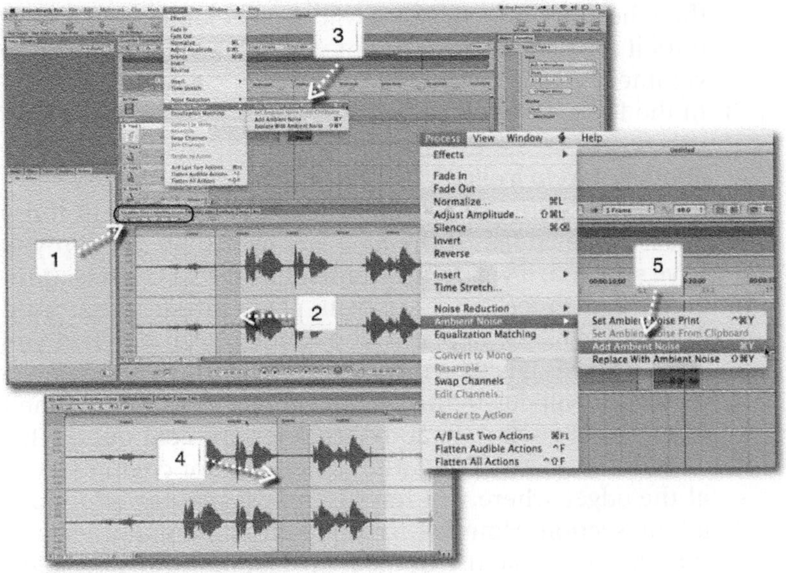

Figure 13-11

Introduction

The Add Ambient Noise feature is a nice tool but I often wish it could work miracles. It seems like such a wonderful possibility to click a button and have ambient noise added to all of my audio tracks. Used in the right way, it can do great things, but you will have to be very careful and listen to all of the results. The key is finding a good piece of ambient noise to use as the noise print. The longer and more consistent the better, and a very short selection will not work at all. The location team should have captured a minute or more of consistent room tone, and this is the best option for the noise print. If you don't have this, it is possible to achieve good results with other selections, but you'll need to try a few out.

Steps

1. Once you have a clip selected, open the File Editor tab in the lower pane.
2. Make a selection of the audio if you are using the currently selected clip for the print source. You can also use the file currently in the clipboard if you have another file you want to take the print from. Make the selection as

long as possible while selecting only consistent sections of the noise. If the ambient noise gets louder and louder, then the new ambient noise will also get louder and louder until it repeats, at which point you will have a large fall in volume.

3. In the Process menu, select Set Ambient Noise Print. This is how you create the source for adding ambient noise to another part of a clip.

4. In the File Editor, select the area where the ambient noise needs to be added. If the area is longer than the clip you have selected, it will repeat until it fills the whole selection.

5. From the Process menu, you can choose either Add Ambient Noise or Replace With Ambient Noise. When you add the noise, it will be mixed into the existing audio. If you replace, it will delete the existing audio. Most of the time I like to have a separate audio track for ambient noise. This is useful when tweaking it to match and for creating fades at the edges where you have to repeat the noise to make a long section. However, creating an additional track and then having to adjust both when mixing means an additional thing to think about. If you have a good selection of ambient noise, I suggest adding it to the clip using the Add Ambient Noise feature first. If it works, then great. If not, you may have to create an additional track and do it that way instead.

12. The Spectrum Selection Tool

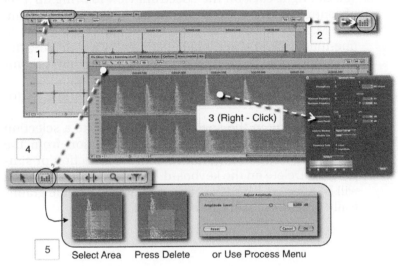

Select Area   Press Delete   or Use Process Menu

Figure 13-12

Introduction

The File Editor has two different views. The first is the Waveform view, which is the most common way to look at audio. The second is the Spectrum view, which is a very different way to look at audio. It shows additional information about the audio such as frequency content. The vertical axis represents frequency while the color intensity represents the amplitude of each frequency. This is very useful for troubleshooting audio problems. You can easily see low frequency rumble and high frequency noise. Additionally, you can use the Spectrum Selection tool to select trouble areas and either turn them down or completely delete them. Don't be afraid of this view if you are new to it. It can be hard to get used to because it adds a number of different pieces of data to an already complex situation. Think of it as a visual equalizer (see Chapter 7, on spectrum effects, for more information). Instead of controlling frequencies using knobs and faders, you get to edit the frequencies themselves. The only way to get used to it is to use it and listen to the results. Experiment by deleting various sections, but try to guess what the result will sound like before you listen to it. I think you will get the hang of it rather quickly.

Steps

1. Once you have a clip selected, open the File Editor tab in the lower pane.

2. Change the File Editor view to Spectrum view.
3. You can right-click on the Spectrum view to bring up a set of controls for the view. The most useful are the Minimum and Maximum Frequency selectors. These allow you to fine-tune what you are looking at. Otherwise, the low frequencies would be hard to work with since they encompass only a fraction of the overall Spectrum view.
4. Choose the Spectrum Selection tool from the File Editor toolbar.
5. Click and drag in the spectrum area to create a selection box. Next, either use the Adjust Level option from the Process menu to change the level of the selection or simply push Delete on the keyboard. Only the audio in the box will be affected. This is useful for removing rumble graphically, or removing unwanted sounds.

13. The Restoration Tools

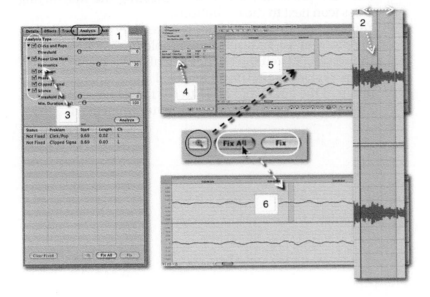

Figure 13-13

Introduction

Restoration tools are available in the Analysis tab. These tools include click and pop removal, power line hum removal, DC off-set removal, phase tools, a de-clipper, and a tool that tells you where any silence exists. Together, they form a powerful set of restoration tools designed to help make your audio the best it can be. The good news is that Soundtrack can tell you when you have these problems. However, it's not always 100% successful when fixing them. Noise reduction is covered separately in Tutorial 14.

Steps

1. Once you have a clip selected, open the Analysis tab in the left pane.
2. Select the area of audio you want to analyze. In this case I have selected an area that has a click/pop.
3. Select the items you want to look for in the audio and then press Analyze.
4. Any problems that are found will be listed in the list below the Analyze button.

5. You can zoom in on each problem by selecting the item from the problem list and then pressing the Magnifying Glass icon next to the Fix buttons.

6. You can Fix All, which attempts to remedy all problems in the problem list, or just Fix the problems that are selected. In this case, I fixed the clipped signal and it created a 'best guess' replacement. Unfortunately, I could still hear a little bump in the audio and I had to cut the whole section out. The other options typically work better when fixed.

14. Noise Reduction

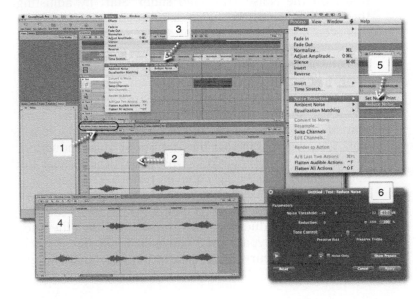

Figure 13-14

Introduction

The Noise Reduction option has been updated in Soundtrack Pro 3. It worked okay in previous versions, but the new High Resolution Noise Print feature produces even better results. I own several very expensive Noise Reduction tools and the Noise Reduction feature in Soundtrack is nothing to sneeze at. It has gotten better with each iteration.

Steps

1. Once you have a clip selected, open the File Editor tab in the bottom pane.
2. Select an area of representative noise. Avoid areas that have additional sounds that may be unwanted but aren't representative of the general noise.
3. In the Process menu, choose Set Noise Print from the Noise Reduction submenu.
4. Select the entire portion of the clip that needs noise reduction.
5. In the Process menu, choose Reduce Noise from the Noise Reduction submenu.
6. The Reduce Noise window appears and you can proceed to reduce various levels of noise. Leave the Reduction

slider at 100%. This helps you hear what is being removed based on the Noise Threshold slider. Start by adjusting the threshold until the noise is completely removed; do this even if it produces a lot of digital artifacts/distortion in the sound. Once you have set the threshold, lower the reduction amount until the digital artifacts/distortion go away. If the audio contains a lot of low frequencies, you might try adjusting the tone control to Preserve Bass frequencies. The opposite is true for high frequency content. Most of the time, leaving the slider in the middle will work fine. When adjusting the amount of noise reduction, you can also select the Noise Only check box to hear the noise signal that is being removed from the audio. If you hear a lot of the sound that you don't want removed, you might have to lower the reduction percentage. You can also bypass the reduction at any time to hear the difference by clicking the Bypass button, which looks like a circle with a dot and a curved arrow inside. Once you are happy, click Apply.

15. Stem Routing

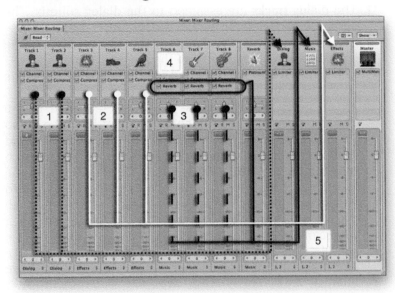

Figure 13-15

Introduction

This might be the most difficult concept to explain using pictures and paper, but I think it is critical to understand. Final Cut is almost exclusively clip-based, meaning that you place filters on the clips and not on video 'tracks' as we can in Soundtrack. Think of track effects as a funnel, and it doesn't really make sense to set up a video funnel that changes everything that passes through it. The closest thing I can think of is a hardware converter box that changes the format of the video as it passes through. Most audio software works in a funnel-type system all of the time. Soundtrack is one of the first that has both excellent funnel effects (real-time track effects) and clip-based effects management (the Actions List); Nuendo from Steinberg is the best at doing both but at around $1500 for an audio-only application it is in a different league. The reason I need to explain this is because the mixer in Soundtrack reflects the funnel approach. Figure 13-15 shows a variety of tracks. The first two are dialog tracks; the next three are effects tracks; the next three are music tracks; and the final track of this group is a bus track that houses a Reverb plug-in. Think of bus tracks as effects tracks that only pass audio through but cannot contain audio clips like an audio track does. Following that are three submix tracks and the final track is the master.

Steps

1. The dialog tracks are assigned to the dialog submix. The submix is funneled through to the master.
2. The effect tracks are assigned to the effects submix. The submix is funneled through to the master.
3. The music tracks are assigned to the music submix. The submix is funneled through to the master.
4. All music tracks have sends which are attached to the reverb bus. A send is the departure point from the audio track and the bus is the destination for the send. The send is effectively a copy machine that sends out a copy of each music track into the reverb bus to be processed by the reverb effect. Right-click in the effects area of each track to add a send to the track. You will be able to choose from all available bus tracks, since that is the only place to which a send can be sent. The reverb bus is assigned to the music submix where it is mixed in with the other music tracks and then sent on to the master (see Tutorial 17 for more on this).
5. Each of the submixes are mixed together at the final stage before leaving Soundtrack through the master.

16. Using the Surround Panner

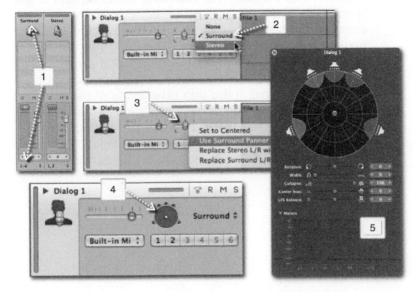

Figure 13-16

Introduction

The surround capabilities of Soundtrack are integral to its overall design. Each track, submix, and master are surround-ready and can be switched to surround at any time. In other words, you don't have to create specialized surround items to use surround; everything is already surround. This example is designed to help you switch a track's panning tool from stereo to surround.

Steps

1. First, you will need to have a surround submix if you want to take advantage of surround on the other tracks. All you need to do is click on the output number at the bottom of the submix track in the mixer and choose a surround output (1–6). This sets the submix to surround.
2. Choose the surround submix you just set for the track you want to be surround. Everything is destination-based. If you set a track to go to a surround submix, its surround capabilities are enabled.
3. Right-click the stereo panner in the track header and choose the Use Surround Panner option from the list.
4. This changes the simple Stereo slider to a mini-surround panner. You can actually grab the panner dot (called a 'puck') and pan the sound around.

5. Double-click on the mini-surround panner to bring up the full surround panner. This has level metering and a few specialized surround panner tools. If your source track contains audio files that are not surround (stereo or mono material), leaving the puck exactly in the center will let the audio pass through in its same configuration (l/r stereo will pass through on the l/r channels). If you move the puck, it will push the stereo audio into other parts of the surround field. Keep in mind that unless you create automation for the panner, none of the moves you make are recorded into Soundtrack Pro. Once you do create automation, you will no longer be able to move it freely. Have a little fun with this!

17. Adding Reverb on a Bus

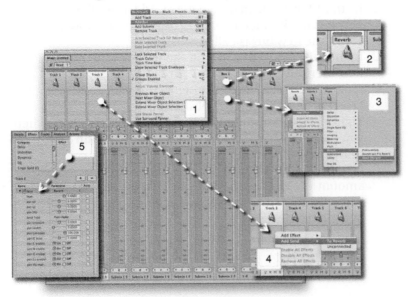

Figure 13-17

Introduction

The use of reverb to mimic the sound of acoustic spaces is a powerful part of audio post-production. Instead of applying reverb to individual clips or on individual tracks, it often makes more sense to set up a single instance of reverb on a special track called a bus. The power of a bus is similar to that of a sub-mix, because it can receive audio from a group of other tracks which are then mixed together and passed on. The bus is different because it can receive audio from other tracks at their send positions. Think of the send as a copy machine that resides on the audio track. The send copies the audio and pushes it to the bus track. The original audio still goes down the track and travels to the submix. If you have a send on a track that is being sent to a bus with no effect, you would end up with two of the audio signals at the destination submix. Placing an effect on the bus is the key, because it changes the audio. The send is located in the same area as plug-ins are inserted on the tracks. The reverb is placed on the bus track and all of the audio in that track is processed by the reverb. The audio is then passed to its selected submix. The strength of doing it in this way is that you can send a lot of different tracks though the same reverb, which helps to create consistency and conserves CPU resources.

Steps

1. In the Multitrack menu, choose Add Bus. This creates a new bus track which is seen in the Mixer window. In Figure 13-17, the new bus is called 'bus 1.'
2. In the mixer, double-click on the name of the bus and give it a descriptive name like 'reverb.'
3. Right-click on the area just below the name and go to **Add Effect** > **Reverb** > **Space Designer**.
4. Right-click on the area below the name of the track where you want to place a send to the bus. Choose **Add Send ⊃ To [name you gave to the bus]**.
5. In the Effects tab in the right pane, you can adjust the amount of signal passed through to the bus via the send. You must have the track with the send selected to view this information.

18. Automating Effects Plug-ins

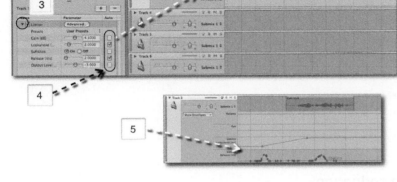

Figure 13-18

Introduction

The ability to automate effects plug-ins is an important part of Soundtrack that was not nearly intuitive enough the first time I tried it. Think of automating as using keyframes or rubber banding in Final Cut. They are only used when you need an effect to change over time to adapt to the audio on the track or to create special effects. You can also record automation by moving parameters on the interfaces when Soundtrack is in an automation write mode. See Chapter 9, on mixing, for more information about recording automation in real time.

Steps

1. Expand the envelope lane for the track you want to automate by clicking on the Expand arrow, located in the top left of the track header.
2. Choose the Effects tab in the left pane to see the effect information.
3. Expand the info area by clicking on the Expand arrow next to the effect's name.
4. The right column, listed as Auto, contains a check box that is used to enable and disable automation for the various effect parameters.
5. The newly enabled parameters will appear in the envelope lane used by the track.

19. Project Music Settings

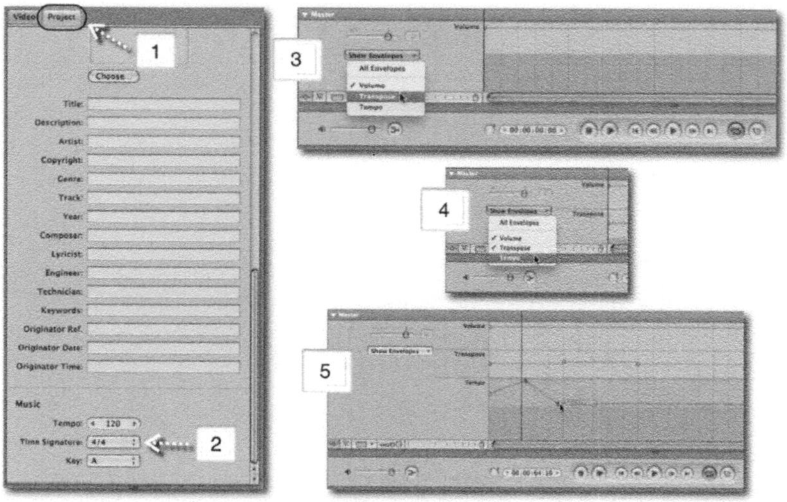

Figure 13-19

Introduction

While Soundtrack is primarily an audio editor, it also has a powerful set of music tools based around the Apple Music Loops file format. While it is not possible to create a completely original musical score using Apple Loops, it is possible to create an in-depth scratch track and sketch out musical ideas. I have used Apple Loops in final productions, but often mixed with original material. When using Loops there are few things to set up. There are also a few useful envelope lanes associated with the master track.

Steps

1. Navigate to the Project tab in the left pane. Besides a lot of other project settings, there is a place to set musical preferences. It is below all of the metadata in the tab.

2. The last parameters in the Project tab are the Tempo, Time Signature, and Key. The tempo default is 120 beats per minute. The default time signature is 4/4, which is what you will be using most often. 4/4 means four beats per measure with the beat on the quarter note. The majority of popular music uses this system. Another semi-common time signature is 3/4, which means that there are three beats per measure; the waltz falls into this category. Polkas have two beats per measure (typically a 2/4 time signature).

The default key, which defines the root note of the music, is A. This is especially critical because the key information transposes the Apple Loops. The easiest way to use them is to pick an Apple Loop you want to use and, before dragging it into the project, set the project settings to match the loop. You will find the tempo and key information in the loop browser (introduced in Tutorial 20). The idea behind Apple Loops is that you really don't need to know that much about music, and to a certain extent it is true. I know a lot of video editors who use Apple Loops by trial and error; they experiment until something works. In the end, you really only need to set a tempo that you like, because Soundtrack will transpose the files and that's not the end of the world. But, if you want to match the key to the primary loop, it will sound better.

3. The Show Envelopes dropdown menu on the master track is where you turn on the Transpose and the Tempo envelopes. Here you can tell the project to transpose Apple Loops and adjust the tempo of the music. You can have the Apple Loops speed up, slow down, and so on. You can create very powerful musical arrangements by using these features.

4. I typically work with all three master envelopes visible.

5. Drawing in tempo and transposition envelopes is as easy as rubber banding in Final Cut.

20. Exploring Music Loops

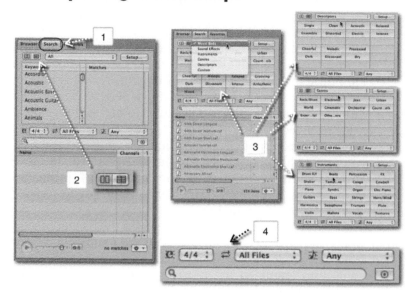

Figure 13-20

Introduction

See Tutorial 19 for more information about setting the project up for Apple Music Loops; this example builds on that information. Apple Loops have metadata that tells Soundtrack about their original key and tempo. When the project tempo and key do not match the Apple Loop's information, Soundtrack speeds up or slows down the loop to fit into the tempo, and attempts to transpose the loop so that it fits the key. The tempo parts seem to work better than the transposition feature, so it is important when working with the loops that you set the project key to match the most important of the loops you will be using. This puts the Apple Loop into its un-transposed key and it will therefore sound the most natural. Of course, it helps to use the loop's original tempo as well, but the project itself often dictates tempo. It would be a hard sell to use an up-tempo piano part during a dramatic death scene, although I'm sure it has been done before. Another useful feature in Soundtrack is the loop browser. This is an efficient way to search through the thousands of different musical files.

Steps

1. Navigate to the Search tab in the right pane.
2. Choose between List and Grid views. I prefer the grid because it provides more information than the list in the same size area.

Printed and bound by CPI Group (UK) Ltd, Croydon, CR0 4YY
21/10/2024
01777094-0010

3. Choose a musical filter from the dropdown selector. Music beds are fully composed music tracks; instruments are individual instruments; descriptors include terms that might help you to find a specific mood; and the last choice, genre, covers the basic musical styles.

4. The search area helps to refine the choices you make in the grid. You can filter by time signature, looping/non-looping files, and musical scale type (major, minor, etc.). You can also type in key words to help with the search. The final search filter is the Target button, which hides all loops except those that are within two semitones of the project key. A semitone is a twelfth of an octave (see Chapter 7) or, more simply, the interval between two adjacent keys on a piano. If the project key is A, you'll be able to see the loops in the following keys: A, B♭/A♯, B, A♭/G♯, and G. This is a great way in which to prevent the overtransposition of loops.

INDEX